THE GRAND EXPERIMENT

The Life and Death of the TTT Program
as Seen through the Eyes of Its Evaluators

Malcolm M. Provus

Edited by Bonnie Herndon

McCutchan Publishing Corporation
2526 Grove Street
Berkeley, California 94704

ISBN 0-8211-1514-6
Library of Congress Catalog Card Number: 74-30961

This work was developed under a grant from the U.S. Office of Education, Department of Health, Education, and Welfare. However, the
opinions and other content do not necessarily reflect the position or
policy of the Agency, and no official endorsement should be inferred.

It would normally be unusual to dedicate a book to its author, except that, in the case of this particular author, nothing was ever unusual. Malcolm Provus died as he lived, in motion and loving it, on the ski slopes of Vermont, January 16, 1975. At the time of his death this book was undergoing its final revision. Mal had approved either the copy or the proposed changes for Chapters 1-7, and had determined the contents of the concluding chapter. On behalf of the Evaluation Research Center and Mal's family, friends, and associates, therefore, we dedicate this, his final accomplishment, to Malcolm Provus, 1928-1975.

Bonnie Herndon
Editor

FOREWORD

This seems to be a moment in education for pause and reflection, a time to reflect on and recover from the tensions and traumas of the late 1960's and early 1970's. More specifically, we appear to be particularly interested in evaluating recent efforts at educational reform for a number of paradoxical reasons. On the one hand, we have the uneasy sense that the results of all the myriad of educational projects and programs of just a few years ago are at best not encouraging. This sense of disappointment, which sometimes reaches a point of anguish, has increased our sense of skepticism and wariness of "bold and daring new plans." Many of us who participated in the "bold new plans" of the sixties are forcing ourselves to look hard at the results of all that frenzied activity with sometimes painful effect.

At the same time we as a profession are also going through a serious reexamination of the evaluation process itself, again for paradoxical reasons. First, because of what I have just said—that there is an increased interest in getting a better sense of accomplishments and effects now that the rhetorical dust has settled. At the same time, however, we as a profession are becoming increasingly concerned about the effects of the evaluation process itself. The sixties brought us concepts like accountability, competence-based teacher education, management by objectives, cost-effectiveness budgeting, and behavioral objectives, all of which put a heavy burden on evaluation procedures. Now we are becoming concerned that we may have a tiger by the tail. Are ideas and programs being held hostage to the demands of evaluation? What are the limits of the art and science of evaluation? Have we sidestepped our leadership responsibilities by channeling creativity into tighter evaluation designs? Most importantly, does our current interest in reexamination and evaluation of the past reflect in part our current avoidance trip to nostalgia or does it reflect a regrouping of our energies based on new and clearer insights that make us better prepared to renew our efforts at educational reform?

Malcolm Provus' useful book on TTT gives us a great deal of information and insight into these questions. On one level, this book is about a remarkable and controversial program, one of the boldest and most imaginatively conceived federal programs in education in this century, and its evaluation. I know of no other federal program with so much money, such wide scope, and such breathtaking hopes that created more furor, controversy, and frustration. That a federal program operated with a minimum of guidelines and not only tolerated but even demanded diversity and creativity was one of the outstanding and almost miraculous features of TTT.

This is, however, no mere presentation of numbers, no arid exposition of technical considerations; nor is it simply a mechanical exposition of bureaucratic handouts. In many ways, the TTT saga can be seen as a metaphor for a significant aspect of American political life in the late sixties and early seventies. The creators and initiators of the program thought and acted boldly and with determination. The scope—nothing short of a sweeping change in the structure of how universities trained teachers was required—was immense. The optimism that allowed participants to actually expect to accomplish these goals seems both bracing and poignant from today's vantage point. This was the essence of liberalism: find the sources of the problem, zero in on it, devise an imaginative and powerful program, and pursue it rigorously. If not solved, the problem was at least on an irreversible course of amelioration. Paradoxically, however, this was also a time when optimism and daring seemed to generate doubt, suspicion, controversy, and bitterness.

Inevitably, the program generated much controversy over virtually every one of its facets, including funding procedures, administrators, guidelines, and evaluation, among others. Perhaps the greatest controversy arose over the so-called "parity" principle, which required that universities, schools, and communities be equally involved in the decision-making processes. At best, this controversy represented a classic confrontation of radical and liberal ideology concerning the allocation of responsibility and power. A great deal of emotion— anger, resentment, passion—characterized discussions on the rights and privileges of lay citizens, particularly the poor, and their relationship to the program. At worst, such questions degenerated into skillful and artful evasions of the requirement or into rather crude political maneuverings. Reading the accounts of these struggles evokes memories of the tense times when these questions were debated throughout our society.

This book deals with another feature of recent educational history: the growing social importance of evaluation. The dramatically increased political and social sensitivities of our time have given rise to the phenomenon of "accountability," a kind of consumer protection plan designed to hold program designers to their rhetoric. Evaluation procedures, then, take on more than academic interest since they are more and more vitally connected to major educational and social policy decisions. The particular requirements placed on evaluating the TTT Program were unusually demanding given its diversity, its loose structure, and the breadth of its goals. The approach adopted by Provus and his associates is an interesting and ingenious effort to measure subtle, human, and intangible qualities. The analysis of this approach raises a larger question concerning the degree to which sensitive, fundamental social and educational policy making should be affected by formal evaluation data.

To me, however, the most valuable part of this book is the way it evokes memories of days of high hopes, intense feelings, deep commitments, and ideological conflict—days of hope, euphoria, and frustration. It is easy and fashionable nowadays to look at programs like TTT as naive, or perhaps even as arrogant. Before we write off such programs, however, let us ask ourselves if the problems and concerns that led people to take action are still present? If so, are we doing anything more than wringing our hands, sighing, and referring to the difficulties of reform? Those who struggled in programs like TTT made a lot of mistakes, but they did struggle. My earnest hope is that those who read this book will be inspired by the imagination and daring of those who struggled and informed by their accomplishments and failures.

David E. Purpel
University of North Carolina, Greensboro

PREFACE

⊙

This book is a fitting memorial to Malcolm Provus, for it is a study of the largest national education program in history, carried out along the precepts of the unique evaluation system he developed. It is indeed fortunate that, when the need arose for a means to evaluate a forty-million-dollar investment in education, this unusual and innovative man was ready with the Discrepancy Evaluation Model, which he had developed and tested, and which he was able to adapt for this complex operation.

The federal program known as the Trainers of Teacher Trainers (TTT) is discussed completely in this book, from its beginnings to speculations on its future impact. As these pages are directed not only to members of the education discipline but to all readers interested in education, we should begin with the reminder that large-scale programs sponsored by the United States Office of Education date back only to the mid-1950's. These experiments in education, so enthusiastically and ambitiously conceived and launched, burgeoned throughout the 1960's. They reached their ultimate growth in 1968 with the establishment of the TTT Program, which, at one time, was spread throughout fifty-eight institutions of higher learning in the United States, and hundreds of secondary and elementary schools.

With the rapid proliferation of federal programs came the obvious questions. How effective were these taxpayer-supported exercises? Was the money well spent? Did education improve as a result? It was obvious that there was a need to monitor their progress, assess their effectiveness, judge their value—*evaluate* them. Enter Malcolm Provus with the Discrepancy Evaluation Model. He and the staff of researchers and evaluators he had brought together at the Evaluation Research Center of the University of Virginia took on the enormous task of evaluating many of the programs, including the largest of them all, the TTT Program. This book, a result of that work, was written from the vast quantities of research and evaluation material they accumulated and tells the story of TTT as seen through their eyes.

Chapter 1 tells why and how the TTT Program was started. It discusses the early political machinations within the Office of Education, the criticisms of teacher training in general, and the desire of educators for a program of national reform, and ends with a description of TTT's goals and objectives.

Chapter 2 deals with the methodology of evaluation. This chapter seeks to measure the extent to which the goals and objectives were achieved. Because of the flexibility of his evaluation system, Malcolm Provus and his staff were able to observe and understand the TTT Program in all its diversity. The evaluation methodology cut through self-serving strategies and deceptions at every level of its design and use. It also helped to spotlight successes that might otherwise have been overlooked.

Chapters 3 and 4 are excerpts from in-depth case studies of TTT projects at two universities. They explain how the goals and objectives of the program were translated into concrete programs involving professors, students, parents, and members of the community.

The last section of the book, Chapters 5 through 7, deals with the achievement of the program goals as seen from various perspectives: those of project directors, evaluation experts, and evaluators from the Evaluation Research Center. A discussion of factors that contributed to failure and what we have learned from the grand experiment follows. The book ends with the author's thoughts and observations on experimental programs and on the future of education in America.

Bonnie Herndon
Editor

ACKNOWLEDGMENTS

This book, a by-product of the Evaluation Research Center's continuing contract evaluation work, reflects the thinking and writing of a great many people. My task has merely been to assemble this material in some coherent form, edit where essential, and contribute new explanatory and elaborative sections wherever needed. As a consequence, attribution of authorship is often impossible, particularly where the original manuscripts from which I worked were in turn the product of earlier joint Evaluation Research Center staff effort. Those of us who work here at ERC have become relatively comfortable with this relationship of joint effort resulting in publication, which is so very different from that practiced at most universities. The disadvantages, such as loss of opportunity for personal distinction, appear to be outweighed by the satisfactions of group endeavor and accomplishment.

On the national level we would like to thank Donald N. Bigelow, Mary Jane Smalley, and Allen Schmeider, who were at one time or another our project officers at the Office of Education. Other OE personnel who were genuinely helpful were Don Davies, Bruce Gaarder, and Iris Garfield. The cluster leaders, who at all times remained responsive to our need for information and who helped to coordinate our project communication, deserve special mention: Richard B. Ford, Herbert Wey, Charles Ruch, William R. Hazard, Eugene E. Slaughter, and Hobart W. Burns. The comments, criticisms, and notes of site visitors Harry N. Rivlin, Harold Cohen, Francis S. Chase, Egon Guba, Ralph W. Tyler, Robert Silvers, Robert J. Kibbee,

A. Harry Passow, John Callahan, and Robert D. Cross contributed significantly to this work, and we would especially like to thank Paul Olson and Erwin Goldenstein, who so graciously wrote the complete history of their project for this book. Appreciation is also extended to co-directors Bruce M. Gansneder and Robert W. Covert, under whose direction much of the material appearing in this book was collected. During the closing years of the program Dr. Covert directed the work of on-site evaluators and the production of material for the technical report as well as for this book. Thanks also to the ERC staff: evaluators Frank Morra, Irene Preston, Charles Hunter, and John Radzikowski; research assistants Carter Allen, Lily Kliot, Wayne Thomas, Robert Brinkerhoff, and Robert O'Connell; and special thanks to our production staff, Linda Meixner and Fred Heblich.

Malcolm M. Provus
November 1974

CONTENTS

INTRODUCTION

A few years ago a young associate professor at Yale University began a book with the question: "What can you say about a twenty-five-year-old girl who died?" He went on to say quite a bit, for the book was *Love Story* and it made the author, Erich Segal, famous.

We begin this book with a similar question: "What can you say about a five-year-old program that died?" We, too, can say quite a bit, and, although we do not expect the book to become a best seller or to make anybody famous, we do hope that, from the history of the deceased program, we can draw generalizations of value to the entire field of education.

The program that died so young was sponsored by the United States Office of Education and was called the Trainers of Teacher Trainers, Triple T, or just TTT. The dream of its originators was sweeping—to change the methods of teaching teachers to teach teachers, to involve people in the community in the learning process on a far more comprehensive scale than ever before, and thereby to improve the quality of education for all the children of the United States.

Whether or not it all came true, the chronicle of so ambitious a dream should be of value to anyone interested in education in America. More specifically, three characteristics of the TTT Program give this story value in the field of education.

 — TTT attempted to influence education with a whole new federal approach. Until 1968 the general practice had been to tinker with mechanisms at the public school level: change courses

1

(new math, for example), create new types of classrooms, build new buildings, obtain new equipment, and lower teacher-student ratio. With TTT, the emphasis was switched to human change in that it attempted to improve the quality of college-level professors who teach prospective teachers. For the first time federal attention was focused on curricula at teachers' colleges, on students practice teaching at teachers' colleges, on the role of liberal arts professors in educating these students—on all of the things that go together to mold future classroom teachers.

— TTT was the first federal program in education to attempt formally the linking of all the individuals and groups concerned with the education of the elementary school child. Dubbed "parity," and groping toward a rough kind of equivalency on the educational scene, this approach was designed to involve everyone from the English professor and the "ed-psych" instructor at the university, through the undergraduate and graduate education student, to the classroom teacher, school principal, and district superintendent, on down to parents and members of the community. Here was something truly unorthodox in educational schemes, a product of the thinking of the 1960's whereby it was held that broad "participatory democracy" should be sought at all levels of society. It brought about almost revolutionary change in federal funding perceptions.

— TTT was one of the largest federal programs in education during the last generation, certainly the most comprehensive program at the university level. It involved fifty-eight institutions of higher education in twenty-four states and the District of Columbia from California (four TTT projects) to Massachusetts (two), from Wisconsin (two) to Florida (four).* And the institutions were, deliberately, heterogeneous: large and small,

---

*Among the institutions participating in TTT were the giants of the teacher-training profession. They included three of the top five institutions in terms of the number of undergraduate degrees granted (Michigan State, Kent State, and Wayne State); four of the five major institutions granting graduate degrees (Indiana, New York University, Michigan State, and Illinois); and the two largest institutions awarding total education degrees (Michigan State and Indiana). Based on *Earned Degrees Conferred, 1969-70* (Washington, D.C.: U.S. Government Printing Office for Institutional Data, Office of Education, U.S. Department of Health, Education, and Welfare, 1970).

public and private, famous and obscure. They included research-oriented universities (Harvard and Berkeley), as well as regional institutions (Appalachian State and George Peabody), both major state teacher-oriented universities (Michigan State and Indiana) and more select schools (Chicago and Wesleyan). On another level, TTT also involved several hundred elementary and secondary schools across the nation since each TTT university worked with at least one school district in its area and usually with a number of different schools. It has been estimated that the program engaged some 42,000 people, 12,000 of them elementary school teachers. The scope was truly prodigious: from ghetto schools in New York to barrio schools in southern California, from high schools in Lansing to primary schools in Florida, from a small Indian school in Oklahoma to rural black schools in Alabama.

These three characteristics of human change—parity inputs and size and scope—made the TTT Program laudable. Four more characteristics added to the scope of the program and made it extraordinary. They were:

- nurturing professional rewards for liberal arts professors working in the education discipline, in contrast to the all-too-prevalent situation in which a professor working with the education department lost status and other benefits in his own discipline;
- providing extensive early field-based training having greater depth and intensity, such as student teachers living in ghettos and "double practicum" (university professors and student teachers both learning in a classroom situation);
- providing courses in methods-methodology (how to teach) simultaneously with courses in substance (subject content), and assigning them equal importance, a departure from the former emphasis on substance courses;
- applying leverage to encourage change in the trainers of teachers and to involve other disciplines, such as the arts and sciences, school personnel, and the community.

An extraordinary program, then, this TTT, in spite of its relatively short duration. As with most valuable experiments, it must be measured not just by the specific results it showed or the revolutions it wrought, but also by the ideas it opened up, the new syntheses it made, the lessons it taught simply in the doing. TTT was no be-all and end-all; nor was it meant to be. It was, rather, a groping, a first step, a foundation, and it is upon that foundation, if the lessons of TTT are heeded, that other more ambitious, perhaps more lasting, programs can be built.

TTT has been described by critics of bureaucracy as a typical example of overpromise, as a modus operandi of the Washington scene. From the unassailable vantage point of the present reviewing the past, it does indeed appear that some proportion of its many expectations were unwarranted. From the same vantage point, however, TTT also materializes as having been different, huge, diverse, and the first—perhaps the last—of its kind. Its leaders expected it to change the world of education. Did it? Or did the dreams become delusions; the grand experiment expire without results?

In its short life, between 1968 and 1973, TTT distributed forty million dollars in federal funds to fifty-eight universities. It had a full and dramatic life which, though it ended prematurely, was eventful. The story deserves not only to be told, but to be told fully and objectively, complete with its beginnings, its frustrations, its successes, its failures, its demise, and its legacy. This responsibility fell to the Evaluation Research Center for the simple reason that ERC was the only entity qualified. In carrying out the assigned task of evaluating TTT in all its scope and complexity, the ERC staff automatically moved into the unique position of being the largest repository of knowledge about the program. As evaluators, it was our task to assess the entire package, whether its contents were impossible dreams or solid constructs. (It turned out, of course, that there were plenty of both!)

ONE

HISTORY OF
THE TTT PROGRAM

1

TEACHERS FOR
THE REAL WORLD

The origins of TTT can be traced to the 1950's and the 1960's, a period during which the education establishment in our society came under serious attack. The launching of the Russian Sputnik in 1957 not only declared the U.S.S.R.'s supremacy in the race for the conquest of space; it also set up a chain reaction which resulted in a demand for better science education programs in the public schools of the United States. The federal government responded by funding a committee in The National Science Foundation to produce new curricula. Called the Physical Sciences Study Committee (PSSC), it was composed of distinguished scientists and educators who worked at the university level developing curricula in physics, chemistry, and biology for secondary schools.

This committee served as a model of cooperative interaction among scientists and educators in producing improvements in teaching at the secondary level. Another group formed shortly afterward produced a method of teaching mathematics known as the new math.

The title of this chapter is the same as that of a book by B. Othanel Smith, Saul Cohen, and Arthur Pearl (Washington, D.C.: American Association of Colleges for Teacher Education, 1969), which was of more than seminal interest for this project.

James Bryant Conant's landmark study, *The Education of American Teachers*, recognized the contribution of the PSSC and urged that all future curriculum development be done in this interdisciplinary fashion.[1]

Then in the 1960's the nation felt the impact of the civil rights movement, the war in Vietnam, and black militancy. National attention focused on the fact that public education was not meeting the needs of our disadvantaged minorities. In spite of all the changes in curricula, inner-city schools remained very much what they had always been—the domain of apathy, low reading scores, and high dropout rates.

American youth, advantaged as well as disadvantaged, were caught in the midst of a social revolution. They were disenchanted with schools and universities and made their protests loud and clear. These institutions strove to meet the demands of the sudden, traumatic changes in society, but the task appeared to be too great. The National Committee on the Reform of Secondary Education, writing about the problem of secondary schools for the education profession, said:

The American comprehensive high school today must be viewed as an establishment striving to meet the complex demands of a society in the throes of social change, at a time when the school system has become too large as an institution and is literally overrun with a mix of young people from inconsistent social backgrounds. The pressure of these forces exhausts the strength of the high school as an organized institution. [2]

The authors of *Growing Up in River City* emphasized the direct relationship between public schools and the alienation of youth from the culturally disadvantaged strata of society:

For the third of River City youth who do not finish high school the way to adulthood is not an easy one. We see that the dropouts have the greatest difficulty in growing up successfully. They are the most vulnerable to delinquency. They get the poorest jobs, if they get jobs at all. They have the most trouble with marriage. The churches see very little of them.

These boys and girls are somehow alien to the society in which they are trying to live. The evidence is clear that they start school with cultural handicaps, they have inadequate help and encouragement from their parents, and they accumulate a record of failure and frustration in school which drives them out of school at the earliest possible date. Early failure in school starts a process of alienation from society that leads them into delinquency and other forms of adolescent maladjustment.

With its present type of program, the school serves these children poorly. As late as a generation ago this group had the alternative of juvenile work leading to adult competence. Now this alternate pathway has narrowed and seems to be disappearing. The school is challenged to create a new and more satisfactory way to adulthood for a third of our youth.[3]

Many educators sharply criticized schools for their failure to serve society. Among them was Mario Fantini, who helped to fund New York City school reform battles with Ford Foundation money and was later a university dean. Fantini decried public education's failure to meet the needs of both advantaged and disadvantaged youth. He said:

. . . public education is failing generally. The most visible failure is in the urban, low-income, racial-minority ghettos. But if one holds education responsible in part for shortcomings throughout American society, education has failed more widely. The shortcomings include such features of contemporary life as the alienation and withdrawal of many economically and culturally advantaged college-age youth and the impotence of social consciousness in mobilizing an adequate response to the nation's domestic crises. Public education's precise share of the blame for these shortcomings need not be calculated in order to assert that it bears *some* share, even a substantial one.[4]

John Holt, a well-known popular writer and former teacher, put the problem even more forcefully. In *How Children Fail*, he said:

Nobody starts off stupid. You have only to watch babies and infants, and think seriously about what all of them learn and do, to see that, except for the most grossly retarded, they show a style of life, and a desire and ability to learn that in an older person we might well call genius. Hardly an adult in a thousand, or ten thousand, could in any three years of his life learn as much, grow as much in his understanding of the world around him, as every infant learns and grows in his first three years. But what happens, as we get older, to this extraordinary capacity for learning and intellectual growth?

What happens is that it is destroyed, and more than by any other one thing, by the process that we misname education—a process that goes on in most homes and schools. We adults destroy most of the intellectual and creative capacity of children by the things we do to them or make them do. We destroy this capacity above all by making them afraid, afraid of not doing what other people want, of not pleasing, of making mistakes, of failing, of being wrong.[5]

This climate, full of antagonism and hostility toward the education establishment, is the one that nurtured TTT.

ORIGINS OF TTT

Precedents

It is unlikely that a section in a book on teacher training would have been devoted to governmental roles before 1960. Only since then has federal activity in teacher education become so highly visible that indeed it appears to hold the dominant role, one that is reflected in universities, state departments of education, and local education agencies.

Assailed as they were by such a deluge of criticism and stimulated by their new role of leadership, successive commissioners in the Office of Education (OE) had increasingly recognized the need for more effective teacher-training endeavors, and, as a first step, encouraged further research into the mysterious processes of teaching and learning.

Under the National Defense Education Act (NDEA), teacher-training institutes were established to bring classroom teachers up to date on new knowledge in the humanities and in the social as well as the natural sciences. Although they were among OE's longest-running and best-supported programs, the institutes nevertheless failed to help teachers reach economically disadvantaged urban students. The PSSC science curriculum reforms also required relatively expensive materials that "turned kids off." It was clear that *how*, as well as what, they learned would have to relate to their own interests and values. What was not clear was how to make this connection.

Programs continued to spring, Minervalike, from the heads of the commissioners and their deputies. There was a period when elaborate, technology-based programs were stressed. Computer-aided instruction is one example. OE spawned large fish which, in turn, produced thousands of small fish, most of which have died. Discussions about their demise have centered on insufficient funding, a need to establish national priorties (if we want to put our children each on their separate moon, we can do it), and ineffective leadership. After the factors of financing, direction, and leadership comes one further consideration: Can the federal government influence the delicate relationship of teacher and child without destroying it? The federal government could decree, could impose its will for reform, but would the cost be loss of individual spontaneity, self-determined choice, and personal initiative?

The quality of interaction between student and teacher is the central and essential learning event in any educational program. (My thought for your smile, or my struggle to understand why you cannot break a word into syllables in return for your continued effort to do so.) Could OE support and advance such activity to the point where social reform through education was possible?

In 1968 Bertram B. Masia and P. David Mitchell, two noted federal evaluators, stated their view of the federal education establishment and its role in teacher training:

The direct involvement of the federal government in teacher training is relatively recent. But the pace of its activity and the degree of its interest in this matter have been accelerating rather sharply during the past few years. As a result of monitoring of these programs by federal officials, of reports from interested individuals in higher education and in the schools, of formal evaluation studies, and of much debate and discussion inside and outside the Office of Education, a number of facts became clear. First, the money managers in Washington felt they were not getting enough return on their investment solely on the basis of the relatively few teachers reached in these programs. Each year only 1 percent of all teachers in the country were reached directly in all programs supported by the Office of Education. Coupled with this was the not surprising finding that the teachers receiving training had, for a variety of reasons, little or no impact on their schools, departments, and colleagues in terms of sharing and communicating what they had achieved and mastered in their training. The designers of the programs were either naive or overoptimistic as to the impact of the training programs on educational personnel back home. At best, the program participant himself had changed in desired directions, but he was either unwilling or incapable or not allowed to spread the gospel. . . . Previous programs to improve teaching skills reached a small precentage of teachers. One problem was how to use limited funds to reach more teachers so as to have maximum impact for the time, effort, and money invested. A possible solution to this problem was to go for the "gatekeepers," the teachers of teachers.[6]

One of the first attempts to reach the gatekeepers was the Tri-University program, a product of OE's Bureau of Elementary and Secondary Education, which was the connecting link between the teacher institutes and TTT. Through this program university professors were retrained with the goal of making the trainers of teachers superb teachers themselves. Liberal arts and education professors were sent to public school classrooms, and classroom teachers were sent to the university to sensitize and stimulate reluctant professor-learners toward change. In its wake, however, the program serendipitously revealed a vast number of community resources for teacher training: community agencies, parents, teachers, custodians, bus drivers, cafeteria help, and principals. From this program came arguments that all participants should share in the decisions that affect a program: liberal arts professors as well as education professors should train teachers and work in the public school classroom; existing local institutions should be utilized to support student-teacher interaction and the training and retraining of everyone connected with the interaction; and, finally, teachers already in school as well as those preparing to go to school should learn from one another and from all other participants in a program. All who learned would ultimately teach others who would in turn teach. This was the basis for the exciting idea that came to be called the Trainers of Teacher Trainers. Seen from the vantage point of the present, it seems a perfectly obvious thing to do, but not until TTT had anyone ever tried to put the idea into practice on a large scale.

Legislative Beginnings

In discussing the legislative origins of TTT, John Merrow[7] wrote:

. . . the Trainers of Teacher Trainers program had its roots in the Bureau of Educational Personnel Development (BEPD). Its legislative mandate, the Education Professions Development Act (EPDA) of 1967 directed OE to identify problems in personnel training and gave it unprecedented authority to design and implement solutions. . . . The central notion behind EPDA is that government ought to be more rational and responsible; that is, if OE had the necessary authority, it would be able to identify specific problems in American education, and use that information in designing solutions, which would be implemented immediately. EPDA encouraged OE to break away from conventional approaches to teacher training. . . . Before the passage of EPDA, a patchwork of programs involved the federal government in teacher training. Dr. Samuel Halperin, then Deputy Assistant Secretary of HEW (Department of Health, Education and Welfare) for Legislation and a key member of the task force that wrote the bill, said:

Under President Johnson, some thirty to forty educational programs had been passed, and only in early 1966 did we . . . realize that, as far as teachers went, we didn't have the desired degree of quality or, in quite a few specialized areas, the quantity. . . . What was missing was the means to determine what was needed, and the flexible, discretionary authority to respond to those needs.[8]

Albert L. Alford, head of the Office of Legislation of OE, and Russell Wood, then Director of Planning for OE, remember essentially the same combination of circumstances: scattered teacher-training authority, a need for a mechanism to assess needs, the lack of flexible authority, and a teacher shortage. . . . [9] But not everyone agreed on a teacher shortage. In 1967 Joseph Froomkin, the Associate Commissioner of Education for the Office of Program Planning and Evaluation (OPPE) published a monograph entitled *Education in the 1970's,* which challenged this idea. In that publication, and in later presentations to BEPD's leadership, Froomkin argued that the shortage would soon be replaced by a teacher surplus. Froomkin recalls that he was challenging the conventional wisdom, and that his was a lone voice. His prediction was generally rejected because, in his words, "everyone tends to project the past into the future . . . ."

In August 1971 Wood, who had played a key part from the beginning, remembered this a little differently. He wrote:

> The surplus situation was clearly foreseen when BEPD was being planned, in 1967, as a result of papers produced for that planning effort by OPPE, and OE. Therefore, all program decisions, and strategy formulations, have been made with this factor in mind.

It is impossible at this time to sort out precisely which version of the story is correct. But it is clear that on this crucial point there was disagreement within OE, and that Froomkin, whose job it was to supervise OE planning, recalls that his advice on the coming teacher surplus was not heeded.

EPDA's congressional sponsors assumed several things: first, that pressing educational needs would be (or already had been) identified by OE; second, that discretionary authority would enable it to meet needs as they arose, and, third, that the consolidation of existing teacher-training programs would eliminate overlap and competition while facilitating efficient and effective training.

There was another important assumption: that the Congress would provide a significantly larger appropriation. With new money, OE could maintain existing commitments while funding new reforms . . . .

The Teacher Corps drew almost all the attention—and the fire—of the Congress, and EPDA emerged essentially as written. After lengthy hearings in the House of Representatives, the Senate, under pressure of time, passed the House version without change.

As passed, EPDA incorporated several major pieces of legislation (Title IV of NDEA, Title V of the Higher Education Act, and Titles V-B and XI of NDEA 1965). Some fifteen other educational manpower training programs continued outside EPDA, and the act called for their coordination.

The Congress specified that no money was to be appropriated for EPDA until fiscal year 1969. . . . The Office of Education embraced the flexible authority and the planning time with enthusiasm.

But the optimism notwithstanding, some portions of the act were restrictive. Its purposes were broadly enough stated (provide a broad range of training opportunities . . . , attract qualified persons into the teaching profession . . . , help to make training more responsive . . .) to avoid any limitations on anyone.

The part of EPDA which provided the most discretion was Part D, which was designed for "Improving Training Opportunities for Personnel Serving in Programs of Education Other Than Higher Education." . . . One congressional intent in Part D was to maintain the popular institute programs at current levels. Teacher Corps and the fellowships and institute programs had administrators and sizable staffs with established operating patterns. None of this was changed by the law. Nor did EPDA disturb OE's traditional practice of funding through universities and colleges. There was more freedom for OE administrators, but much inherited baggage, which was brought together under one roof when OE decided to create a new bureau.

That the planners in OE, intent on making maximum use of EPDA's flexibility and discretion, should have created a BEPD which left little authority in the hands of its new director, Don Davies, was the major irony of the story.

Davies, who had been the executive director of the NEA's Commission on Teacher Education and Professional Standards (TEPS) and before that had been a public school teacher and a university faculty member involved in teacher training, . . . arrived in BEPD with the notion of reforming teacher education itself—principally by loosening up the requirements for teacher certification, diversifying the education professions, and recruiting new members to them. He also wanted to reduce the almost exclusive OE reliance on universities as the locus for and source of wisdom on teacher training; Davies wanted to get the public schools more involved.

Also, he arrived as head of BEPD just as the full impact of the civil rights-black upheaval washed over city schools and the federal education establishment. The riots of the late 1960's brought about pressure to turn more of OE's resources to the problems of the disadvantaged, and to recruit minority OE staff to help create and manage these efforts. Davies recalls that he arrived with a general sympathy toward these ideas, "not a ten-point checklist of new programs."

Between the passage of the EPDA law in June 1967 and the setting up of the bureau in February 1968, there was a flurry of activity in USOE and in the schools of education around the country . . . .

Commisioner Howe set up a task force within OE, under the direction of Wood, to prepare for implementation. A Planning Coordination Committee was established outside OE, under the leadership of Dwight Allen, then of the Stanford University School of Education. The committee was told to explore all the possibilities for EPDA, regardless of political constraints.[10] Allen's group consisted chiefly of educators from colleges and universities; this makeup was a conscious decision by Howe and Allen to exclude those involved in traditional teacher-training programs, and instead to search for new ideas.[11]

. . . The Allen Task Force also strongly recommended clear guidelines with specific examples, lest "the whole program . . . degenerate into an amorphous and unadministrable heap."[12]

While the Allen Task Force was examining the broad possibilities, Wood's group, calling itself the "EPDA Think Group," was grappling with more practical problems. . . . The group's primary job was "to translate the broad goals and priorities agreed upon . . . into program regulations and guidelines."[13]

The Wood Report "recommended" in December what had been decided upon earlier: a Bureau of Educational Personnel Development within OE. . . . Wood's "Think Group" proposed the creation of four divisions within the bureau: one of them was the Division of Program Administration (DPA), with responsibility for all ongoing programs. . . . It contained all of the operating authority of EPDA except for Teacher Corps. It was headed by Donald Bigelow. . . . In preparation for EPDA he had developed and funded (under NDEA) a program to train teacher trainers; it was to become the new bureau's first program, the Trainers of Teacher Trainers.[14]

The Role of the Office of Education

Bigelow, as the Director of the Division of Educational Personnel Training, had already begun to move toward bringing the benefits of the new legislation into the Office of Education, and, ultimately, into his own division. During June 1967 Bigelow arranged a conference on the "Programmatic Consideration of Teacher Education." "Bigelow admits to arranging the conference in 'anticipation' . . . that EPDA would arrive safe and sound in OE, and hopefully perhaps, even in DEPT (Division of Educational Personnel Training), Bigelow's own division in BESE [Bureau of Elementary and Secondary Education]."[15]

An early disciple of the reeducation of teachers and university professors, Bigelow administered the seventy-eight-million-dollar programs that included NDEA's Summer Teacher Institutes and the Experienced Teacher Fellowship Program. Also a creator of BESE's Tri-University program, he was in a good position to recognize the new legislation as a significant opportunity for creating a program much greater in scope than had generally been anticipated. The strategy for TTT as an immense national program, then, came largely from Bigelow, who, as director of the programs for the bureau, now had responsibility for lasting action.

Bigelow also wanted the program to move away from an emphasis on teaching teachers the content of science or mathematics to an emphasis on "how to teach" these subjects and toward taking the learner, his values and ideals, into account when teaching anything. Bigelow's background, that of a university history professor, meant that his interest was understandably at the college level, but he related the problems he saw in college to all levels of education.

What's happening, or so it appears to this bureaucratized historian, is that the campus revolts are beginning to add up to the first great protest of modern times against the academic community at large. They are really announcing to one and all, it seems to me, the failure of the university to serve adequately the society which supports it. The student protest movement is a protest against nineteenth-century educational methods being applied to students who will live much of their lives (and whose children will live all of their lives) in the next century. It is a protest against colleges and universities which remain places where the professor's education may continue, while the student's may not start; it is a protest against the Ph.D. credit card which is validated by scholarly ghosts of the nineteenth century and universally accepted as a criterion of excellence in the twentieth; it is a protest against teachers who go to "think-tanks," to foreign countries (yes, even to Washington), in order to serve their country while not always serving their students. Finally, it is a protest against teachers who do not teach, a protest against those who are unable to unite "the young and the old in the imaginative consideration of learning."[16]

Bigelow's own feelings about the importance of teacher reform at the highest level were reinforced by the words and actions of other educators. He felt that some national group was needed to decry the recent emphasis on teaching teachers for the disadvantaged only. He asked the American Association of Colleges of Teacher Education (AACTE), a group of reform-minded educators, to come up with new ideas for training teachers, and from their efforts came *Teachers for the Real World:*[17]

The burden of this book, especially as it relates to colleges and universities, is that there must be two major shifts in the field of teacher education: (1) A far more orderly and systematic procedure must be created for the preparation of the teacher in relation to the tasks of teaching. (2) This can best be accomplished by adopting procedures that are clinically and case-study oriented. In short, the study calls for a movement toward clinical training and an end to courses dominated by lectures and discussion. It also challenges colleges and universities to develop a systematic body of information, including audiovisual material, that will help prospective teachers analyze their behavior, clarify concepts, and interpret situations.[18]

As John Merrow has summarized: "The planners of TTT adopted a strategy based on two major assumptions: first, that the greatest leverage for affecting change was to be had by focusing efforts and resources on those who prepare the trainers of teachers, and, second, that the teacher's training should not remain the major concern of just the faculty of the schools of education, but should interest members of college liberal arts faculties, school personnel, and representatives of the community. It was this kernel of thought which Donald Bigelow, the originator of the program, and his associates were to sow, fertilize, and nurture when it sprouted in the spring of 1968 as the Trainers of Teacher Trainers Program."[19]

TTT, then, owes its existence to new federal legislation and reorganization in the Office of Education, plus creative action by Alford, Wood, Davies, Bigelow, and others. All elements were responsive to a public demand from the community, educators, and professional education organizations to improve schools in the latter years of President Johnson's administration.

From the men involved, discretionary authority newly offered by EPDA, and different leadership in Washington emerged the program that would be a remedy simultaneously applied to American pupils and teachers in both public schools and universities. There was also a growing belief that a reasonable, courageous new effort, based on an honest admission of problems and a forthright dedication to their solution, just might work.

THE PROGRAM

Planning

The program planners were aware of the odds, yet they firmly believed that money and expertise would make a difference if the right people were involved and the right conditions were ensured. They planned their strategy to get to the source of the problem. What was wrong with the schools could largely be controlled by reforming teacher-training institutions and practices. Nothing less would do. The planners of TTT intended to deal with the entire beast by exercising control at some vital point.

It was TTT's purpose to make schools more responsive to pupils who would normally drop out—especially those in the inner city where cultural deprivation might be greatest and the presence of failure and frustration, overwhelming. This was to be accomplished by changing the kind of teachers who went into these schools and the ways they related to their students, and it was this vital point that was to affect the whole institutional structure of universities. B. Othanel Smith provided a graphic explanation of the necessary changes in his *On the Preparation of the Teachers of Teachers*. He stressed the need for cooperation between pedagogical and nonped-agogical faculties stating: "It is the work of these faculties that we are primarily concerned about when we discuss the preparation of teachers."

Smith also pointed out that graduate faculties were concerned with turning out research workers:

These individuals, while they are trained to do research and prepare papers for publication, typically find themselves employed in institutions where they are responsible for training teachers at the preservice level. While thus engaged they try to carry on research or to write articles and books that will help them to escape from this assignment as early as possible and to climb to the level of the graduate faculty where they themselves can engage in the process of preparing individuals to do research who will in turn be employed to train teachers. . . .

The purpose here is not to deprecate in the least the importance of research in any field whatever. . . . [but] it is important to note that the knowledge of a discipline can be used for some purpose other than the production of further knowledge. And it is this point that we wish to make here in connection with the training of the teacher of teachers. . . .

But, to be effective teachers, Smith said:

. . . It goes without saying that the program of preparation for the teacher of teachers must include systematic work in various aspects of pedagogy such as human development, learning, deviant behavior, curriculum development, socio-logy of education, philosphy of education, and other aspects. . . . These are the tools that the teacher trainer uses as he interprets and modifies the behavior of his students, who are prospective teachers, and thereby trains them to do likewise with their own pupils . . . .

Smith then addressed a key point of the TTT Program—moving the university professor out of his own domain and into the public school classrooms:

. . . To perform this job [of teacher training] is to know the classroom work of the teacher—what he does from day to day, from moment to moment; it is to know the structure and dynamics of teaching behavior; to know how to direct the prospective teacher as he improves his teaching behavior; it is to know what the teacher does outside the classroom in the school and community; and to be able to shape the prospective teacher's behavior to the requirements of these extra-classroom duties. . . .

He concluded with a view of the preparation of teachers as a cooperative venture:

. . . The graduate faculty can neither design the program nor carry it on alone. The graduate faculty in all the disciplines, including pedagogy, is isolated. Its members know little about teaching in the common school, and the faculty of the common school is equally removed from the work of the graduate faculty. The undergraduate faculty, which gives the bulk of preservice training, is suspended between the two with little support from either side. In consequence the current teacher-training program typically consists of nonpedagogical courses in the prospective teacher's field of specialization plus a few courses in pedagogy, capped with student teaching. . . .

The only way to break this system of compartmentalization and isolation is to develop a mechanism for bringing these three faculties together to consider their common problem, to work out a plan for dealing with it and for sharing in the development and execution of the plan.[20]

Lloyd Trump, a man who has spent his entire professional life trying to improve classroom practice, is widely known as the father of team teaching—a way of getting teachers to cooperate within the school building in order to improve instruction. He was in basic agreement with Bigelow when he spoke about the teaching of children.

Only if teachers stimulate and expect more personal responsibility for learning from their students, spend more time teaching students how to learn, and make effective suggestions as to how students may research beyond their given assignments, only then will the independent study resulting from large-group instruction be better than today's homework and their special projects, which students copy from encyclopedias and illustrate with pictures cut from popular magazines.[21]

Roy Edelfelt, spokesman for improved teacher training for the one-million-member National Education Association and a former TEPS Commission colleague of Davies, had long been critical of existing methods of teaching potential teachers. In exhorting his associates to specific action, he cited six problems: that schools of education are largely standard and traditional; that the teaching profession tends to impose conformity; that preservice and in-service training should be improved; that few schools in the nation have programs of individualized staff development; that new curriculum projects designed to be exciting new concepts turn out to be merely the same old methods with changes in subject content; and that almost nothing exists on different orders of teaching. He concluded:

If preservice and in-service teacher education are to prepare teachers for new developments in curriculum content, new concepts of school (e.g., nongraded school, open school), and new staffing patterns, these six problems present some hellishly difficult roadblocks.[22]

Bigelow put it in a somewhat different form:

I believe I can say with reasonable assurance that hardly anyone ever jumped out of bed in the morning and said with gusto, "Bully for me; I'm a trainer of teachers of teachers, I am going to work today." However, there are a host of people who might, it they chose, say precisely that. Besides university professors in schools of education and liberal arts, many people are actively engaged in the task of training teachers who teach teachers. For example, there are librarians, educational media specialists, critic teachers, school administrators of every rank. . . .[23]

Objectives

The three original TTT goals, as conceived by Bigelow and his colleagues early in the program, remained fairly stable:
— to develop more effective programs for training educators, both in institutions of higher learning and in the schools;
— to increase the competency of persons currently serving as trainers (TTT's) both in institutions of higher learning and in the schools; and
— to identify recruit and train qualified individuals as Teacher Trainers (TT's) and Trainers of Teacher Trainers (TTT's).

The planners of TTT expected that a coalition of all sectors of the educational process—teacher education, colleges of arts and sciences, public schools, and local communities—would share responsibility for achieving these three goals.

The principle of parity, implied as a fourth purpose, leads into another of TTT's major intents, although one never stated as a program goal: the promotion of cultural pluralism. As Dr. Mary Jane Smalley explained:

The emergence of cultural pluralism as a central concern of the Training of Teacher Trainers program is not surprising. When the TTT began in December, 1967, there was not an explicit commitment to the concept of cultural pluralism and its implementation in all projects. There was, however, insistence upon another kind of equity basic to teacher training: "decisional" pluralism among all the groups and agencies affected by or affecting the training that teachers receive. It was this sense of equity which, by the course of its development, made inevitable the emergence of the demand for cultural pluralism which was first noted in early 1970.[24]

By late 1970 the TTT Program had two more objectives: to institutionalize program effects within the funded training agency, and to extend these effects to other nonfunded institutions. Thus, by November 1970, the TTT Program had five major goals:

— to focus projects on the identification, recruitment, and training of TTT's;

— to find a balance (parity) among the consumers concerned with the training of educational personnel;

— to include in the program the best of recent educational developments and deal with critical current educational issues;

— to institutionalize improvements resulting from TTT projects; and

— to develop strategies through each project that would achieve a maximum multiplier effect.

In reaching toward these goals, TTT planners selected and worked within certain constructs.

Constructs

Teacher-Training Institutions. The first and most important of the constructs was the reform of teacher-training institutions. To reform these institutions, three groups of people, in addition to education professors, were slated to be used differently: liberal arts professors, public school personnel, and parents and community members served by public schools. These groups would give powerful input to the problems of teacher training and to the design and execution of new kinds of training programs.

Gatekeepers. To carry out this work and involve all of these people simultaneously in the reconstruction task, a second construct was called for: teacher-training institutions could be changed only where existing institutional leadership welcomed such change. New institutions were not to be created; instead, existing apparatus was to be modified and used to carry out the teacher-training experiment. To effect the necessary accommodations and produce the long-lasting changes required, Lewin's concept of the "institutional gatekeeper" was verbalized and employed by Donald Bigelow. All university administrators up and down the ranks have the power to say "no" to new programs. TTT attempted to locate and to work with those few administrators who had the power to say "yes"—the institutional gatekeepers. Change, then, was to come through the status hierarchy and the authoritative leadership of existing teacher-training institutions. To have ignored this leadership would have increased the risk of failure at considerably higher dollar costs. In addition, these institutions could be changed only where leaders could persuade their followers that traditional behavior was dysfunctional and that new behavior might be helpful. This, of course, required change in the existing reward system.

Problem-Solving Orientation. The need for changes in organization staff behavior drew attention to a third construct, equally a part of the reform desired by the architects of TTT. If teacher training was to be reformed, a definition of education for students and teachers alike was needed, with emphasis on inquiry rather than knowledge, on problem-solving ability rather than academic facility. Clearly, the education that students and teachers alike had been receiving had failed to solve the real problems existing in everyday classrooms and in urban living. TTT was to establish teacher-training programs for "teachers for the real world," which proved to be a forth construct.

The Real World. This was the world meant to be addressed by teachers at all levels, and it differed from the white, middle-class, goal-oriented one most of them know. It was, instead, a world of diffident learners, ethnic minorities, and disenchanted youth who, in large part, were found in urban pockets of social discontent. TTT sought out those people who understood the character of life in inner cities through firsthand experience, who had learned to teach in public schools rather than university classrooms, and who were "turned in" to the concerns and needs of urban America.

The explicit constructs of TTT, then, were to find those gatekeepers of existing teacher-training institutions willing to involve liberal arts professors, public school people, and community people in the task of training teachers through a new kind of educational experience aimed at the problems of contemporary America.

Since guidelines for specific activities were never set out, separate projects continued to vary and grow over time. The major strategies, or groups of activities, employed by the different projects ranged from the relatively traditional to the novel. And project directors, unhampered by any rigid guidelines, were freed to accomplish the five very general goals in any way that seemed reasonable and likely to succeed.

Thus, individual projects took off like particles of matter in an

expanding universe, each spinning off satellites. The field of education had rarely seen so exciting a phenomenon, or one so rich in
promise. At the same time it must be recognized that problems, such
as the attrition rate of projects, were already visible on the horizon.

In May 1968 sixty-five universities had drafted proposals for the
U.S. Office of Education to consider. Fifty-eight were funded for the
academic year 1969-70. Within one year, this number dropped
dramatically—to forty-three projects; by the end of the academic
year 1970-71, only thirty-three remained. Slightly more than half
the original number of projects (thirty-two) were funded for the year
1971-72, and by the final year, 1972-73, only twenty-nine projects
actually remained in operation. The program's extreme diversity,
rapidly reaching exponential proportions, posed another severe
problem: How was such a problem ever to be observed, studied, or
reported upon?

2

EVALUATION
PROCEDURES

Fortunately a method already existed by which TTT could be examined: evaluation. Although the role of evaluation in educational and social programs is relatively new, it was in existence as far back as the 1930's. At that time evaluation consisted of little more than simple observation—how many new jobs were created, how many public works were completed. There was little concern for using demographic data or determining the effectiveness of national programs. National data on education did not exist at all until 1940, and only within the last few years has it come to be accepted as reliable.

There was a dramatic rise in the importance of the role of evaluation during the fifties and sixties, as principles of systems analysis and business administration came to be applied to national social and educational programs. During the prosperous sixties a wealth of programs were created to foster changes in individuals and institutions. Thus, the concept of evaluation became part of the TTT Program at a time when members of the executive branch of government at both the state and the federal levels began to question the usefulness of educational program expenditures generally and of teacher-training programs in particular.

Public officials demanded proof that specific goals had been established for TTT and, if they had, that they had been attained. Because the program was subject to new scrutiny, managers of the program were concerned that local determination of project affairs would come under attack. Evaluation as a means of monitoring project progress toward stated objectives became attractive. In fact, in a program as enormous and amorphous as TTT, evaluation was the key component.

TTT management wanted the program evaluated, but on an internal and casual basis. No clear directive was ever issued, however, and OE's Office of Program Planning and Evaluation, which evaluated all BEPD programs, stepped in and forced the bureau to have TTT evaluated during the period 1970-71, using outside technical assistance.

EARLY EFFORTS

Since OPPE initially felt that federal programs could be evaluated only on the basis of local impact, this first official evaluation effort sought to develop and obtain measures of effect on classroom teachers and students, an approach that assumed a rather direct relationship between the program and its consumers. Instead, the programs were quite complex and heterogeneous, and this complexity minimized the usefulness of the notion of product evaluation. Consequently, there were never any guidelines or requirements for assessing local projects. "Most proposals did not reserve any substantial portion of the budget for monitoring purposes, and it is open to question whether the TTT administrators would have accepted any that did."[1]

The next attempt at evaluation began when the Leadership Training Institute (LTI), within BEPD, was charged with "assessing the effectiveness of the TTT Program as a whole, and disseminating available pertinent information."[2] In November and December 1969, and later in May 1970, LTI-TTT, at the request of BEPD, conducted a series of site visits to TTT projects. The timing was particularly unfortunate because no project director knew whether the project was to be funded or discontinued. The directors all suspected, despite official and unofficial denials, that the visits were actually a cover for an investigation on which funding decisions would be based. Although these site visits proved to be a major source of information for TTT, their usefulness was compromised by such suspicions.

The general picture of TTT that emerged from LTI site visits was somewhat cloudy. Ultimately site visits proved to be a poor means of providing the kind of feedback desired by the individual project directors. A third of the directors stated that the data contained in the site visit reports was useless, and about two-thirds felt that the reports had made no difference in what their projects had been doing.[3]

Since TTT's efforts at self-analysis lacked both the clarity of purpose and the careful organization generally associated with more formalized schemes of evaluation, objective evaluation was attempted. This approach also presented problems. The first attempt, a study conducted by Bertram B. Masia and P. David Mitchell during the planning session of 1968-69, was primarily descriptive in nature, recording the manner in which TTT took shape and was implemented. Masia and Mitchell made no provision for feedback from project personnel, relying, instead, on their own staff for observation and interpretation. The staff, in turn, relied heavily on official documents to construct its picture of TTT.[4]

The next attempt was begun by Thomas Hastings of the Center for Instructional Research and Curriculum Evaluation (CIRCE) at the University of Illinois in February 1969. Although the first *Aperiodic Report* of the CIRCE group clearly stated that "the project level is where the degree of success of the TTT Program is determined and certainly our greatest evaluation efforts should be at this level," they chose to do otherwise in practice,[5] and focused their major efforts on an analysis of the TTT clusters and LTI site visits. According to Donald Bigelow, the Hastings methodology and content "didn't meet bureau needs and didn't have bureau approval."[6] As a consequence, the CIRCE analysis was terminated by the TTT administration before completion of its first year.

ERC ENTERS

It was at this point that the Evaluation Research Center stepped in. As director of the center, the author had worked with BEPD to draw up a design for a bureau-wide evaluation. TTT was not described in this initial plan, however, because it appeared too complex for the time allotted to the task. Yet TTT was intriguing. If the ERC staff could systematically evaluate such an amorphous conglomerate of functions, it could analyze virtually any federal program. Our proposal was sent to Mary Jane Smalley, Chief of the TTT Branch of OE, and to Donald Bigelow, and, in mid-1970, the center was awarded a contract for the evaluation of TTT. Because of its experience with the theory and development of the Discrepancy Evaluation Model (DEM),[7] the ERC staff chose this method of evaluation. Its design was adaptable to even the confusing polymorph that TTT became. By using the results of the study made by the ERC staff, we can attempt to describe the grand experiment so that others may study, understand, and assess it.

Before proceeding with a report on TTT, some attention should be directed toward the concept of evaluation itself and toward a description of the discrepancy evaluation method. By understanding concept and methodology, the reader is in a better position to understand our conclusions about the program in general.

Evaluation is a controversial subject. The following extract from an OE memorandum written by Donald R. Tuttle of the TTT staff represents no small part of the project's and staff's disposition toward evaluation in general, and ERC's evaluation in particular.

There is something about evaluators and evaluations that frightens me. Although in theory I agree that we ought to attempt to determine the worth of our programs and projects, erroneous evaluations promulgated with awesome solemnity and specious authority can destroy good programs and projects. Secondly, evaluators inevitably produce what I call a "straight-jacket" effect because it is easier to evaluate projects comparatively if they are all alike and static.

You can see the iron hand closing down on the project directors as the document progresses. Page 3, item B, paragraph 2, sentence 2, under *General Statement of Work* asserts, "This work will also insure that the individual project evaluations are not *counterproductive* to the total TTT Program evaluation." (Italics mine.) Now what does counterproductive mean? Does it mean that the director can't find out anything about the results of this program not in the general evaluation? Or worse, if the evaluation designed by the local director is likely to develop data that might challenge the conclusions of the central investigation, at all costs must it be suppressed?

Next paragraph: if TTT is developing something new, must it nevertheless be measured by adapted or existent instruments?

Even more restrictive is item 6 under *Specific Statement of Work* ". . . the proposer's staff will produce a set of *Proposed Guidelines,* which will ensure that *any new project proposals will conform to the evaluation design.*" (Italics mine.) Here we have progressed to evaluator thought control indeed!

And of course this is what regularly happens in American education. The object comes to be to do well on the test rather than to educate children. Put an evaluator to work on a program designed to produce change, and he will soon bind it so that no further change is possible. If you can stop change, you can get more valid data.

Again the mailed fist smashes nonconformity in item 2 under *Remedial Project Design and Monitoring Work:* "The proposer's staff will meet separately with a small team from *each* (italics the proposer's) project to consider revisions in the evaluation section of each program. Sections which are *counterproductive to the total program evaluation effort will be removed.*" Again what does this mean? That the directors can find out about the effects of their programs only those things which the proposer & co. want them to know? The whole tone sounds highhanded to me.

The next item (3) reinforces the limitations on the director's freedom to study his own project, for "the proposer's staff will work with each project team to *insure* (italics mine) that all instruments used in each *project* (italics proposer's) evaluation are not counterproductive to or do not duplicate those in the *program* evaluation."

The aim appears to be to make the director completely powerless to defend himself from an evaluation design that does not appear to fit his program.

Tuttle was correct in his view that all local project directors would be under pressure to use "program design" language. Comparability of terms and a comparable level of specificity of detail across projects is essential to any evaluation of a national program.

But comparability does not have to mean conformity. The use of a common set of categories to decode local project activity need no more limit that activity than use of the terms yards, feet, and inches limits the length of a line. It is not the classification system or the ruler, but how it is used that is the determining factor. If national program expectations had been used to establish categories for describing and then for judging the adequacy of local projects, Tuttle's worst fears would have been realized. If, instead, local expectations were used to establish descriptors and local project expectations as well as national program expectations were then used as the basis for judging local success, both national and local interests could, in effect, be served. To stay with the yardstick analogy, if one bolt of cloth were described only in terms of length and all bolts were evaluated according to this single criterion, such qualities as color and weave would be unimportant. If, each time a new bolt of cloth was examined, its qualities were first described and then established as criteria for judging all bolts, a dazzling array of criteria—width, texture, pattern—could then be created.

In order to evaluate TTT it was necessary to determine minimal, essential conditions for which each local project could be held accountable with regard to both national and local criteria. This did not mean that local criteria could not change; it simply meant that such changes had to be explicit and public.

Evaluation is always, however, the instrument of management, and, since management existed at both the local project and national program levels, it was entirely possible that national management would impose national program criteria and not permit local project management to revise them. It appears that Tuttle feared national program authority rather than evaluation per se. Tuttle, like so many of Bigelow's OE staff, was determined that new ways to educate the trainers of teachers be explored and directed through local initiative. The challenge of evaluating TTT was to serve and protect that initiative while taking national management needs into account.

SELECTING AN EVALUATION PROCEDURE

There are two kinds of evaluation, summative and formative. The primary aim of summative evaluation is assessment, and this is the purpose usually identified with the word "evaluation." The primary aim of formative evaluation is program improvement, and it is designed to discover whether a program is operating as it was intended. Formative and summative evaluation complement each other, the second following logically upon the activities of the first in developing programs. Without the foundation provided by formative evaluation, it is virtually impossible, both technically and politically, to produce high-quality summative evaluation. Evaluation has for too long been viewed by educational practitioners as a negative, constricting, threatening activity to be tolerated only under duress. Evaluation can, however, be its own best reward, and both types—formative and summative—are essentially constructive activities.

The Discrepancy Evaluation Model developed in 1966 served the dual purposes of providing information for program improvement and for program assessment. The DEM is particularly appropriate for use with new and innovative projects. It is sensitive to the natural developmental stages (planning, installation, early operation, stabilization) experienced by such programs and provides evaluation activity appropriate to each stage. Information obtained through evaluation is designed to help the administrator make timely and defensible decisions that change and improve programs in initial stages of development and operation.[8]

The model, based on the primary assumption that evaluation must involve the comparison of performance against a standard, uses any discrepancy between the two as a unit of measurement. DEM includes five major stages: program design, program installation, program process, program terminal products, and program cost-benefit analysis. All stages except one could be applied to the national program and to some forty local projects. It was clear from the beginning that a cost-benefit analysis would be impossible without functional budgeting at the project level, and to install and enforce such procedures seemed impossible given the self-determination of the project managers. Stage V, therefore, had to be dropped. The four stages contributing to the evaluation of either the national or project level of the TTT Program are outlined as follows:

	Levels of management	
Stages	Local project	Federal program
I. Design	Projects designed with technical assistance	Aggregation of project designs as basis for design of the national program
II. Installation	Project installation measures obtained	Aggregation of project installation measures
III. Process	Field work in selected sites and site visits; participant views of project outcomes	———
IV. Product	Outcomes documented and analyzed	Generalization of outcomes

The evaluation activities were enormously complex, each having many subparts and involving hundreds of thousands of people. Each activity required its own methodology and compromise based on conceptual, human, and dollar constraints. Almost immediately two question arose: To what extent would the limited resources available for evaluation permit such diverse activity? What accommodations would have to be made?

One of the problems with evaluating TTT was the view the

planners had of their own program. They firmly believed that this was a grand experiment, one that would revolutionize the education profession in the United States. So great were their expectations that evaluators could not fail to perceive that the goals might well prove unrealistic. At that point, however, any suspicions as to the quixotic nature of the program to be evaluated were deliberately not mentioned.

Some years later, in an informal discussion of the beginning of the evaluation, the question was raised as to whether the evaluators were not as naive as the planners in that they seemed to accept the program in its entirety, dreams and all.

"It is not our modus operandi to prejudge a program," I explained at that time. "There are some other evaluation groups in which evaluators listen to the unrealistic ideas and cut them off cold turkey. We don't do that. We don't throw cold water on a client's values. We start with their values. If it's a grand design, we go along with it. But as we work with a client, we ask more specific questions. We did it in TTT in three ways: through project management, OE management, and field training. We had them check their resources and check their processes. Once they had done that, they themselves began to take a more realistic stance."

While ERC's staff was working with OE management and its perception of reality, it was also tailoring its evaluation questions and goals within the reality of what could happen.

Stage I: Project Design

The ERC staff provided project staffs with design forms in order to facilitate processing of project design information and to achieve consistency of format. These forms required the project to employ the taxonomies in describing the activities, the participants, and the objectives of the project activities. They were designed with an eye toward developing a rational progression of project details and also with concern for transferring design data to a computerized information system.

Analysis of project designs

ERC's staff analyzed the designs for structural adequacy (how well our procedures were followed), and to see how well the projects met apparent TTT Program goals: identification, recruitment, and training of TTT's; parity representation; inclusion of the best of recent educational developments; institutionalization of improvements resulting from TTT projects and the multiplier effect. The purpose of the structural adequacy analysis was to determine how accurate evaluative inferences could be. If the individual taxonomy were to be used incorrectly, for example, a later count of the number of TTT's in the project, based on the taxonomy categories given, would likely be wrong.

To determine the structural adequacy of a project design, the classification of elements, participants, receptors, and change variables on the design forms were compared with narrative descriptions and the previous year's proposal. Where questions arose, extensive phone conversations and, in some cases, face-to-face meetings aided clarification.

The second phase of the preliminary analysis was to extract from the design the numbers of different types of people and institutions listed as participants for each element, information that would help the evaluators assess the achievement of the goals. These analyses were done for both the current year (1970-71) and the proposed year (1971-72). From the analyses it was determined that there were over 27,000 participants engaged in almost a thousand different activities.[9] Students and community people were most numerous (more than 17,000), but there were also more than 4,000 teachers, almost 5,000 teacher trainers, and no less than 1,500 TTT's, the people the program was originally aimed at including and changing.

The scope of activities, too, was enormous.[10] There were 233 courses involving 24 kinds of course work opportunities, and 230 practicum offerings in 33 different categories, ranging from encounter group sensitivity training, clinical experience, and living in an ethnic neighborhood different from that of one's origin. There were also eight teaching centers and nine resource centers focusing on media, bilingual education, and history. At the University of North Dakota, the New School, where the objectives had been the upgrading of less-than-degree teachers and the institution of open classrooms, merged with the university's School of Education to become the Center for Teaching and Learning. Under TTT it expanded its activities to include OE's Follow Through program for disadvantaged youth, and the Future Indian Teachers program.

Thirteen different projects had a total of twenty-seven courses in community and contemporary problems, including seven at the

University of Minnesota. There were fourteen math courses alone in five different projects, and several projects had large mathematics components consisting of several parts. In the mathematics methods class at Michigan State University the teacher candidates were required to plan a lesson for a small group of elementary children. "Subsequent observation of this lesson," according to codirectors Joseph Vellanti and Leland W. Dean, "was conducted by the same methods class professor. Later the professor and student evaluated the lesson together. Thus the tasks of teaching math methods to a student, then requiring that student to plan, implement, and evaluate the lesson, were carried out by one professor with each student in the methods class."[11]

Ten projects set up short, self-contained activities to train people who could not be reached otherwise. Fordham University, for example, hosted a conference on bilingual education that involved several two-year and four-year colleges; the University of Washington had a conference on Indian education and Southeastern Oklahoma State College hosted a conference for college and university English department chairmen and faculty.

To bring participants closer to the real world of the classroom, all projects included at least one learning experience in practicum and moved methods instruction to the schools. By integrating methods instruction with student teaching, school staffs were involved and had an opportunity to learn new techniques, giving TTT's and TT's an opportunity to sharpen their skills in a real situation. Again, at Michigan State, the professor teaching an elementary-reading methods course designed her classroom as a model classroom illustrating the implementation of an individualized reading program. The teacher trainees pursued learning activities within this methods class according to individual needs, pace, and interests, just as their pupils might function one day.[12]

Many schools planned curriculum projects in such fields as history, psychology, geometry, elementary education, and geography. In addition, several projects set up formal activities to develop new curricula for training teachers of TT's. Indiana University, for example, had an activity designed to develop an entirely new curriculum for elementary teachers.

Each project had some activities directed toward managing the project and coordinating it with other TTT projects, schools, or federal agencies. In line with program guidelines on parity, projects include representatives from the fields of education, liberal arts, the sciences and from the community and the school. Each group had its own special emphasis: for TTT's and TT's it was special courses, seminars, and management; for community participants, it was management and planning.

Emphasis on special course work and clinical experience was expected; however, it was interesting to note that participants also wanted to be part of planning and management. Whether it always worked or not, the concept of parity through involvement in decision making was taken seriously in all projects.

ERC's staff finally pulled together all of the information and wrote a short report on each project; in the reports TTT goals were discussed. These were the reports that were submitted to OE prior to the time that re-funding decisions were made. As the program design work was completed, it became apparent that local projects would not be re-funded. The grand experiment was already losing ground. There would be little opportunity to use discrepancy information in Stage II (program installation) or Stage III (program process) to aid local development work. For that reason feedback was given to project managers and their staffs without the benefit of comparing it with that of other projects. Two major outcomes of the Stage I evaluation work were the development of a design for the national TTT Program and the development of more sophisticated taxonomies for future reference.

Stage II: Installation

Selecting activities for evaluation

In November 1970 each project submitted its design, including a description of major elements or activities, the persons who were to be involved in each activity, and the changes (both individual and institutional) that were expected. It is not always possible to accomplish all the intentions of a program design; the ability to live up to the intentions can, however, either reduce or increase a program's success as more realistic plans are formulated. The major purpose of Stage II was to determine whether or not project intentions had become realities: Had major project activities been implemented? Had project personnel been recruited and retained in accord with the plan? What were the racial-ethnic and other characteristics of persons involved in the TTT Program? (This question was the result of special interests expressed by OE staff.)

Because there were hundreds of elements in the TTT Program, it was impossible to collect information on all of them. Rather, the evaluators selected a sample of sixty-six activities (two per project) on the basis of focus on major TTT Program goals, and varied types of persons involved. Each element had to fulfill four criteria, determined through mutual agreement with project officers on the TTT Program staff. They were:

— that the element be identified as a practicum;
— that the element be intended to function at that point in time;
— that the element involved cover, wherever possible, the range of types of TTT participants including education TTT's, TT's and T's; arts and sciences TTT's, TT's, and T's; school TTT's, TT's, and T's; and community persons; and
— that the element be judged important to the attainment of TTT Program goals by program management staff and ERC staff.

TTT was also developmental, not prescriptive. As a result, projects revised, dropped, and added objectives and elements between fall 1970 and June 1971. It was essential that ERC's staff capture all of these program changes as they occurred. Further, rather than adhering to the accomplishment of original project objectives, evaluators had to collect data on the attainment of new as well as old objectives as they emerged over time. Our staff had to establish a credible and low-cost method for estimating the attainment of hundreds of diverse project intentions to change individuals and institutions. Initially, the ERC staff depended on local staff to indicate which objectives were reached, but verification had to go beyond self-interested reports. This later resulted in on-site visits by highly skilled evaluators.

Installation Measurement Instrument 1

During the winter of 1970-71 ERC's staff developed Installation Measurement Instrument 1 to answer many sets of questions.[13] It focused on the ability of the projects to implement activities and to recruit and maintain persons. Each project director was sent copies of the instrument and a letter that explained its purpose. The ERC evaluators asked the project directors to return the instrument by February 22, 1971, but some, even after repeated phone calls, delayed until mid-April. Three of the thirty-three projects never did forward all of the information required.

The results of this first instrument showed that projects were moving from the university out into the community. The largest increases in terms of personnel occurred among public school-teachers and administrators, undergraduate students and community people. These changes may indicate not only an increased focus of TTT projects on the nonuniversity setting, but also an increased success in developing a sphere of influence in the nonuniversity realm. And the people involved were predominantly white, followed in number by blacks, Puerto Ricans, Mexican-Americans, American Indians and Orientals.[14]

It would appear from this data that local TTT directors did an admirable job of installing their projects, with the possible serious exceptions of not involving as many TTT's as expected, nor as many minority participants as might have been expected in a program that, after all, emphasized the training of teachers for children from disadvantaged neighborhoods. It appeared, from the results of the first Installation Measurement Instrument, that expected project operations were well underway, but what about the more subtle thrust of the TTT Program? Were education professors, liberal arts professors, school staff, school administrators, and community people working together in the field in accordance with the TTT idea?

The TTT Program intended that there be parity at the local level of involvement between the personnel and institutions training teachers and the trainers of teachers. The adequacy of this balance could not, of course, be judged in any prescribed way. Rather, the participants themselves had to determine and judge what optimum cooperation meant. To examine these perceptions, a number of questions were asked: What institutions did participants see as involved? How equal was institutional participation? How were various individuals to be affected? What effects would there be on various institutions? To answer these questions, ERC's staff of evaluators examined Installation Measurement Instrument 2.[15]

From this instrument, the ERC evaluators determined that the participants surveyed felt that, as institutions, schools and universities were deeply involved; the community was not.[16] As individuals, respondents felt that personnel in public schools and schools of education were truly involved; members of arts and sciences departments and community persons were far less involved. Similarly, when participants were asked whether these four groups shared equally in discussion, in control and direction of an activity, and in evaluation of an activity, university professors were seen as being dominant. From this data, it appeared that the program was successful in achieving school-university parity, but not successful in achieving parity with people in schools of arts and sciences and community persons.[17]

The second instrument also determined that the TTT Program would have its greatest effect on education professors: what they taught, their teaching methods, and their relationships with students, school people, and liberal arts professors. Respondents even felt their relationships with the community would improve.

In addition, although the persons involved thought the activities were intended to have some effect on school and university personnel, few felt that the activities were intended to change the role of community persons. The statistics also showed that little change was anticipated with the gatekeepers: less than half of the respondents felt that the activities were intended to affect university professors in the arts and sciences or university administrators.[18]

Lastly, the second instrument determined that most respondents felt that the activities were intended to affect public schools or school districts, also colleges and graduate schools. Few, however, felt that the activities were designed to affect state education agencies, teacher organizations, or parity boards.[19]

In order to get at least an indirect estimate of the multiplier effect of the activities, persons involved were asked if they intended, as a result of each activity, to go back and effect changes in their home institutions and, if so, what institutions they intended to change. Of the 734 respondents, 435 answered yes, and 423 named the institution. Most intended to change either the graduate institution or its components, or the local education agency or its components. Only 6 percent named a four-year college, and less than a single percent intended to change the community. The last of these percentages undoubtedly reflects the small number of community persons who returned the instrument. If 59 percent of the persons involved in the TTT Program actually did go back and bring about some change in their home institutions, the program would have been very effective, indeed.

Stage III: Process

Far-flung and complex projects

When they reached Stage III, the evaluators realized it would have to be deferred, for it required a comprehensive study of thirty-three[20] far-flung, highly complex projects. Such an effort would have consumed more resources than were available for the entire evaluation. The evaluators decided to go directly to Stage IV, which would not only determine what projects had produced, but would also compare them and rank them. That way they would identify a few projects in which the considerable expenditure required to study Stage III would most likely be fruitful. ERC's staff would then be able to conduct a limited version of Stage III in those selected sites.

Federal management activities impossible to evaluate

Description of performance, or discrepancy information regarding Stage III, was not attempted at the federal level. Normally this would have involved OE staff descriptions of that part of their work that was essential to the control of resources, the monitoring of project activities, the collection of data on their management performance, and discrepancy reports. Changes in staff (three directors in two-and-a-half years) and in policy concerning TTT, however, were so rapid as to preclude meaningful evaluation of TTT management functions at the federal level.

Stage IV: Product

Phase 1, Perception of trainees and participants

Beginning in May 1971, the first phase of the fourth stage of evaluation work—collecting evidence of local project success—was undertaken. The ERC staff developed a comprehensive instrument, consisting of seventeen scales, that focused on the attainment of major program goals deduced from project designs developed during the preceding year.[21] Each scale permitted the comparison of at least three perspectives on the question at issue.

Different forms of the instrument were developed for each of five respondent groups: faculty, trainees, school staff persons, school administrators, and community persons. An attempt was made to remove "jargon" and tailor response procedures to each group. The instrument was eventually sent to 1,922 participants by direct mail.

An initial "tryout" mailing did not include return postage and had a low response rate. When return postage was included, the percentage of returns went up, but most of the additional returned instruments were from persons who said that they were "not involved' in TTT. (They must have felt that, as long as there was a stamp on the envelope, they might as well return it.) A number of explanations of this phenomenon might be advanced. "Involved" may be an ill-defined term. The staff at ERC assumed that this meant people who were directly involved and on whom the TTT Program had been intended to have an effect. In some projects, persons may have been involved, but they were unaware that they were involved. A few project directors mentioned that at times it was not "political" to inform people that they were involved in TTT. In one project the activity chosen was actually quite separated from the TTT project. In another project, two activities (conferences) of extremely short duration were selected. A final explanation, perhaps, might be that project directors did not know who was really involved in these activities.

By November 1971 the staff at ERC began looking for answers to some of their questions. For example, were training objectives being realized:

- in the areas of curriculum design and development?
- with regard to supervision and educational program evaluation?
- in the areas of knowledge of learning and child development?
- in community factors and skills in teaching?
- in attitudes toward minority groups?
- in parity concept, institutional cooperation, and education research?
- and likely to be institutionalized?

Participants' Perspective on Attainment of TTT Goals

The TTT participants themselves hoped to bring about many changes through TTT programs. Cutting across four major categories of knowledge, skill, attitudes, and relations with others, their list included the following areas: relationships between students and faculty; individual teaching; recognizing the problems of ethnic groups, whether blacks, Chicanos, or the poverty-ridden people of Appalachia; the use of sophisticated aids, such as videotape and microteaching in the classroom; receptivity to change; and a cooperative relationship between professors of education and members of public school staffs.[22]

The major change all participants desired was the kind of knowledge that would make for better classroom performance. In the category of skills, public schoolteachers wanted more skill in classroom work and communications; administrators and university personnel wanted more skill in management, supervision, curriculum and research. All participants desired a change in attitude toward the other groups involved—education professors toward school and community, liberal arts faculty and community toward the teaching profession.

The primary purpose of each project was to restructure both formal and informal relationships between education faculty, arts and sciences faculty, school personnel, and the community-at-large. It was hoped that bringing these groups closer would result in an interchange of ideas and an improvement in the educational system. The data indicated that courses and clinical experiences produced changes in knowledge and skills, but a more surprising conclusion was that TTT projects, through participation in management and planning activities, tended to change attitudes and relationships.

Program participants also desired institutional changes and placed major emphasis on improving the relationship between university, school, and community, on introducing revised courses, on improving internal communications within the project, and on providing practicums for TTT participants or in-service training for school personnel.[23]

There was considerable evidence that almost all of the major parties to the TTT Program reacted positively and agreed as to specific benefits of TTT at the local level. The exceptions were:
- students did not perceive benefits in the research training they received;
- community, school personnel, and university professors disagreed as to the extent to which parity, or equal participation in local projects, had been achieved.
- community, school personnel, and university professors disagreed as to the extent to which changes in general institutional climate had been realized.

The evidence from this survey pertaining to community participation in TTT and to perception and realization of change as a result of the program confirmed the negative findings the ERC evaluators had found in their analysis of the earlier installation measurement instrument. In most other sectors, TTT's intended goals were generally endorsed by staffs, trainees, and other participants.

The following conclusions were drawn from examination of ERC's data on participants' perceptions and attitudes toward TTT's national goals:

Goal one: New roles. Many new roles were learned in TTT projects, and participants were generally satisfied that they learned the skills and knowledge essential to the conduct of these roles. In the areas of "child learning," trainees felt more instruction should be provided in a practicum setting. A variety of things about the community, the student, and the factors in his environment that affect his style and ability to learn were taught in the program, and all parties felt that this information was often useful and would improve the quality of interaction between producers (teachers) and consumers (public school students) of education. Trainees, however, felt that there was room for more and improved instruction in this area.

Goal two: Parity. It may be inferred from the impact questionnaire that the low response rate of the "community" sector showed there was less involvement and cooperation here than in other sectors. Analyses of selected responses of those community participants who did answer the questionnaire bear this out. Neither the community nor other groups believed that the community would continue to be meaningfully involved in the training of teachers; nor did they believe that they had an equal voice in making decisions affecting teacher training. Further, there was a clear, positive relationship between the decision-making power of the respondent, as conferred by his institutional role, and his perception that all parties to a local project had equal influence. Community members saw themselves at a clear disadvantage compared with other parties to teacher training.

Goal three: New educational methods. Most of the participants in TTT felt that global changes in teacher training occurred as a result of the TTT Program. Faculty members felt this most strongly, and public school staffs, somewhat less so, with the opinions of trainees and school administrators falling between the two. Community members, however, felt much less positive about such change taking place. Apparently those closest to the university, and the training of undergraduate and graduate students, see much institutional change while those farthest away see little.

Goal four: Institutionalization. When asked about specific changes in institutional policies or practices, all five referent groups agreed that at least one significant institutional change had occurred. The fact that "community" respondents agree with university professors on this matter suggests that the community's negative (or less than positive) belief about the institutional effects of TTT may be part of a general attitude toward the universities in ability to change.[24]

Goal five: Multiplier effect. There was considerable evidence that trainees were enthusiastic in their belief that they would be able to secure jobs and eventually have a significant impact on the institutions that employed them because of the training they received. In short, they felt like, and intended to be, change agents.

Phase 2, Evidence of goal attainment

At the completion of the first phase, project directors were asked to relate the attainment of these goals to project activities. This twelve-step procedure became Phase 2. It was during this period of data collection that ERC's staff encountered additional problems, the most important being the unavailability of "hard" data to support project successes. It was one thing for them to say they had been successful. ERC's evaluators demanded proof. It was this problem that led to the cross-project analysis.

CROSS-PROJECT ANALYSIS

Of major interest to both OE officials and ERC evaluators was disinterested, verified evidence of project success. Only on-site visitors could come close to satisfying this ultimate criterion. Since only limited funds were available, it was decided that they should be used to investigate those sites in which there was a preponderance of convincing documentary evidence that TTT outcomes of consequence had occurred. Then Stage III—site visits—could be conducted to verify outcomes and explore the reasons for project success. The method ERC evaluators used to compile this evidence was cross-project analysis.[25] This made it possible to determine, at least from the viewpoint of participants, whether project processes related to the goals of the TTT Program were actually underway. Nine criteria, which further defined the five program goals, were developed. They enabled the evaluators to describe the program at the projects, determine the project's ability to initiate major activities, and assess the opinions and feelings of participants about the meaningfulness of project processes.

Cross-project analysis also determined differences among projects as to the type and validity of evidence submitted; it analyzed project differences with regard to clarity of the change statements, emphasis toward major TTT goals, current educational practices, types of institutional changes, types of institutions changed, and types of individuals changed; it compared criteria validating the evidence in support of the change. Supporting evidence was examined from several perspectives, and the final set of interproject comparisons was made only for those changes where there was strong supporting evidence. Then projects were compared based on their orientation to the TTT goals.

What was accomplished by this extensive analytic work? First and foremost was a way of estimating a local project's attainment in terms of its own goals and its own evidence. Though projects might overstate their accomplishments, on the one hand, cross-project analysis would reveal small, local successes that might be overlooked, on the other. It was also possible to determine where projects had fallen short of their important intended outcomes, if they showed no evidence of success. Further, where evidence submitted by a project was not credible, some presumption of doubt as to attainment could be entertained.

The application of these criteria to twenty-nine eligible projects resulted in rankings on forty-nine variables. After discussion with OE staff, these variables were weighed, and one additional variable of importance, geographic location, was added. The seven highest-ranked projects were then selected for site visits, and Stage III, in-depth case studies and site visits, could begin.

TWO

CASE STUDIES

The final strategic steps in the evaluation of TTT, site visitations and in-depth field work, elicited possible causal relationships among project success, conditions, and experimental variables. The sites selected for visitations were Michigan State University, the University of Nebraska, Clark University, Appalachian State University, Northwestern University, the City University of New York, and Texas Teacher Center University. While the team of experts made their site visits and prepared their reports, ERC evaluators prepared their in-depth case studies.

Clark University had the distinction of being that project where interdisciplinary cooperation reached its highest point. This goal, identified in Chapter 1 as "the focus of projects on the identification, recruitment, and training of TTT's," was only minimally achieved in other projects. Chapter 3 is an overview of the Clark University project, with emphasis on achieving the goal of interdisciplinary cooperation.

City University of New York (CUNY) is the major teacher-training institution for New York City; 50 percent of its graduates become inner-city teachers or enter related educational fields. TTT was introduced at CUNY in an attempt to deal with the problems then facing inner-city teaching and teacher training. One notorious problem was the proximity and strength of a variety of political factions and the inability of educational institutions (public schools, colleges, and universities) to deal with these forces constructively. As a main goal, therefore, the CUNY-TTT project strove to create—with surrounding communities in general and poverty communities in particular—continual joint parity participation in teacher education: "an equal sharing in both the production and consumption of educational 'goods.' " Chapter 4 examines the TTT project at CUNY.

3
CLARK UNIVERSITY

The TTT project at Clark University in Worcester, Massachusetts, had one major purpose during its four years of operation: training new Ph.D.'s in geography, history, and economics. Doctorates were to be taken within the disciplines, but experiences and courses that would give the candidate considerable knowledge of the problems of teaching and the schools were to be included in the program. It was envisioned that, upon completion of their work, the candidates would take employment at institutions where substantial numbers of teachers and teacher trainers are prepared; they would then be in a position to advance both new ideas in their subject matter and new methods for teaching. As a result of intense experiences in the schools during their doctoral training, these TTT-Ph.D's would have credibility with teachers and students preparing to be teachers.

These TTT-Ph.D's, having completed all requirements for the "traditional" doctorate, would also enjoy full "credibility" within their disciplines and be able to influence colleagues toward more involvement with education and the schools. This ambitious undertaking rested on some key assumptions:

— the candidates would accept the program which required Ph.D.

Excerpted from the in-depth case study by ERC evaluator, Frank Morra, Jr.

work in the disciplines along with intensive experiences in education;
- the faculty would be willing to participate enthusiastically in the coordination of discipline- and education-related activity to make the program feasible;
- the educational community would open itself to the TTT-Ph.D. candidates to permit them to gain the experiences necessary for their work; and
- the Ph.D. degree itself is the currently accepted requirement for employment in the disciplines, and, with the existent surplus of Ph.D.'s it was assumed that any new degree, such as a Doctor of Arts in Teaching, would not allow the candidates access to positions that would permit them to act as agents of change.

This description makes the Clark project seem heavily university-oriented; the reverse, in fact, proved true. In order to place the candidates in situations where they could gain meaningful experiences, the university had to open itself to the schools and the community. The result of the program was that the Worcester-Clark project employed an organizational structure that facilitated experimentation while keeping to its initial purpose. At the same time, the organization always included persons with the ability to interrelate knowledge and trends at the national, university, and local levels. Within this structure, roles were intentionally "blurred" to permit free and open interchange. The result of these three factors was a structure remarkably similar to a living organism. There were two basic roles: *homeostatic,* which kept the project moving toward its stated goals; and *evolutionary,* which sought modifications to suit changing needs. The project grew within this structure and gained recognition at every level: at the national level it consistently ranked among the top TTT projects; within the university it gained support from many related departments; in the schools it was recognized as a source of exciting and innovative curricula. Much of the responsibility for this can be directly traced to efficient management coupled with a sensitive response to needs at the three levels. Richard B. Ford, a codirector of the project and a professor of history at Clark, primarily performed the former role; Irving Schwartz, from the Worcester school system, the latter one. Not all projects achieved the kind of creative tension wrought by these two men and their staffs, but, because of it, Clark may have been more successful than most participating institutions.

MAJOR PRODUCTS OF THE WORCESTER-CLARK PROJECT

Seven "products" were selected from the work of the Clark project during the years from 1969 to 1973. The criteria used were:

- the product had to stem directly from TTT work (that is, it had to be attributed to TTT funding);
- the product had to have been developed and refined over a period of years so that it could be considered "proven";
- the product had to evidence integration of scholarship and action research; and
- the product had to be in existence, so that it could be viewed directly and allow the viewer to form his own opinion.

Three of the products stem from work done as a part of the "TTT core." Each met the four criteria above, and, in addition, each formed the basis for a dissertation prepared by a TTT fellow. The remaining four products are examples of curricula and instructional arrangements that build directly on work done by TTT fellows and faculty in the educational community.

THE TTT-PH.D.'S

There were a total of seventeen TTT fellows. Of these, thirteen have left Clark to work in other institutions, ten at the university level and three in the public schools. These fellows were trained in two groups: the first entered in the summer of 1969; the second, in the summer of 1970. There were history and geography fellows in both groups, but economics was represented only in the second.

These TTT-Ph.D.'s are the principal products of the Worcester-Clark project. It is difficult to speak of people as a product; we would rather view them as the seeds of TTT. In a sense, the efforts of the four years covered in this report can be viewed as preparing the fellows to go out into the educational world and "be fruitful and multiply." At present, we can only examine the flowering and cross-pollination that produced the TTT-Ph.D.'s. Most of them began work at their job sites in September 1973, so we can also begin to describe the ground upon which these seeds fell. Any other effects are, unfortunately, beyond the scope of our investigation.

At present, thirteen fellows are involved in teacher training (two are cooperating teachers in the schools). The college-based people have an opportunity to influence from ten to thirty undergraduates per semester. These fellows, as a group, may be estimated to influence around 110 to 330 students per semester. Once more data is available, it may be possible to use a sophisticated epidemiological model to estimate the diffusion of effects of these TTT fellows.

WORK RESULTING FROM THE "TTT CORE"

Three projects were born in the interdisciplinary seminar that brought the TTT fellows together to design new methods for integrating social science theory with educational practice.

Autobiography Seminar

The fellows evolved a seminar based on the creating and sharing of the autobiographies of the participants, which served two broad goals. First, relations among participants were considerably eased and enriched, enabling professors, graduate students, and students and classroom teachers whom they met later, to break down social barriers and establish new bonds of trust and friendship. Second, it taught the students basic principles of social science methodology: that material is selected subjectively as well as objectively and that a person telling his life story faces the same problems of choosing items from a phenomenological field that a scientist faces.

The initial tryout of the autobiography seminar proved to be quite successful. As one student teacher said: "The important thing about meeting [my cooperating teacher] and becoming friends was that once I went into the school and had any problems, there was immediate support available . . . we became a team working on a problem instead of separate individuals."[1]

The process proved so successful that it became an organized part of the project, was made an official part of the Clark curriculum, and is now ready to be disseminated elsewhere.

Curriculum in Ethnic-Urban Migrations

This work dealt with the history of Italian, Irish, Jewish and black minorities as they migrated to America and its cities, treating the stresses to which the emigrants were subjected and the subsequent accommodation. The inquiry combined both scholarly research and activity in the field, with the city of Worcester serving as a laboratory. A model of the social, economic, and political structure of the city was developed and used as an analytical framework for their work. In keeping with the philosophy of TTT, the group sought to extend this method into teaching.

In particular, they sought to involve the community, that is, people actually from the various ethnic groups, in the design of the course by working with the Worcester Career Opportunities Program, a program that brings disadvantaged persons into the schools as paraprofessional aides and helps them earn degrees and certification while they work. The course in ethnic-urban migrations was taught on an experimental basis to fifteen participants in the Career Opportunity Program, several of whom had already been connected with TTT on planning boards or in summer workshops. Participants received college credit for the course, and, as prospective teachers, they assisted the TTT fellows in evaluating the course.

The experiment was successfully completed and led to the development of a course implemented at Worcester State College. The work at the college represented the flowering of Dr. Vincent Powers' work in ethnic-urban migrations, and the academic year 1972-73 was set aside as a planning year to develop a four-year sequence in "urban affairs." The program derived quite a few features from TTT, such as interdisciplinary background course work in history, sociology, and geography, plus a working internship. There were four tracks—education, law enforcement, planning, and welfare—in the program headed by Powers. This is a good example of TTT-type inquiry, and the research, which is interesting, produced dissertation topics for several fellows. Without TTT it might have ended there, but the TTT emphasis on educational applications led to an investigation of the curricular implications of such work.

In-service Training Program in the Use of Local Resources

This was a series of workshops to build skills in expanding the classroom to use community resources in education. An example might be the integration of a visit to a steel mill with science lessons or local architecture with state and local history. Again, the work grew out of the research interests of three TTT fellows. It has since been tested at Montpelier, Vermont, and Norfolk, Virginia, and it has led Clark University and the Old Sturbridge Village Association to cooperate in developing workshops for using museum resources in the classroom.

WORK RESULTING FROM EXPERIENCES
IN THE EDUCATIONAL COMMUNITY

The following projects represent extensions of TTT ideas into the community. All of them have been institutionalized (that is, they are not dependent on TTT or other federal funding). They illustrate that the Clark TTT project could, and did, make a significant contribution to the educational community even though the overall purpose was the training of TTT Ph.D.'s.

Independent Studies Program at Tahanto High School

Several TTT fellows worked closely with a selected group of students to guide them in independent study. For example, each student did a research paper and each group made a presentation. The spirit of the papers generally showed that the students went out into the world to dig out information about a topic of interest to them. Given this rough start, the groundwork was laid for scholarly touches to be added later.

During the summer of 1970 a group of students and Vincent Keane (the program's leader) wrote a proposal entitled "School as a Microcosm of Society," which was funded for the sum of $1,800 under ESEA, Title III, as a special purpose grant. The money was used to buy videotape equipment in order to produce tapes of activities such as class meetings and city council meetings. These recordings were subjected to analysis using Edward Fenton's *Comparative Political Systems*.[2] This work developed five concepts: leadership, ideology, institutions, citizenship, and decision making. Thus, the students would have experience in analyzing political systems that are both familiar and unfamiliar to them.

The Tahanto activity showed the TTT multiplier effect in action: a "seed" planted during 1969-70 was able to gain independent funding. In addition, two other teachers besides Vincent Keane became involved with the work. As Keane explained, "During my first year I felt threatened and unreceived. Then [another teacher] became involved and I felt more support . . . other people have expressed interest . . . there is [slow] movement toward some kind of change."[3]

The independent studies program has continued along these lines since 1971 and is now an integral part of the Tahanto curriculum.

Doherty Memorial High School Psychology Course

Several TTT fellows and faculty were able to assist a secondary school teacher in realizing his dream of creating a course that would make the ideas of psychology, a science usually left out of school curricula, available to his students. The course had four units aimed at confronting the major problems of youth (at the time): the generation gap, alienation, and the search for meaning in life.

The first unit focused primarily on the generation gap by exploring the political, social, and economic events of the years from 1930 to 1940. Through the use of audiovisual materials, periodicals, and newspapers, it was possible to re-create a portion of the social forces that shaped their parents' generation. In his evaluation of the unit, Robert George said, "In addition to making the students' past more meaningful for them, the young people were afforded an opportunity to see their parents as people for the first time."[4] The second unit, a survey of adolescence in Samoan, French, Russian, Japanese, and American societies, was intended to demonstrate that social conflict is part of maturation in any society, and the third one was devoted to the physiological aspects of adolescence, treating growth, intelligence, and socialization from a more or less traditional framework.

Unit four dealt with identity formation, using the theories of Erik Erikson, and contrasted existential psychology with behaviorist and Freudian positions. The aim was to give the student an opportunity to reflect on his philosophy of life—to give him a framework on which to hang questions about the meaning of life.

The four units comprise a psychology course that is tailor-made for adolescents. In the words of Robert George, his course was "a vehicle which will aid students in uniting the forgotten self of yesterday, the bewildering self of today, and the unpredictable self of tomorrow." The course has been a regular fixture at Doherty Memorial High School since the fall of 1970.

The Clark University Training Complex

Clark University has no undergraduate department of education. In spite of this, it produces eight to ten highly competent public school teachers every year. This is accomplished through what is called the

Training Complex, which is basically a series of seminars that permits an undergraduate majoring in a noneducation discipline to receive gradually increasing experiences in the schools, finally culminating in a semester-long internship experience. The Training Complex arrangement benefits all parties concerned:

— undergraduates gradually gain experiences that permit them to decide upon their desire to enter the profession early in their academic career, rather than waiting until their senior year before they actually face children in the classroom, which occurs in traditional programs;

— public school teachers benefit in that they are involved with undergraduates over a protracted period as teacher trainers, a role they are often denied except for a brief period as a cooperating teacher, and in that they receive additional help in the classroom from interning undergraduates;

— the university receives an added perspective from the public schools, and there is an opportunity to do on-site research in the schools.

The program has been in operation for two years and has received favorable comment from all levels. A sophomore felt that he had "come to understand my reactions to people a lot better . . . . I can deal with the pressures I find academia placing on me."[5] An apprentice teacher commented that, through the Training Complex experience, his "tolerance has increased . . . you begin to concern yourself with *their* [students'] needs, *their* frustrations; you begin to put yourself in their place, rather than setting the priorities on your own and going on an ego trip at the expense of what they're concerned with."[6] And, a TTT fellow saw the overall interactions in the Training Complex as involving "a diverse population and each person can bring a different set of skills, different perceptions, different insights . . . a freshman's idea of what it's like to be a teacher comes from the other side of the desk, what it's like to be a student."[7] People reacted to the diversity of participants and the multiplicity of interactions. The Training Complex was perhaps best summarized by Robert Morrill, assistant to the director:

I think that the [Training Complex model] in terms of student teaching [undergraduates going into the public schools] is so obvious that I wonder why it hadn't been thought of or put into effect before . . . . You get a team of potential resources that can be pretty effective . . . .The reason is that you have a cooperating teacher and a student teacher who have spent some time together and have gotten all kinds of issues resolved between them, so they know each other when they begin working.[8]

The Training Complex, a "downward" extension of the TTT-Ph.D. program, took students completing their training in liberal arts and offered them "add-on" course work and educational experiences so that they could gain certification as teachers. Through this approach, TTT was able to inject new personnel, ideas, and roles into the schools.

The Adjunct School

The Adjunct School was set up to offer an alternative to traditional forms of instruction. This learning community, different and apart from that of the regular high school, blurred the usual roles of students and teachers. The school was planned by a committee that included all parties concerned with the work: Clark University faculty, school administrators and teachers, Training Complex teachers and students, TTT fellows, and high school students. The program, according to a research study, attracted staff members who had a deep concern for the "whole" student, that is, for both affective and cognitive growth. It also showed the progress of several "problem students" from alienation and hostility to interest and creativity. On the other side of the coin, the study showed weak points in the structure: low attendance, lack of serious reflection on issues by some students, and decreased participation by teachers in the regular North High program.

The school eventually, however, won the commitment and support of the Worcester school system and has become one of the parts of TTT institutionalized into the schools. In the opinion of Dr. Ralph Tyler,

The Adjunct School . . . and the autobiography seminar seemed to me the most significant of the strategies employed by Clark University in its TTT program. In my talks with the undergraduate students and with the high school participants, I found excitement and thoughtful reflection on the role and values of the Adjunct School. It has captured the interest and energy of the undergraduates as well as the high school students and the school personnel involved. The undergraduates said that, as a result of this experience, they did not feel that they were expected merely to conform to prevailing school practices, and instead, their imaginations appeared to be stimulated, and they were enthusiastic about developing new approaches to meet school problems.

The success of this school seemed to be greatly dependent upon the excellent cooperation between the school staff and the project leaders. Both groups were greatly interested both in the success of the Adjunct School and in understanding its dynamics. The relationship appeared to be an open and cordial one. Hence the undergraduates found no significant barriers to their participation and they were treated as colleagues in the enterprise. The success of the school was greatly enhanced by the success in getting the active participation of the high school students enrolled.[9]

"Although the evaluation of these many community activities is, at best, subjective," codirector Richard Ford wrote in a letter to the center in 1974, "I think it added a new dimension to the disciplines, at least in the minds of our TTT graduate students, which they will carry with them into the undergraduate classrooms where they are presently teaching." A chronological examination of the Clark project helps to show how such programs are created and what the problems are in educational innovation.

The first year: 1969-70. The TTT project used the first year to get itself together, both by reexamining the Ph.D. program on its own and by making contact with others in the Worcester educational community. As a part of the latter effort, a summer workshop was held, which resulted in the development of tentative bridges between Clark and two Worcester schools (Burncoat Junior High School and Tahanto Regional High School) and two local teacher-training institutions (Fitchburg State College and Leicester Junior College).

During the academic year professors from the participating disciplines engaged in serious and extended debate about the TTT-Ph.D. program. Since the project depended on federal money, it was difficult to persuade many faculty members to move from scholarly research into education, or to "compromise" any of the requirements for the Ph.D. program by allowing candidates to substitute experiences in the public schools as a requirement. There were many arguments during Clark faculty meetings, and only after lengthy debate was a three-point plan finally established for the graduate program: the candidate had to perform successfully in course work within his discipline as well as in a special set of "TTT core" courses; the candidate had to be examined in four areas, three from the discipline and one from an interdisciplinary area; the candidate's dissertation had to show both competence in the discipline and improvement in the teaching of that discipline. In other words, a TTT-Ph.D. candidate had to meet all of the requirements for the traditional degree, and, in addition, gain educational experience in the classroom.

Within the "TTT core," a social science seminar provided the setting for the presentation of general social science theory by faculty from a wide variety of departments. An attempt to involve TTT fellows in active research got off to a good start, but it was not completed because of the student unrest following the Cambodian invasion and the killings at Kent State University in the spring of 1970.

Problems relating to the gap that existed between the university and the schools produced certain frustrations at Burncoat, Leicester, and Fitchburg State. (A successful independent studies program was, however, installed at Tahanto). Out of these problems TTT leaders evolved the concept of "neutral ground" as a guide to institutional relations. Gaps, such as the perceived difference in status between high school teachers and university professors, were bridged by emphasizing a horizontal rather than a hierarchical relationship, thus stressing an area where differences could be blurred and collegiality sought.

The second year: 1970-71. During the summer of 1970 three workshops were held to design new courses for the coming year: geography for newly arrived Spanish students, high school psychology, and an alternative to ancient history as the ninth-grade social studies requirement. Another workshop emphasizing "interaction" continued to promote ties between the university and the local schools. Summer signaled a large rise in the status of the TTT project within the Worcester schools; in fact, three of the workshop activities were begun at the initiative of the schools themselves.

During the academic year, the "TTT core" was highlighted by the development of four major innovations in the social science seminar and the urban migrations curriculum, all of which stemmed from the educational experiences of the participants during the previous year and which were translated from experience to curriculum, a process that proved to be one of the most valuable TTT contributions. During this same year the TTT project involved its fellows in a wide variety of schoolroom experiences: participants were able to rescue a disastrous course in law enforcement at Chandler Junior High by transferring it to Worcester State; an urban migrations course used community people as a valuable resource; the Tahanto independent studies program continued to be successful, gaining Title III funds for videotape equipment; and the psychology course was received with great enthusiasm at Doherty Memorial High School. One of the TTT professors summarized the sophomore year of the Clark project this way: "If you want creative, free people, you have to give them those kinds of experiences in which they are forced to demonstrate and practice those skills of looking for alternatives and making the best of situations." This the project certainly did.

The third year: 1971-72. During the summer TTT held six workshops, three of which were for the further refinement of topics that had originated in the social science seminar of the previous year. These workshops attempted to translate new ideas and methods into the school curricula, a venture showing TTT creativity at its best. The other three were to develop two broad curricular innovations: redesigning the whole social science curriculum in two Worcester schools (McKay Laboratory School and Elm Park School) and using the resources of the museum at Old Sturbridge Village. Of these efforts, only the work at Old Sturbridge Village flourished. The failure at McKay, once the school year started, was due to bad institutional relations that predated TTT; the failure at Elm Park was the result of a difference in educational philosophy between two members of the TTT staff.

During the school year the Clark TTT graduate program came to maturity. Two waves of graduate students had completed their required courses and were busy completing their exams, internships, and dissertations. The rash of new ideas ceased, for the most part, and the emphasis turned toward consolidation. Creative work was still, however, being done at another level—in the undergraduate Training Complex, where TTT ideas were adopted, examined, and expanded. Although much TTT work this year was simply a continuation of earlier years, there were two new developments. At Doherty Memorial High School, and later at Fitchburgh State College, TTT participants began plans for an alternative to the social studies requirement which was called SITE (for Students Interested in Their Education), a program that involved the participation of prominent figures in the Worcester community, including lawyers, doctors, educators, and politicians. And, thanks to a series of visits to Poland by some of the geographers in the program, new cooperative work was undertaken on an international scale, resulting in a monograph, two dissertations, and an undergraduate honors project.

The work of this year was characterized by increased recognition from educators and the community, projects with greater scope and responsibility, and integration of past knowledge into coherent wholes—all characteristics of the mature TTT project at Clark University.

The fourth year: 1972-73. At the beginning of this year the project was notified that the national TTT Program was being terminated and that no more federal funds would be available beyond December 1973. The project, as a result, began to wind down its operations and to concentrate on institutionalizing its benefits with other funds. Summer workshops were concentrated, for the most part, on developing the Adjunct School in an attempt to pull together the many different themes that had developed over the past three years of TTT and also to draw the Training Complex closer to TTT efforts. There were quite a few growing pains during the summer, to be sure—chiefly around issues of curriculum, leadership, and evaluation, as with most experimental programs—but by the end of the summer, the Adjunct School had been planned and was to become the major focus of TTT efforts in the final year.

Inevitably problems arose, and, for the most part, were met. The initial design called for a school population representative of the general North High population, which the Adjunct School was to serve, and, when this did not happen, some questions about the school's purpose and identity were raised. The design also called for the creation of a "learning community" of teachers and students within the Adjunct School, but this tended to isolate the Adjunct School from the main school and to create unfortunate tensions between the two. On top of that, the Adjunct School ended up with a skeleton staff of two public school teachers when six were called for originally. In spite of its problems, most observers agreed that the Adjunct experiment proved successful, offering interesting new courses and building a challenging "living" curriculum.

Other work, of course, also went on. TTT fellows continued to operate in the school. One, for example, did some imaginative things as liaison between the Training Complex and the Adjunct School, while another contributed to staff development courses for the Worcester school system. And the SITE project went ahead full steam at Doherty Memorial High School, where it was becoming increasingly popular.

The Clark University TTT project, in four brief but adventuresome years, proved an exciting, albeit limited, experience. Its primary job, training a new kind of Ph.D. who could bring the liberal arts together with education to improve the schools, was realized. Along the way, TTT participants also learned the necessity of accepting public school teachers and administrators as coequals in planning and executing projects, and of involving the entire educational community in the graduate-training process.

The products of this work reflect this involvement. Dissertations at Clark are not abstract volumes gathering dust in the library; they have been turned into actual curricular developments at both the college and the school levels. The work of the TTT-Ph.D. fellows shows the scholarship necessary to work within chosen disciplines, but it also shows the added and equally important dimension: an understanding of and a dedication to teaching. Within the local school system new courses and techniques have been adopted, and still more will be generated through the sustained efforts of the Training Complex and the Adjunct School, which now enjoy local funding. Of course, the scope of the activities has been reduced with the demise of TTT as a national program, but the major ideas generated by TTT have survived. The Clark project, despite flaws, emulated the basic spirit of TTT at its best: it wrought a small revolution within university walls and then moved out from there to touch the community and to set a model for interinstitutional cooperation.

4

CITY UNIVERSITY
OF NEW YORK

New York, a city of approximately eight million people, has changed radically in the past few decades. The city once had numerous upper- and lower-middle-class families, as well as substantial numbers of transient, upwardly mobile immigrants. The new inhabitants, coming from areas in the South or territories such as Puerto Rico, are non-white with lower incomes, and their family styles and cultures differ greatly from those of white middle-class society. Their one million children attend more than eight hundred public schools and are taught by fifty thousand teachers, and they are not happy with the education their children are getting.

In the words of the management staff at the City University of New York (CUNY):

The black and Puerto Rican communities have given forceful expression to their dissatisfaction with the quality of education available to their children. To a considerable degree, the failure of the education establishment has been associated with presumed or real insensitivity and/or incompetence on the part of educational personnel. To an equal degree, condemnation of the schools reflects the inability of the poverty community to identify with—to feel part of— the education establishment. [1]

Excerpted from the in-depth case study prepared by Irene Preston, ERC evaluator.

The City University encompasses Hunter, City, Richmond, and Brooklyn Colleges, and it is the major trainer of new teachers for New York City. Of the graduates, 80 percent become inner-city educators or enter the education-related fields of school administration, counseling, and special services. Each year more than forty thousand students participate in teacher education programs.

The TTT Program, introduced at CUNY as an attempt to deal with the challenges facing inner-city teacher education, focused on the development of personnel especially trained for service in New York's inner-city schools. The participating schools were near the depressed areas of Harlem and Staten Island, and each project stressed the relationship of education to poverty-stricken communities. As one overall objective, CUNY's program was to create continual joint parity participation in teacher education, with communities-at-large and with poor communities in particular. CUNY's TTT sites, therefore, stressed the creation of curricula especially suited to minority groups and the urban poor—black history, bilingual (Spanish-English) education, open education—as a means of teaching students with diverse backgrounds.

The TTT programs at all four CUNY sites were administered by a central office. That office coordinated activities at sites within the overall structure of CUNY and with the schools and communities each served; it designed and improved TTT activities, such as curriculum and parity, and developed guidelines congruent with the policies of CUNY, the City University Research Foundation, and the U.S. Office of Education. The programs at Hunter College and City College are examined in greater detail because they demonstrate the problems of teaching and learning in an area as populous as New York City.

HUNTER COLLEGE

The project that began at Hunter College in 1969 was seen as a way of expanding a commitment to urban education, and it was part of a reform movement within the Division of Teacher Education that had been going on for a decade. TTT provided the incentive and the support that enabled the college to provide large numbers of their faculty and students with firsthand exposure to the day-to-day problems of the public school system. A major strategy of the project was to move student teachers out of the college environment into the public schools.[2]

Liberal arts instruction at Hunter was combined with teaching instruction and practicum at one of Harlem's six elementary schools. Each year another scholastic year has been added to the program. Members of the first four-year graduating class received their degrees in 1972. Except for juniors who transferred in 1969, these students received the first TTT diplomas granted by Hunter. By 1973 there were representatives of TTT at each of the four undergraduate levels. There was, however, no graduate program, and undergraduate instruction was limited to the field of elementary education.

As implemented, the Hunter project was designed to function at three levels: the college, the inner-city schools that participated in the project, and the communities surrounding the schools. At the college level faculty and students were exposed to conditions prevailing in the Harlem schools, which enabled both teachers and students to relate textbook material to the real world. At the level of the participating elementary schools, teachers were aided by student teachers in the classroom, and both faculty and students were exposed to the wide range of arts and sciences disciplines possessed by undergraduates and faculty members. With respect to the communities, prior to the advent of TTT members of the community had little influence over what was done in their schools. The principle of parity, introduced as part of TTT, permitted them to voice opinions in ways that school policy makers could not ignore.

The TTT Student

The initial enrollment in the TTT project during the 1969-70 school year was 100 students, primarily freshmen and some juniors who had transferred to the program. By the time the program ended, there were 270 students. One of the major differences between CUNY's TTT project and others throughout the country was the teacher candidate himself.

Many of the students, recruited from the ghetto areas of the city of New York, were themselves disadvantaged. Of the 270 participants, 80 percent were eligible for financial aid under federal guidelines.[3] The project's open enrollment guaranteed inclusion of up to 50 academically deficient students each year (the actual number never exceeded 40). A number of minority students (currently 70 percent), especially black and Puerto Rican males (hitherto "untapped") also became involved in the program. In 1971 minorities constituted 25 percent of all Hunter TTT students. This figure has now dropped to 15 percent, but, when one considers that Hunter was known as an institution for white, middle-class women, even the smaller percentage is significant. Charles Coleman has stated that there is a "much higher proportion of black and Puerto Rican males involved in TTT than has been in any similar program in New York City, including open enrollment."

The students involved in TTT during the first year were described as self-disciplined, mature young women in their late twenties.[4] Their exceptional success was due both to the program, and, according to other students, to the high quality of the students involved. They were succeeded by younger, less mature students who could not cope as well with the lack of structure in the project or use the diversity of the program as effectively as earlier classes had. The students, especially those recruited through open enrollment, eventually caused problems. Liberal arts and education faculty were confronted with:

— absenteeism (up to one-third of TTT students tended not to attend field-based classes when other school work interfered);[5]

— lack of preparation before class (Mrs. Lippman and several liberal arts faculty stated that they gave TTT students class time to prepare work previously assigned.);

— lack of developed verbal and mathematical skills, requiring additional support in areas where Hunter College's resources were already overtaxed (These resources included a federally funded program that provided assistance for approximately one hundred freshmen each year in reading, writing, and mathematics, as well as an Office of Academic Services, which dealt specifically with open enrollment students and provided help in credit and noncredit courses.).

Although CUNY's TTT students may have differed from those in other projects, its strategies and activities were similar to those at other sites.

Strategies and Activities

Hunter's major strategies were manifested through their major activities, which included the establishment of field-based teacher-training centers, the involvement of liberal arts professors, the development of the core curriculum, the use of open classrooms, and the concept of parity.

Field-based teacher-training centers. The development of these centers was a central strategy of Hunter's project from the beginning.[6] The TTT field centers, located in six Harlem elementary schools, trained a total of 279 students. The teaching staff assigned to each school consisted of a college instructor, a graduate assistant, and resource personnel from the school and the community. The students attended college classes and teaching seminars, observed techniques, and conferred with their instructors. They also instructed individual pupils or small groups of students.

Through this program students could test their teaching ability and decide whether to pursue a career in professional education. In addition, they became familiar with school politics, curriculum, teachers, pupils, and parents. Approximately 10 percent dropped out. The program helped college faculty members by identifying individual student needs, maximizing individualized instruction, and providing continuous feedback on their own teaching. This was valuable since many of them had had little firsthand experience with teaching in the New York City schools. The program also enabled parents to be trained to work as paraprofessionals in the schools.

The practicum for the freshman year included classroom teaching, community study, and child development. During the second year the student practiced language and mathematics instruction. The third year included science and social science work, while the fourth year centered on creative arts and included an entire semester of apprentice teaching.

Field-based training had existed at Hunter College before TTT, but it was limited in scope. TTT made it possible for Hunter to incorporate a field-based training program into its Division of Teacher Education.

Involvement of liberal arts professors in teacher education. Participants in this program included Margaret Mead (lecturer-consultant), and Mary Dolciani (mathematician and author of textbooks). Indeed, Mary Dolciani was motivated to create elementary textbooks employing a nonverbal approach to teaching mathematics as a result of experience in TTT classrooms.[7]

This program began in 1969 when thirty members of ten college departments were granted released time, facilitated by TTT funds, to plan courses together, and to participate in activities designed to implement them. Educators were aware that courses in liberal arts, comprising almost 75 percent of a prospective teacher's studies, were not designed to relate to teaching. It was possible, however, to have joint liberal arts and education instruction in science, anthropology, language arts, and mathematics. During the spring semester of 1972, for example, TTT sophomores took an interdisciplinary science content and teaching methods course at Public School 168. Until TTT entered, the school had not had an organized science program, and there was little equipment for teaching it. The lab created by TTT provided equipment, an instruction room, and the resources of student teachers and liberal arts and education faculty. TTT students learned course content and studied the teaching methods of the instructors, pupils at Public School 168 were introduced to more sophisticated equipment and instruction, and regular science teachers participated in the program. The total experience benefited all who were involved.

Core curriculum. During the academic year 1969-70, the main focus of Hunter's TTT project was on curriculum planning. At a meeting of college faculty, attended by representatives from the student body, the community, and the Harlem public schools, a pilot curriculum for up to four hundred students was planned. It included new subject matter and methods courses for education students, and liberal arts and teacher education courses were integrated into a single teacher-training program. The program consisted of three years of basic requirements in arts and sciences, electives, and courses in the student's major field, with a concentration on methods courses and student teaching in the fourth year. Practicum experiences in teaching parallel subjects spaced throughout the four-year curriculum gave prospective teachers simultaneous command of subject matter and related teaching methodologies.

One example of actual core course work would be the community studies course, which focused on methods of sociological investigation. Students were taught to observe, record, and analyze community needs, resources, and group interaction patterns, initially, by studying a city block. After that information was compiled, inferences were drawn concerning the nature of the community and its changes of direction. The needs of the community were then analyzed in relation to availability of such resources as housing, health, child care, education, and welfare. Several basic courses—music, art, anthropology, urban affairs—were related to this study, and each year students used these resources as they taught and worked with parents. Throughout the program, students were encouraged to participate in community activities and to help with parent programs at the schools.

Open classrooms and role models. Open classrooms, an underlying tenet of the Hunter TTT program, served as the vehicle for field-based teacher training. Previously this concept had been heavily supported within the Division of Teacher Education at Hunter; now the TTT program made possible its implementation, as field-based training guaranteed the presence of many adults (teachers, teacher trainers, student teachers, and paraprofessionals) working in one classroom through field-based training.

The open classroom project at Hunter served to isolate and define the roles played by all classroom participants, from aides to clinical professors, and was important for three reasons: first, it provided black and Puerto Rican children with classroom adults, community people with whom they were already familiar, as role models; second, it convinced teachers that valuable use could be made of classroom participants at levels beyond custodial or clerical, which was especially helpful where bilingual aides were involved; and third, since paraprofessionals received general studies credit from Hunter, or equivalency high school diplomas, it helped ensure the continued recruitment and participation of minority people.

Mae Gamble, a curriculum professor at Hunter, taught a course in open classroom methods to a group of teachers at East Harlem's Public School 168. Her course was designed to encourage a positive attitude toward open classrooms among those teaching in the public school system and to bolster confidence in their ability to use open instruction with minority children in large urban classrooms. The format of her course was, in fact, similar to the open classroom approach she urged her students to adopt. Her message to them was not to impose a rigid system in the classroom. Using a problem-solving technique and citing personal experiences as examples of what worked in particular situations, she urged her students to rely on certain human values when dealing with children and parents and then do what they thought would work.

Dr. Gamble, a superb teacher who relates well to students, recorded her own impressions of the impact her course had on her students in a paper presented at Hunter College:

First, I discovered that there were far fewer "bad" teachers in the public schools than one is led to believe. It is true that schools are failing to meet the needs of many children, but the fault lies less with teachers and their personality characteristics and more with their preservice training (which has not prepared them for the problems they meet), and the bureaucracy of a large city school system with its limited funds, and the difficulty of meeting the increasingly bewildering demands of children living in today's big cities, which may be described as overcrowded, uncomfortable and stress-producing in many ways, and culturally disintegrated. Teachers, on the whole, are conscientious and hard-working and anxious to be successful in their jobs. They want school to be a happy place where children learn and live well together. They do need help in obtaining their goals, even the most experienced of them. . . .

I also discovered that helping teachers become more competent is a more difficult and more rewarding matter than simply giving them the "right answers." Being in the school on a regular basis, I found that if I make a suggestion to a teacher and it doesn't work, she can tell me about it the next day. Then it is necessary for me to follow it up with a deeper analysis. Going into the classroom and finding out why it doesn't work, usually means working with the children and diagnosing their needs. Sometimes I have to go to other people, books, etc., and do more research on the problem. This all makes for a much more satisfying experience, both for the classroom teacher and the professor, than teaching in-service graduate courses on campus, where the instructor is beseiged with teachers' problems but, due to unfamiliarity with the actual classroom situation, finds diagnosis and solution very often to be a shot-in-the-dark. . . .

. . . I gradually have begun to feel less and less like an expert; I have become instead a resource person, a facilitator, a counselor, and a friend. Many times I am only a messenger. The staff of the school sees me sharing in their goals and objectives. . . .

The teachers are also gaining from the experience. They have started talking to each other more and more about curriculum, about learning and about teaching. As they discover there are no easy solutions and as they gain confidence from my recognition of the hard work they are doing, they slowly have begun to reveal their problems, their fears, their failures. They also have begun to approach the task of educating youngsters as a team effort. They share ideas, materials, new learnings, etc. Some have done demonstration teaching. Others have volunteered to go into classrooms and help diagnose learning problems. They argue and they talk and work out mutually satisfying solutions to problems of concern. They observe each other. The cooperative spirit I have witnessed growing in the school, has been one of the most satisfying aspects of my TTT experience.

Parity. At Hunter, parity evolved in an atmosphere of increased student demands influenced by the Harlem riots. Parity representatives gained voting rights on four general types of TTT management decisions:

— the selection of new personnel with regard to both TTT- and college-funded positions;

— the development of new curricula, especially in the core areas of science, mathematics, English, Spanish, art, and the social sciences;

— recommendations on new methods and materials used in TTT classrooms;

— requests for new funds and the allocating of existing funds, within established guidelines.

Through parity, the role of TTT students and their decision-making powers were considerably magnified. Millie Efre, a TTT student interviewed on May 1, 1973, said:

Parity as a means of decision making has made a lot of students aware that they do have the power to change things, and they will have the power in deciding how they are going to learn. They take part in the hiring and firing of teachers. Not in the direct ways of saying, "we don't want you around," but we have a vote on the steering committee meeting, and that's the meeting that basically decides what needs to be changed . . . . In 1971-1972, there was a linguistic course. The syllabus was good; but the students felt that much of the teacher's orientation was racist in nature. Also, we felt that we need a less theoretical and more practical approach to linguistics. We brought the problem to the steering committee and the teacher was fired. It may not have been solely because of our recommendation, but I'm sure we influenced the decision.

Effect on Individual Participants

TTT precipitated a variety of changes in project participants. The 1972-73 Hunter College funding proposal cited changes in faculty and students at Hunter College and in cooperating teachers and pupils from the public schools as follows:

Liberal arts and education faculty. For the twenty-four liberal arts and education faculty who participated in TTT, the project wanted to bring about the following specific changes:

— increased knowledge of the resources of the Harlem communities to improve teacher education;

— increased knowledge of the background of black and Puerto Rican peoples, their needs, problems, contributions, and aspirations;

— higher degrees of skill in using innovative methods of teaching: microteaching, team teaching, practicum, field work, and use of simulation materials;

— increased rapport and empathy with the communities the college serves;
— extension of knowledge of latest research on methods and materials of instruction that have been successful in urban classrooms;
— increased ability to work as team members with people from other disciplines, from the schools, and from the community;
— establishment of better rapport with the student body, especially with students from minority groups.

What TTT seemed actually to bring about was a general change in the orientation of participating faculty members toward teaching. Whether the specific changes desired would be equivalent to this general change in orientation seems indeterminable. It is also possible that the global changes college faculty saw in themselves as a result of TTT would not break down to the predetermined goals. Perhaps the best standard for assessing success for faculty participants is found in the opening paragraph of the 1971-72 funding proposal:

Hunter College's TTT program is designed to enable a significant number of liberal arts and education faculty to gain new perspectives and skills that will result in better preparation of teachers for black and Puerto Rican youngsters in New York City public schools. This goal without doubt has been reached.

Mae Gamble, who feels she is living proof of this, said:

I thought for the first time this morning how TTT had changed me. When I went into the program, I really lacked confidence in my ability to decide what I should be doing as a teacher. I found myself looking at other people's outlines, seeing what they are covering in them . . . always judging myself by someone else, and wondering how I should conform here and how I should conform there. I realized this morning that I approach things much differently now, having been involved in planning and developing the program. I now approach things with the attitude that I can do it, and I sit down and make up my outline. I have confidence in my own ability to solve a problem. I have grown a lot, and changed feelings about myself as a person, as a teacher of others, as a decision maker. I have a lot more power than I would in a traditional program, which is a very significant thing.[8]

Undergraduates. For undergraduate participants, TTT's goals included the following changes in undergraduate students:
— a greater role for students in planning their educational experiences;

— greater knowledge of Puerto Rican and black history and culture;
— ability to communicate in Spanish with pupils and parents in local communities;
— most extensive knowledge of the community and its resources;
— skill in studying a community;
— skill in teaching individuals, small groups, and entire classes in East and Central Harlem;
— development of a continuing relationship with a school district;
— extension of cultural horizons of students from ghetto communities.

Like the faculty participants, students saw the changes in themselves brought about by TTT as being generally more global in nature than the specific goals listed above. They tended, for instance, to cite such developments as greater awarenesses, feelings of ability to change the situations in urban schools, and personal changes as examples of the most common results of TTT. The majority of the students interviewed (fifteen) cited "increased awareness of the educational environment and its social and political contexts" as the single greatest change they experienced through the program. "I didn't realize how political education is," Veronica Moore, a sophomore, told us, emphasizing that you "have to fight for what you want in the school system." The next most frequently cited results of TTT were personal changes in students, including the development of a sense of responsibility and self-reliance, both as teachers in the classroom and as students at Hunter College.

"One of the biggest results of the program for undergraduates was actually a side effect," Milton Gold claimed in 1973. He went on to say:

We enrolled students, a third of whom perhaps had inferior academic ability as compared to the normal Hunter average, and these TTT students have succeeded far better than any other similar group at the college, and maybe better than any group at the university [CUNY]. We have hazarded certain guesses to explain this. One is that the students' concept of themselves as both learners and teachers has been enhanced through TTT. Another reason for this success may be the "family" arrangement of TTT, a small group of fewer than 300 students in our mammoth institution of 12,000 day students. The people in the project show very close relationships. They know each other very well now. The most important issue at City University right now is how to bring up the youngsters with poor academic backgrounds. TTT has been able to succeed very well here.[9]

Most TTT students were themselves products of the urban school system, and some of them, especially open enrollment students, had not been especially successful as pupils in inner-city schools. Because of her experiences in TTT schools, Julie Wood, a junior, could "see why minority children lack a good education. I have observed what the teachers in urban schools do not understand about the children, namely the results of combined social and educational problems. By observing these teachers, I have come up with my own ideas and implemented them in the classroom. While my success has not been fantastic, it has been fairly good."[10]

Project goals for cooperating public school teachers were:
— closer relationship to college faculty;
— increased knowledge of methods and materials leading to individualization of instruction and development of self-concept;
— increased skill in working as members of teams in planning and teaching;
— increased skill in supervising student teachers.

It is more difficult to document the attainment of specific project goals in the case of cooperating teachers than it was for either college faculty or students. Dean Gold has said that many cooperating teachers, even in the last year of TTT funding, were reluctant to take the initiative in relations with liberal arts and education faculty, and also, to some degree, with students, even though these people were working in their classrooms with their pupils.

Participating teachers, however, were affected by TTT in their everyday activities. They were called upon to play supervisory roles with student teachers, and they were exposed to liberal arts and education faculty working in the schools. The ideas of some cooperating teachers about education and special projects in education, such as TTT, changed after the program began. "In 1969, we really had to struggle to get teachers to accept TTT students," said Sidney Schwager, principal of Public School 168, but by 1973 "there was only one teacher from the staff who said 'I do not want a TTT student.' Others may get disgusted for one reason or another, but most teachers are very anxious to have TTT students. And most of them are using TTT staff as real teaching assistants."[11]

Inner-city pupils. Pupils in cooperating classrooms were also affected by TTT, although the major recorded changes involved attitude toward schooling, rather than skills acquired or knowledge learned.

Social changes have also taken place; for example, through the program's practice of recruiting paraprofessionals, black and Puerto Rican children have been provided with classroom adults as role models. "Their behavior is better and their willingness to learn seems to have increased," Dr. Gamble said in 1973.

"The children look forward to classes now," Artie Galaskewicz, a junior, said. "They are openly affectionate with TTT students. While they may or may not actually be learning more, they come to school more eagerly and depart with greater reluctance. This new situation must eventually lead to increased learning."[12]

Six out of eight cooperating teachers at Public School 168 believed that their children were learning at a somewhat more rapid rate. Resource teacher Sheila Evers told of a math workbook she introduced through TTT. It was so popular that she caught children smuggling it home so they could work in it at night.

Despite termination of the TTT Program by the federal government, Hunter continued its project. All major activities were funded except for two: the use of parents and graduate assistants in the schools and coordinating time for liberal arts and education faculty. The activities that were maintained were largely financed by Hunter College through credit hours generated by the 350 TTT students enrolled in 1974. While the loss of federal funds caused some problems, other potentially negative effects of institutionalization also emerged.

Some TTT graduates, such as Jimmy Borrero, a student teacher at Public School 168, said that "when TTT becomes funded by Hunter, it will become less innovative and possibly less exciting."[13]

Students like Borrero feared that Hunter's project was already too permissive and too unstructured for today's students. Rather than helping the situation, they saw TTT's funding by Hunter as a negative force.

Not all the effects of institutionalizing the TTT project are known. The degree to which TTT-sponsored activities will be continued is largely a matter of local option. If the intensity with which both students and faculty members searched for a new location for the campus TTT office is any indication, however, Hunter TTT will not be permitted to die.

CITY COLLEGE

The central intention of the City College program was to improve education in Harlem elementary schools directly, through personnel, equipment, and modern teaching techniques. This, however, was only a step toward the ultimate goal: the development of "exportable" techniques through experiences gained at the Harlem schools and from the training given by knowledgeable, experienced teacher trainers. In the words of Vivian Windley, the project director, City College intended to "effect changes at teacher-training institutes and in the public schools that will result in better education for children."[14]

A major strategy in the City College project, as in all TTT projects, was promotion of the concept of parity. The City College TTT project probably made more extensive use of community persons than the other CUNY-TTT projects. According to Allen Freedman, TTT Program director at CUNY, "a major thrust of Dr. Windley's program has certainly been her training of paraprofessionals."

The TTT Program was implemented at City College through the combined efforts of the college, the graduate center at CUNY, eight public elementary schools in Harlem, and the related school communities. As a primary strategy to meet TTT goals, a classroom model was developed to reform both the content and the structure of education in New York's inner-city schools. Open education, the model's rationale, was the vehicle for preservice undergraduate education, in-service training for classroom teachers and educational auxiliaries, and support for liberal arts and education professors in increasing their skills.

Open Classrooms

Background. The City College project began in 1969 with eight open classrooms in Harlem elementary schools and expanded soon thereafter to thirty-two classes. Eventually, fifty open classrooms involved over five hundred participants: four hundred public school pupils, seventeen student teachers, and approximately one hundred teachers, instructors, advisers, auxiliaries, and other personnel at both the public school and collegiate levels.[15]

The cooperating partners in City College's program were Public School 154 in Central Harlem, Public School 192 in West Harlem, the local school districts, the school communities, City College, and the City University of New York. Advisory services were provided through the program for six other Manhattan elementary schools. The pupils served by TTT comprised a good balance of black, Puerto Rican, Oriental, and white children.[16]

The impact of open education on American schools has been widespread; many programs like TTT have seen it as a solution to educational problems, including the current crisis in urban schools. Educators have come to realize, however, that open education cannot succeed without adequate support from the schools, from the community, and from teachers thoroughly prepared to teach in such environments.

Open education in New York City has received this kind of support since it began. At a meeting at City College in 1968, open education-minded legislators, educators, and community representatives selected New York City's District 4 as the place to provide the necessary classroom training facilities for the TTT project. Included were such school and community personnel as cooperating teachers, clinical instructors, educational auxiliaries, social workers, and guidance counselors.

At City College, the director, eight student teachers, and consultants from the liberal arts faculty and the school of education created, in conjunction, a ten-credit tuition-free course for the cooperating teachers at Public School 154. It was initially designated as the Teacher Training Center, with all seminars and workshops housed at Public School 154. Community field work also was an intended part of the model, for, in an urban setting, teachers needed firsthand knowledge of the communities they served. Therefore, cooperating teachers, student teachers, and clinical instructors worked in such community agencies as the Harlem Youth Center, the Urban League, and the Under-Achiever's program as part of their professional training.

The creation of open classrooms, and the model they provided for teacher training, marked a new movement in teacher education at City College. A preservice program for college juniors and seniors was developed, and the in-service training of teachers and educational auxiliaries, together with liberal arts and education faculty, was implemented. The public schools also assumed increased responsibility for both preservice and in-service training by creating a new position, that of clinical instructor, to be filled by a public schoolteacher, trained at the college level, who would supervise student teachers.

Classroom models. A classroom-based model for open education develops a laboratory environment in which all participants work toward individualizing learning in its truest sense.[17] Teachers relinquish their traditional roles as dispensers of knowledge and are recast as guides and stimulators of children's personal learning experiences.[18] Children regain the status of central participants in their own education. Classrooms are reorganized into learning centers filled with a variety of materials that provide novel subject matter, much of which is drawn from children's own interests and environment (jars of soda bottle caps for mathematics, substituting the telephone yellow pages for a dictionary to give practice in looking up alphabetized words). Children also learn at individual rates, free from the traditionally competitive classroom atmosphere. A child's work is compared with his own previous achievement, not the progress of others in the class.

Vivian Windley used the British Infant School (for five- to seven-year-old children) as her open classroom model. Theoretically, the model is based upon Piaget's stages of child development and upon Montessori's and Dewey's notions of designing education to fit the particular needs of each stage of children's growth. "However," Dr. Windley said, "all teachers are not right for open education, nor do all want to make the transition, nor should they. One teacher at P.S. 192 left the program this year. She said she just didn't have the time or energy."

Resources for the open classroom model included teachers and advisory-consultant staff, as well as the physical facilities of the public school, educational materials, and the community. Advisory-consultant support for teacher training had two levels: the advisers, who were liberal arts or education faculty, community persons or parents, and the parent liaison staff, which consisted of a parent at each school who acted as liaison between the TTT project and the school community.

In addition to support from college faculty and community persons, involvement of the participating school administrators in the project was crucial. According to Vivian Windley, "if the teachers who were using open education didn't have the support of the school administration, their morale would have been low and their success limited."

In terms of the model, greater interaction between teachers, student teachers, paraprofessionals, and college faculty was also crucial. After it was attained, these groups planned together, shared ideas, talked about children, reassessed, and diagnosed so that each knew where the other was, what the other was thinking. This communication is a central part of open education.

Open classroom goals. The central goal of the open classroom model was to humanize education for children. Specifically included under this model were the creation of decentralized schools (making the American version more like the British), and individualized instruction (children given tasks to do independently at their own pace or along with other children having similar learning abilities).

The second goal was an open environment. The key to open environment is the freedom it gives children to socialize, to learn from each other. TTT had a big effect on public school pupils in this respect, for, to quote Vivian Windley again: "Children can now work together, talk to each other and plan and learn from each other, replacing the traditional system under which the only talking was between the teacher and the child."

In addition, an environment creates a laboratory experience. As children are free to interact, so public schoolteachers and college faculty can experiment with their ideas. "The real experiment is a new way of looking at children and a new way of viewing teaching-learning experiences. It involves parents, teachers, and student teachers working with education and liberal arts faculty, testing ideas, and exploring."[19]

The third goal of the Windley model was dissemination of the open approach to education, and this goal has already been met. "We started in one school, now we are in eight," she said in 1973. "Parents come to us continually asking how to implement open education in their children's schools. . . . In addition, hundreds of visitors come each year to see our program. Many of us have been invited around the country, especially to California and on the east coast, to talk to teachers, administrators and parents. I've also been to England to talk about the model. To disseminate the material I use slides and videotapes of classrooms and meetings."[20]

TTT's open education model affected the school lives of approximately four hundred classroom children. The major changes noted were affective: project children seemed more willing to come to school and not as anxious to leave. Although there is not yet conclusive evidence that children learn more in open classrooms than in traditional ones the pupils' preference for open classrooms was evident from their comments: "If I had a child, I would want him placed in a TTT class because you can work on your own, and there are lots of things to do"; "I like the TTT class because the teacher doesn't stand up in front of the room and talk all the time"; "I like the TTT class because we have lots of people in the room to help you."

Open classroom centers. An integral part of the classroom model was an instructional materials center, housed in each project school and developed through the collaborative effort of all project participants. The center contained new instructional materials—audiovisual materials, books and magazines, and other instructional resources. Some of these materials were available from commercial suppliers, and some were created by participants. Parents and community persons were encouraged to use the resource centers.

In 1972 there was a movement at City College to design special centers for open education. Sixteen City College architecture students designed seventeen different models for the new education environment, but, thus far, their work has been limited to the redesign of existing classroom areas, using wall space, cabinet dividers, and lofts. The chairman of the school planning committee of the board of education has promised Vivian Windley an old school building of her own, if one can be found in the area. Then several of the more radical architectural proposals could be enacted and a school-wide open education center could be constructed.

Involvement of liberal arts and community persons. Liberal arts faculty from five City College departments, as well as community persons, became partners in teacher education for the first time at City College through the open classroom model. From 1968 to 1970 a growing movement at City College toward interdisciplinary teacher education had resulted in better relations between arts and sciences faculty and the department of education. Liberal arts shared responsibility for joint teacher training correlated with the development of TTT, and professors saw it as a way of ensuring their participation in teacher education. Liberal arts participants became deeply involved in the program. One example would be Robert Perrault, the poet, who continued his work with kindergarten children, without pay, even though a move to New Jersey made it necessary for him to commute to the school. This example is not atypical.

Community persons have also assisted in every phase of development. They shared experiences with college faculty, thereby providing insight into what children need from schools to grow up in Harlem as well as to succeed in a larger world. They served as a communications link between the program and the communities and as both teachers and participants in community seminars.

The City College funding proposal for 1972-73 cited as major project goals:

— the involvement of parents, community leaders, student teachers, administrators, and education and liberal arts faculty in the planning and implementation of the program;

— the development of a teacher education laboratory-type training model that will provide fruitful insights for liberal arts and education faculty, administrators, teachers, and community people as well as improve teacher education.

Goal 1: Parity. The first goal has been met. The scope of the project was large, and the participants were varied. TTT change agents included 127 participants, including one school district superintendent, nine graduate faculty members in education, nine liberal arts graduate faculty members, one public school-based supervisor of cooperating teachers, nine college administrators, and two doctoral students in psychology. These participants were involved in the program as trainers and as members of either advisory boards or steering committees. Participation by public school people expanded these figures to seventeen teachers and supervisors, fourteen student teachers, eight educational auxiliaries, and five hundred pupils, community persons, and parents, bringing the total number of participants to more than eight hundred.[21]

Parent and community participation is being continued under City College's funding of major TTT components, and this includes two of the most successful project activities specifically related to community persons: the four-year program of seminars and workshops for students, parents, and educational auxiliaries, and the career-ladder degree program for parents and educational auxiliaries. The third major community activity, parent workshops, has been continued through the advisory service that City College provides for public schoolteachers in cooperating schools.

Continued funding of courses for community persons is by no

means assured, however, and there is an air of pessimism concerning the future. Vivian Windley, in the spring of 1973, even questioned her own future participation in federal projects because of the disillusionment that programs tended to foster in community participants. At that time she felt that community persons had been "used," especially with regard to the scarcity of follow-through provisions for sustaining community input and the "lack of federal commitment to support community-involved activities. In essence," she said, "these programs are perpetrating a fraud on the community."[22]

Delphine Downes, a community resource adviser, saw a reduction in the involvement of community persons: progressively fewer educational auxiliaries were being used for open classroom work. Mrs. Downes felt that student teachers were being used as classroom replacements for community persons because they were not paid for their services; also, they generated credit hours for City College through their classroom work.

There has been difficulty in maintaining parity at the relatively high level of earlier years. In some cases, the earlier level has simply not been maintained. The problems of developing or maintaining community-institutional relations centered on the training of community people, the staffing of project positions by community people, and institutional "rewards" for both the community participants (career-ladder degrees) and the college faculty for "nontraditional" project activities (coordinating, community training, and others).

Problems in training and staffing are closely related and may be described as "the displacement of community persons in projects through time." There were instances where positions meant to be staffed by project participants came to be filled by persons on a "higher" level. For example, at City College, the special training program that ended for educational auxiliaries was still being conducted for student teachers and teachers. Consequently, the educational auxiliaries took over the more informal parent workshops, which had been created originally to train parents to aid their own children with their schoolwork. Because this made the workshops unsuitable for some participating parents, the training of nine educational auxiliaries in these workshops reduced the number of participating parents from sixty to forty. A second part of the "displacement" problem was the tendency to replace educational auxiliaries with student teachers in classroom situations.

Institutional rewards for community participants in City College's TTT project were salaries and credits toward career-ladder degrees. Since the goal of most of the educational auxiliaries was to become teachers, both rewards were meaningful. The career-ladder program was not, however, a complete success. Some community persons' salaries, as previously noted, were discontinued with the replacement of educational auxiliaries by student teachers. It also became apparent, as Vivian Windley observed, that community people "are getting some credit, and they have been taking courses, but no one has *ever* graduated . . . because it takes a long, long time. It is nonsense to go through forty years to get a degree."[23] Participants with high school diplomas earned one credit a year toward college degrees. Those without a diploma earned no credits. The length of time required to earn a degree was discouraging, and it prevented all but the most youthful from ever becoming teachers. These facts seem to indicate that there was a discrepancy between the ideal and the real roles played by community persons in TTT.

Goal 2: Open classrooms. The laboratory training model (the second goal) was developed, implemented, and partially disseminated. It is difficult to determine whether participants received the "fruitful insights" mentioned in the proposal. Project participants did generally claim to have greater insight into children, their stages of development, and optimum learning environments. Specific objectives for 1972-73 included:

— restructure and institutionalization of the undergraduate program in teacher education, staffed by an interdisciplinary team of liberal arts and education faculty, and including both study and practicum experience;
— the development of an intensive training program for a cadre of public schoolteachers;
— workshops for public school administrators to familiarize them with the purpose and basic philosophy of the TTT project and, thus, to enlist their support for institutionalizing TTT innovations in the public school system;
— identification and isolation of specific competencies needed for the open classroom approach;
— development of a program of interproject activities for greater articulation between the City College and Hunter College TTT projects in an effort to satisfy the needs of both programs through

the pooled resources of students, faculty, and physical facilities; and

— utilization of the expert opinion and knowledge of community leaders, community resource assistants, and parents in the training of teachers and teacher trainers, particularly as they relate to community problems and issues.[24]

By 1973, only four of the twelve open classrooms at Public School 192, the site of City College's TTT project, were staffed by the full "classroom team" (teacher, student teacher, and educational auxiliary). In the other classrooms, undergraduates filled the dual roles of student teacher and educational auxiliary. Yet, as designated in the proposals, the "team" was an integral part of the City College project.

In an interview in May 1973, Benjamin Rosner spoke of TTT's influence on the university:

I think that my office has really benefitted from its involvement with TTT. I think it has enabled teacher education at the university level to interact with people throughout the city to a greater degree than might otherwise have been. The opportunity for maintaining the input of community-school, each organization and group, is there, whether or not these groups retain their interest. I don't know to what extent the community, and the schools will be willing to invest their energies into things they regard as important, but not of the highest order of priorities for their respective efforts, when external funds to support them in some way are not available. We have reason to believe that the teacher groups, some of the community groups, and certainly the school system as a whole, will continue to be very much involved.[25]

THREE

PERSPECTIVES

The energy and activity generated by the TTT Program could not fail to produce an enormous amount of verbiage ranging from an amorphous mass of raw data to precise, well-written reports. And yet, for all of the material that was available, one segment was lacking; there was no complete history of the project written by its own directors. Erwin Goldenstein and Paul Olson, directors of the University of Nebraska project, agreed to fill this gap. They had been involved in the program from its very beginnings in the Tri-University project, grappling with its daily problems and frustrations and rejoicing in its successes. As they themselves said, they "had almost no sense of educational politics, of theory of institutional change within communities," but they persevered until the program ended. In order to provide additional viewpoints, excerpts from letters and final reports written by project directors from various parts of the country follow the definitive report by Goldenstein and Olson.

Site visitors, who reported on what they observed at various project locations, provide a second perspective, and, finally, ERC evaluators, who used data gathered from taxonomies, instruments, and cross-project analysis, provide a third one. All three perspectives are based on the attainment of TTT's national goals.

5

PROJECT DIRECTORS

UNIVERSITY OF NEBRASKA

Beginnings and Goals

The idea for the Nebraska project really came into existence in 1966. In February of that year, the University of Nebraska conducted an OE conference concerned with training elementary teachers and the teachers of elementary teachers in English, linguistics, and reading. This conference led to a report and a memo written by Paul Olson urging USOE to initiate work of a "TTT" sort in old language arts areas which would encourage them to take cognizance of new work in structuralism and linguistics. At about the same time, Donald Bigelow, who was then director of NDEA, Title XI, began to work on details of the transition to the new Bureau of Education Personnel Development. Included in the planning for that bill was a program

The University of Nebraska portion of this chapter was prepared by Erwin H. Goldenstein and Paul A. Olson, former directors of the University of Nebraska TTT project, and it is dedicated to Professors Joe Aguilar, Gene Hardy, and Royce Ronning, three directors in the TTT enterprise without whom the work would not have progressed.

for educating or reeducating those who educate teachers. About a year later, as the thinking about the bill crystallized, Bigelow and Nolan Estes, who was director of OE-ESEA programs, invited representatives of three universities to work on programs for training the teachers of elementary teachers. These programs were to serve as precursors for Parts D and F of the Education Professions Development Act, which by that time was under serious consideration. The University of Washington was to handle social sciences; the University of Nebraska, English and linguistics; Yale University, the behavioral sciences. (Yale was later replaced by New York University.) The English program discussed between people from OE and those from Nebraska was to emphasize:

— structuralism (transformations) in the understanding of children's development in language and their ability to create literature, play, and fantasy by using their imaginations;

— double practicum, whereby teachers in the project were to use theory to illuminate practice with children in clinical schools and in the field, and college "teacher trainers" were to learn practical applications of classroom theory through work in clinical schools and with teachers who were examining their own work with children;

— institutional change at the participants' institutions, which would allow both teachers and teacher trainers brought into the project to return to their home institutions to transform the teacher education process, making it more sophisticated (reflecting modern findings in developmental psychology, linguistics, and structuralism) and more responsive to environmental conditions. Similar reforms were to take place at the host institutions, though the obligation of the host institution was not clarified.

Prominent members of the group planning the Nebraska Tri-University (TTT) project had attended or been influenced by the Anglo-American Dartmouth conference on the teaching of English that took place in 1966. A group of very distinguished British educators demonstrated the power of the British education reform movement with its emphasis on open classrooms, on concern for the child's inner self as a social construct and for his capacity to relate to a community, and on the part education plays in subtle organic processes of development. The Nebraska group had long been interested in the work of Chomsky and Piaget, in which more subtle forms of self-directed or open education were promoted.

The Nebraska project represented an attempt to fuse educational theory and practice and to reform teacher education. The leaders, though they were respected at the university, lacked knowledge of educational politics. They were unable to deal with the subtle or not so subtle opposition that accompanies structural change in any institution, and structural change was what Bigelow, Estes, and the new EPDA bill were seeking. It is also particularly important to know that the planning group, the director, and the staff had almost no contact with the school administrator's community and only tenuous connections with the teacher's group, the Establishment, and the minority communities. Plans were formulated to change the University of Nebraska and the client universities and colleges from which participants might come, but there was no attempt to relate the plans to operations already set up to handle planning, budgeting, governance, and political interaction. The entire project, involving hundreds of thousands of dollars and dozens of people at three universities (plus nationwide recruitment of program participants), was mounted from February through April 1967, which meant that the program had to be set, a staff secured, and participants chosen, all within a couple of months.

It is revealing to compare project developments in Nebraska with those in North Dakota, where a New School in the Behavioral Studies was considered by the legislature, the university, and state and national centers in an attempt to analyze the need for further training for elementary teachers, the need for a new structure, and the availability of state and university support after federal funds disappeared. All of this was done *before* significant amounts of federal money became available. That a new structure appeared in North Dakota under TTT auspices was not surprising; what was surprising was the form of education which the structure promoted.

The North Dakota project, an insider's project, used institutional means to secure educational change, but it became, increasingly, an "outsider's" institution because of the form of education it supported. In contrast, the Nebraska project was mostly an "outside" attempt to influence the school establishment, the Teachers College establishment (Nebraska University's school of education), and the arts and sciences-oriented groups. The Nebraska project seems to be somewhat like the picaro—the beggar in the sixteenth-century rich man's house (the university). Much time is spent trying to win the master's favor by sleight-of-hand tricks, juggling, angry assaults, or wild appeals to the master's sense of humor and his need for security. In the picaresque novel the master does not always care for his tricky slave; nor does the slave always love the master whom he is trying to relieve of his burden of wordly wealth and power or to reform and please simultaneously.

The original goals of the Nebraska project in 1967-68 were a modest appropriation of goals articulated for the whole project by OE:

— to foster the application of structuralist developmental approaches toward understanding the process of education, particularly the children's and the culture's imaginative and linguistic forms;
— to foster the development of open educational formats that would permit learning to follow the excitement and inquisitiveness of children, teachers, and teacher educators in liberal arts and education;
— to foster a sensitivity to cultural differences as these differences appear in the language, dialects, and conventional writing forms of various groups, in play and informal fantasy structures, and in formal literary, mythical, and religious structures;
— to move the primary site of the education of teachers to the streets and the schools where children actually learn and to encourage a more thorough "immersion" of teachers and the educators of teachers in the school-community process;
— to encourage a total institutional commitment to the improvement of the education of teachers, including both arts and sciences and education staff, and to make that commitment a full four-year one, including early field experience.

The reform emphasis which the project had at its inception was reinforced by those invited to lead discussions of educational reform at the first conference: John Holt and J. McVicker Hunt represented the area of schools and children's growth; Herb Kohl and Alton Becker, children's imaginative and linguistic development; Douglas Oliver and Robert Hess, schooling and human culture. Minority concerns, the uses of anthropology, open classrooms, and the need for courses in psycholinguistics and developmental psychology were at the center of the discussions. During the conference it became apparent that behavior modification would be a primary issue when J. McVicker Hunt attacked both it and Louis Bright. Bright, then head of the Bureau of Research, was preparing to institute behavioristic Competency Based Teacher Education (CBTE) using his "Elementary Models" program for educating teachers. As minority school issues and culture-based education were discussed, it became equally clear to at least some of the people attending the conference that parents and their worlds could not be ignored. Although this first conference was exceedingly abrasive, the project did move, at least for several years, insistently in one direction. The emphasis was on community initiative, culture-based education, "open" ways of learning, and developmental-structuralist analytic tools.[1] These were the principles that were being promoted as EPDA was passed and the national TTT Program unfolded. Parent and community participation in determining what kinds of people were to educate their children became a sixth goal during the first year (1967-68), and it was explicitly stated as a goal thereafter.

TTT in Its Middle Years

The movement toward open classrooms, culture-based education, and community initiative was a slow one. Open classroom work progressed somewhat in 1967-68. There was also some concern for culture and some effort to become acquainted with the community. These efforts gained momentum in August 1968 with the Tri-U Minneapolis conference, from which came the publication, *A Pride of Lions.* This conference, eloquently led by community people who stated forcefully their need for a role in the education of their children, had some effect on TTT administration set up at the national level. That conference following closely on the controversy at Tucson in 1968 over whether community participation and a "power to parents" focus was required by the sketchy TTT guidelines, crystallized the community participation issue. That these community participation concerns did indeed fall within TTT guidelines gradually came to be accepted.

As for the participants, there were college trainers of teachers from English departments and education departments all over the country, teachers from many public schools, preservice undergraduates, and some graduate students aspiring to be teachers of teachers. These people knew they had been picked by a community committee made up of parents of children attending an elementary school that had been selected to serve as the clinical site. The committee included blacks, American Indians, and low-income whites.

Some years the program began with a review of the community at the clinical site or of other communities made up of predominantly low-income people where the schools were clearly in trouble, such as schools on the Nebraska Indian reservation or in the predominantly black North Side community of Omaha. The first in-depth experience might have included a live-in, talks by members of the community, or visits to community agencies. James Johnson, an architect on the community committee, developed a computer programming technique to represent demographically the effects of disease, old age, death, poor housing, racial isolation, and limited play space. This form of representation was applied to Lincoln, and the results were offered to participants as an aid in understanding the children and the parents in the clinical school.

Both participants and staff spent a great deal of time, initially, in determining what people wanted and needed to learn and what skills could be offered by the total group. Theoretical learning was to coincide with work in both the community and the school. If, for instance, a group of participants chose to work on "structuralism and theory of play and childhood fantasy" as set down by Brian Sutton Smith, Bob Georges, Roger Abraham, and others, the members would videotape or take field notes on children at play, individually and in groups. One participant might spend a weekend accompanying a young boy, whether in and out of pool halls, on his paper route, to the barber shop, or to the neighborhood "dozen's" group. Out of these activities a picture of how children learn, what they learn, and what they might learn next would form. During the early years of the project there had been too many staff-initiated courses and projects. The middle years, particularly those under Gene Hardy's and Royce Ronning's leadership, saw more and more staff-and-participant, staff-community committee, and participant-participant activity. Although it is not clear just when the emphasis changed, the discussion sequences became reality oriented.

Participants and staff were likely to be learning, along with other staff members and participants, the importance, for schools, of:
— black dialects and reading;
— authority relations on Indian reservations and bridging the gap between school and community;
— Christian allegory in children's literature and the writing and symbolism of children raised in orthodox homes;

— developmental theory as it affected children's mathematical-logical learnings and their development as writers and organizers of prose.

At any one time, there might be from twelve to fifty such groups organized in the project.

At the same time, participants were likely to be:

— helping to organize open classrooms in Randolph school, a blue-collar school;
— working with the Winnebago tribal council on a tutorial for Indian children;
— working with tribal councils for correct audits of Johnson O'Malley and Title I funds;
— working to open Chicano cultural awareness centers in pre-dominantly Chicano neighborhoods;
— setting up a printing press and editing and publishing children's poetry and prose;
— working on aides in a community preschool and technical center organized by a strong group of black mothers in Omaha or working with other agencies to obtain funds;
— picking up Omaha folklore from a street dweller who represented himself as a "doctor of winology" and who knew the scene.

These activities were pulled together in formal and informal discussion-and-assessment sessions designed to ask how to educate, what to teach, and how to prepare those who would teach in totally different milieus.

It should be observed that project participants, staff members, and community representatives frequently disagreed both within and between groups. This was not part of any conscious design. Some sensitivity sessions were held, but they proved relatively unsuccessful. Rather, it appeared that the very intense political-educational issues at stake in the project encouraged strong reactions.

The participants represented a wide-ranging spectrum of political and educational interests, and many came from outside Nebraska, a state that constituted a somewhat intractable medium. Because many of the participants spent such a short time in the local environment, the changes brought about were not always obvious. It is perhaps more helpful to look at some of the functions of participants, staff, and community members in terms of the six goals, beginning with the community-oriented ones and moving backward.

Goal VI: *To secure parent participation in, or control over, the education of children and determining who is to educate them.*

In this area the best-known work of the project was its pressure on the national TTT Program to enforce the "community participation" rubrics vaguely set down in the original TTT guidelines, agreed to at the Tucson TTT evaluation, and strongly urged at the Minneapolis "Pride of Lions" conference. More important achievements were, however, developed by participants and community contracts. For example:

1. Theodore Johnson of the community committee raised nationally the issue of the parents' "right to know" about the use of Ritalin and other behavior control drugs, which led to a congressional initiative and new Office of Child Development guidelines to control the use of behavior control drugs contrary to parent intention.

2. Reuben Snake, Louis LaRose, Leonard Springer, and other members of the community committee initiated a series of actions that led to Harrison Loesch's placing Nebraska's Johnson O'Malley funds in the hands of Nebraska tribes—the first such action in the United States.

3. Alice Neuendorf, a 1968-69 Navajo participant, later directed the administration of several million dollars from Johnson O'Malley funds to be used in New Mexico and helped establish the right of native American groups to secure independent audits of these funds.

4. A Chicano group that came together under TTT auspices asked the first serious questions about the teacher-training process at the University of Nebraska as it related to Spanish-speaking peoples and eventually encouraged the university to undertake its own affirmative action examination and generally scrutinize its responsiveness to the Chicano community.

5. Several participants organized, participated in the organization of, or worked in "free schools" that parents had formed and that had an open, community base. These people included Phil Medcalf (the Illiahe School in Eugene, Oregon, and another learning community in Guyana); Mark DuPree (The School Around Us in Kennebunkport, Maine); Bob Frangenberg (the defunct Lincoln Free School); John DeFrain (the Little School in Seattle); Loretta Butler (a New Orleans "free School"); and Ken Haar and Carol

Baumert (the Omaha New School). Other participants furthered
projects for alternative systems allowing maximum parent participation within publicly supported systems: Myrliss Hershey (the
Wichita parent-developed public alternative schools proposal);
Sister Eileen Neville (a series of successful efforts to transfer
control of public and parochial schools to the South Dakota
tribes); Ruth Vaughan (parent work at Randolph School); John
DeFrain (parent control of educational work going ahead at the
University of Wisconsin, Madison).

6. Lawrence Freeman, Paul Olson, and Ron Cramer also worked to
   to develop guidelines and sites for the BEPD "School Programs,"
   TT Early Childhood projects located at nine universities (Oakland,
   Rochester, Syracuse, New York University, New Mexico, Kansas,
   Utah, California State, and Colorado), which emphasized, at several
   sites, community participation in teacher education through parent
   parity at the practicum site and in the training of the "Early
   Childhood" teacher-educator. Some of these projects (Oakland,
   Syracuse) were chosen as model projects by significant agencies.
   The Nebraska Confederation in Early Childhood Education, which
   fostered, and for a time coordinated, the nine projects during the
   planning and action period from 1968-1972, was a direct outgrowth of the Nebraska TTT project.[2]

This list by no means exhausts the actions by Nebraska participants
to achieve Goal VI; it simply indicates the variety.

Goal V: *To encourage a total institutional commitment to the education of teachers, including arts and sciences and education,
and to make that commitment a four-year one.*

1. Three participants in the Nebraska project have become deans or
   assistant deans of arts and sciences colleges: Gerald Walton (University of Mississippi); Max Larsen (University of Nebraska); and
   Vivian Robinson (Paine College, director of humanities). All have
   contributed to revising their institution's programmatic concerns
   and management in order to bring about a better fusion of arts
   and sciences and education in their particular institutions.[3]

2. A fourth participant, Melvin George, member of the TTT arts and
   sciences task force and former dean of the arts and sciences college
   at Nebraska, was until recently academic head of the experimental
   "Open University" located at the State University of Nebraska
   and has participated in an effort to organize the Council of

Colleges of Arts and Sciences deans and the land grant colleges arts and sciences deans to assure more effective participation nationally in the education of teachers.

Goal IV: *To move the primary site of the education of teachers to the streets and schools where children learn.*

1. Several members of the Nebraska staff worked on the Nebraska University Secondary Teacher Education Project (NUSTEP), which moved secondary teacher education at the University of Nebraska to clinical sites. Pat Brose worked with experimental clinical schools at Chico State that led to more permanent reform there. Ron Cramer in his Early Childhood clinical school work developed community school-based work in tough areas of Detroit and adjacent cities. Ron Lundeberg worked in clinical schools at the University of California, Berkeley. Myrliss Hershey did field-based teaching and teacher education work in Wichita, Kansas, which is depicted in *The Teacher Was a Witch* (Philadelphia: Westminster, 1973). Evelyn Wiggins (education) and Pat Gardner (English) worked with Ned Bodily to develop school-based teacher training for Utah State University at Mendon and in other Utah towns in in the Logan area.

Goal III: *To foster a sensitivity to cultural differences as these differences appear in the language, dialects, and conventional writing forms of various groups, in play and informal fantasy, and in formal literary, mythical, and religious structures.*

1. Several arts and sciences faculty members assumed leadership roles in developing the scholarship and school experience necessary for effective participation in this aspect of the process of educating teachers. For example, William Anderson (English, San Fernando Valley State College) worked for several years in black and Chicano practicum schools and developed English courses in genre studies and children's literature. He wrote, with Patrick Groff, a standard higher education introduction to children's literature and literary analysis (Anderson and Groff, *A New Look at Children's Literature* [Belmont, Calif.: Wadsworth, 1972]) based on his experience. Lawrence Evers taught in the Macy (Omaha tribe) public schools, encouraged the introduction of Omaha literature and language to the Macy public schools, participated in some of the first teaching of native American literature related to the school curriculum at

the University of Nebraska, wrote a soon-to-be-published collection of Omaha literature for schools (using present and older Omaha materials), and now occupies a role in teaching native American literature (English and anthropology) at the University of Arizona. Ralph Grajeda organized several Chicano cultural awareness centers related to the reform of schooling in Nebraska, developed new modes of literary approach to Chicano literature written in both Spanish and English and to the Pocho figure, caught between the Chicano and the Anglo worlds. He was hired in the University of Nebraska ethnic studies and English departments to work on literary criticism and contacts and resources in restructuring Chicano literary programs in schools. Fanonian in ideology, Mr. Grajeda is also the only Chicano presently involved in the American Association of Colleges' project for reform in the liberal arts. Curt Rulon (North Texas State College, English and linguistics) wrote about, taught, and developed transformational linguistic approaches to the study of black dialects, reading, and dialectical miscue analysis. Sophia Nelson, chairwoman of the department of English at West Virginia State College, labored vigorously to improve the black studies component in the literature curriculum for teachers in her school, developed a useful set of black studies readings (Lettie S. Austin *et al., Black Man and the Promise of America* [Glenview, Ill.: Scott, Foresman, 1970]), and participated in several collateral moves to improve the black community's voice in the education process for teachers.

2. Similar work was done by other persons in arts sectors at their home institutions: Dave Brumble (English TTT at the University of Pittsburgh) worked in iconology, medieval literature, and children's drama in the schools while the Pittsburgh TTT project was in progress; Vern Torczon (Louisiana State University, New Orleans), in black history and culture of New Orleans; Dick Zbaracki (Iowa State University), in English genre theory in schools; Gene Hardy (University of Nebraska), in genre theory and children's literature; Leslie Whipp (University of Nebraska), in children's and adults' fantasy structures and ordinary daylight experiences.

3. There is a similar history of work by people in education using the theoretical structures, commonly asserted to be the possession of arts people, to develop school materials, school policy, and better

teachers: Mildred Gladney (University of Nebraska and Chicago public schools) used black dialectical structures to develop language experience and reading; Ron Cramer (Oakland), developmental psychology and linguistic studies to develop community-based education; Virginia Jones, structural linguistics and phonemic-graphemic relations to train teachers of Alaskan natives; Patrick Groff (San Diego), literary theory to teach children's literature. There are many more examples.

Goal II: *To foster the development of open educational formats.*

1. In addition to the free schools, open educational formats—some used for the clinical training of teachers and some not—were developed in schools. Open classrooms which had uses in inservice or preservice teacher training were developed. The character of these efforts to open up the school and to provide decent environment-specific education to teacher and child are epitomized in an article by Diane Divoky:

> . . . The children who go to school here [in Appalachia] do not look or act like the children in San Jose or Brooklyn or St. Paul. The teeth are often dark with decay, the too-small shoes have no laces, the faces are pasty-pale from a diet of beans. Most often the school clothes are provided by a $25 allowance from the privately sponsored Save the Children Federation, which also buys equipment for the schools.
>
> The children come from homes with no television or books. They cannot tell you the name of a major league baseball team, or what country has windmills and tulips, or what year they were born. An 80 IQ is no rarity here. . . .
>
> Since 1937, Juanita Witt has been a teacher in these schools, a dispenser of ideas, in many ways, the only link to the world outside. She took some time off to raise six children and help her husband—a badly disabled World War II veteran—with their farm chores. She also found time to commute to Berea College to finish her degree in 1969 and travel out to the University of Nebraska in 1969-70 to take a master's at an [EPDA-] sponsored institute. She has been put down by local school officials for being "a little too rebellious," forced to beg for whatever books and materials she has collected, and been disappointed by the meager results of great efforts, but she has never given up on the children of Appalachia.
>
> For the past two years, Juanita has been a Title I remedial reading teacher assigned to the seven one-room school houses still remaining in the country. Well Hope enrolls 16 students in grades one through seven. (Until the road was paved last year, students never "went out" from Well Hope to high school. It was the beginning and end of their education.) Juanita hauls the filmstrip projector and record player up the muddy slope into the dilapidated school. Their entrance is greeted by shy smiles. Juanita has brought a book

with bright-colored pictures of Indians. "I saw it, and you know, children, I couldn't resist."

... High-interest projects are the technique Juanita uses to turn her students on to using their imaginations, to get them to talk and read and write without being self-conscious about it. Last year she guided her class through projects on animals and Kentucky history, subjects with a natural attraction for her children. The animal unit resulted in a booklet of animal poems, and the history unit in letter writing to officials in every county in the state . . . .

Her stock in trade is a dogged optimism and firm belief in the potential of the children. "These children just don't have the opportunities or the materials; it's not that they don't have the mental capabilities," she insists. Her year with other hand-picked teachers in Nebraska was a big boost. "I learned that urban teachers have problems, too, and that I wasn't as far behind in my thinking as I had thought I was . . . "

Mostly, she is a source of reassurance and confidence for the children. "I try not to crowd them too much," she explains. "The big thing is to make them feel good about themselves. If you've done that, then you've done most of your teaching. Sometimes I get to feeling hopeless, but then I see a child who's interested and I feel good again." (*Learning: The Magazine for Creative Teaching*, 1 [November 1972], 13; copyright 1972 by Education Today Company, Inc., 530 University Avenue, Palo Alto, CA 94301; reprinted by permission.)

Juanita Witt is not rare among Nebraska TTT project teachers. The environments in which many of them work for reform are harsh.

Goal I: *To foster the use of structuralist approaches to children and their various cultures, particularly the imaginative and linguistic forms.*

1. This work has been advanced by the activity of Hugh Rudorf, Ron Cramer, Vergie Grambrell, Mildred Gladney, and Curt Rulon (linguistics, reading, black dialects) and has resulted in published research, reading materials, and teacher education devices. Ray Jung used structuralist techniques to do rhetorical analyses of children's writing. Alice Neuendorf (University of New Mexico) analyzed Navajo literature and language. Ernest Bradford is doing a structuralist exegetical analysis of black liberation literature based on the Bible and its relation to black education. The work of Evers, Brose, and others, mentioned above, could as well appear here.

Evaluation

The Nebraska project was evaluated by Gabriel Della-Piana at the University of Utah. This evaluation was based on the notion that any "change" produced by the project would immediately be apparent. Measurements taken during the first year to see how the participants had changed their institutions and their own practice did not allow for the difficulties in achieving educational reform, the necessity of working through clumsy bureaucracies to gain approval for reform, the risk that some participants might be fired or have to relocate to secure reform. Hence, they did not show what we have learned across almost a decade of following people about how much people will do given time and just a bit of a chance. The Whitmanesque catalogues above do not exhaust the efforts of participants to achieve project goals. Most participants tried to change things at their home institutions. Some gave up. A few—precious few—treated the program as the John Hay Fellows Program, where "one could spend a year sitting on a rug with Vivaldi playing stereophonically and just audibly in the background" (Donald Bigelow's description). Few people neglected the program while they were in it, however, or were lazy about reform when they returned to their old places. That is perhaps more a tribute to their guts than to the strategy used, which was too brief and lacked focus on the participants' home environment. Future OE strategies to educate change agents should not only educate participants but also provide an opportunity to analyze change in terms of the home environment and provide support, information, and "news" for at least a decade after they return to their home institutions. Participants should also come together periodically to discuss their work as change agents.

Institutional Change

The Nebraska project was also supposed to "change" the host institution. That goal was scarcely mentioned in the original mandate, save in Donald Bigelow's vague talk, delivered with the help of overhead transparencies in 1967, in which he suggested that the project should "capture the graduate colleges" of the host institutions. It became clear in time that effective work with the participants required an effort to change the University of Nebraska. How could participants gain practice as institutional change agents in an open situation except through attempting to change their own environment—the University of Nebraska and the communities in the area? Before assessing that effort, it is helpful to examine the position of the university and that of the state from 1967 to 1969, the first years of the project.

   As the project got underway, Nebraska was in the closing stages of a centralization process that had eliminated thousands of rural schools, but this was occurring later than it had in most other states. Conventional educators in the state's department of education and various colleges of education had worked steadily to develop a rating system for quality schools, to get state aid for education, to guarantee some sort of minimal standards for the "backwater" rural areas. In the 1940's and the 1950's educators in the department of education and at the University of Nebraska Teachers College, who had fought the "liberal arts elitists" to a standstill and kept at bay repressive forces in some communities, such as the American Legion, had been replaced by more pragmatic administrators willing to make peace with liberal arts and liberal arts-controlled curriculum reform efforts. Community education, considered important by educators in the fifties (especially Vaughn Phelps, Dale Hayes, and Walt Beggs), was lost in the rush toward standardization, quality control, curriculum reform, and teacher retraining. This was also a period of adjustment within certain sectors of the Nebraska populace. Eldridge Cleaver came to Omaha, Malcolm X's birthplace, to speak at a park which the black people of Omaha had renamed Malcolm X Park. The American Indian Movement (AIM) was organizing on Indian reservations. And Corky Gonzalez' Crusade for Justice was being formed on behalf of his sort of cultural nationalism in the western Nebraska Chicano communities along the Platte, particularly Scottsbluff. Almost all of this activity ultimately focused on the human service agencies in the communities where minorities lived: the OEO (Office of Economic Opportunity), the schools, the health agencies, and police protection agencies. From 1967 to 1970 student power also hit the state (later than in most states) and expressed itself in student pressure for self-determination within the university, for educational reform of a decentralized, nonnormed sort, and for student resistance to the institutions seen as serving Vietnam and the draft (Reserve Officers' Training Corps and harsh grading systems). Though about one in fifteen Nebraskans were members of minority groups, the university had less than fifty minority students among its fifteen thousand students, and there were almost no representatives from minority groups on the faculty. In 1967 prominent university and state officials claimed that Nebraska had "no minority problem because it treated its minorities right." Scottsbluff, Gordon, Wounded

Knee, the Omaha riots, and student demonstrations and strikes had not yet split the state.

There was even more reason for complacency as older generations of Nebraska statesmen gained national political prominence. President Nixon several times received his largest margin of support from Nebraskans, and he had many close Nebraska advisers. He appointed Clifford Hardin, at that time chancellor of the University of Nebraska, to be Secretary of Agriculture. By the late sixties Nebraska saw itself as the center of mid-American prosperity and stability— "religious," increasingly prosperous, and old—proud of having surmounted the ravages of the depression and the period of "bad schools." Yet, almost one-third of the state was poor in OEO terms; Indians, on the average, died at the age of forty; Indians and Chicanos dropped out of schools at rates well over 50 percent; and black schools in Omaha were, to all appearances, both segregated and unequal, a matter that the Justice Department has since pursued in the courts. The Circuit Court of Appeals in St. Louis, in June 1975, declared the Omaha schools to be segregated schools and ordered elimination of segregation—root and branch. Yet, in 1967, the notion was that all was well.

The first TTT proposal setting forth goals aimed at changing the University of Nebraska was the one for 1969-70, and the goals were almost identical with those developed earlier for and with visiting participants, except that two items significant for the participant portion of the program were dropped from the "home institution" reform goals: the emphasis on structuralism and developmental perspectives, and the exclusive emphasis on elementary education. The latter is self-explanatory; it was the total University of Nebraska program that was to be altered, not just the elementary sector. The concern for structuralism and developmental perspectives involved controversies that paralleled those between Bright and Hunt at the first conference. At Nebraska's Teachers College the notion that reform might be accomplished by applying principles of behavioristic psychology and systems theory to the total institutional program had been discussed. Since that type of reform was already being discussed, it seemed best to omit the question of psychological and administrative theory from discussions of the "home institution" reform goals in the hope that a variety of alternatives would spring up.

In retrospect, it is clear that the Nebraska TTT project was thrown up to bridge the chasm between the "haves" and the "have-nots," but the structure was fragile, indeed. TTT was regarded as dangerous and radical by the haves (one site visit report on the project by a famous evaluator reflects that view), and, by some have-nots, as a cautious organization that played at school reform and culture-based education while the real issues, transfer of political power and revolutionary change, went unattended. When efforts to institutionalize reforms sought by the TTT project were made part of the day-to-day action of TTT project personnel, suspicions were further heightened. Project personnel, at the request of fellow faculty members, served on committees that selected D. B. Varner as president and Peter McGrath and Robert Egbert as deans. They successfully pushed minority concerns and education reform (particularly the improvement of undergraduate teaching and its evaluation) as selection criteria for the men who were to occupy these positions. Project members also privately raised a quantity of money to support the court cases of minority persons seeking educational and political reform, persons unjustly arrested. This action helped project participants see how technical assistance could convince people of the political viability of conventional institutions, but it did little to ease Establishment discomfort.

When the Cambodian-Kent State crisis occurred, the Nebraska TTT was encouraged both by campus "radicals" and by university administrators to open a campus forum to discuss these events and their meaning for educational reform. This forum, which included representatives from the administration, from the reserve officers' program, and from the groups opposing the war in Vietnam, established some communication between the right and the left on the campus and conveyed some sense of the educational and civic reforms needed. An independent citizens' group appointed by the university and made up largely of businessmen and lawyers (the Spelts Commission) applauded the project for its assistance and imagination during the crisis, but the local community was not entirely happy with what TTT had done. The action was thought to have caused a strike. No action for social-educational change, no effort to counter oppression where oppression has existed, can altogether eliminate the anger, frustration, and retaliation of those whose interests are not directly served by the effort.

To bring the home institution effort to the point where enduring actual reforms could be made, four task forces representing the community, the school, liberal arts, and education were set up in 1969-70. At the end of 1970 each task force presented plans for the reform of teacher education at the university and the reform of education as it affected each area. The community task force report recommended changes in community participation in the teacher education process, a "field" or community component to provide political education for all teachers, intense training in the history, language, art, and ethnoscience of Chicano, Indian, and black children, and heavy emphasis on improving teachers' abilities to teach reading and provide a general sense of self-esteem. None of these suggestions were welcome ones.

By fall of 1970 the institutional reform segment of the Nebraska TTT project had reached a crossroad—perhaps, more appropriately, a series of crossroads. Pro- and anti-Establishment forces created one such situation. Another developed between those who favored a behaviorist model for educational change and those who favored a developmental "open" model. The alignments that resulted from these polarizations could have been predicted with some accuracy.

Establishment forces were heavily supported by public school and Teachers College personnel. Anti-Establishment forces were more often aided by representatives from the academic disciplines and from the community, especially ethnic minority groups. It is perhaps surprising that some conservative rural supporters of one-room schools were forced to take an awkward anti-Establishment stance as a result of the school reorganization (consolidation) movement promoted earlier by influential educationists. While they had much in common with reform elements seeking decentralization and community control, they were, for the most part, relatively passive onlookers in that they did not always identify with the style of minority-oriented reformers or with minority causes. Hence, the TTT project in Nebraska did not benefit the white people in the less wealthy rural areas of Nebraska as much as it should have. It is curious that both directors of the project, who wrote this chapter, came from rural one-room-school or small-town backgrounds. Yet both were more successful in organizing reform related to urban and minority efforts than in those related to rural areas. There is no easy explanation for this.

The concept of parity also became troublesome. Teachers College and public school personnel tended to see it as an unwarranted intrusion into areas in which they were, presumably, the acknowledged experts. In some cases they supported all of the reforms sought by anti-Establishment forces, with one notable exception, the concept of parity, which they saw as a threat to the control they had achieved through a century-long struggle for "professional" status. Although liberal arts scholars no longer derided education courses as they once had and younger scholars were concerned with humane, individual, and liberating approaches to schooling—concepts to which now skeptical educationists had long paid verbal tribute—some of the old condescension remained. Because community members, particularly those with minority ethnic backgrounds, found the schools wanting insofar as their needs and those of their children were concerned, the more vocal and aggressive ones welcomed the opportunity to participate in educational decision making. Many other people, although they favored greater community involvement, were suspicious and reluctant to devote the necessary time and energy to activities which, they were convinced, would not change bureaucratic procedures. School personnel saw all of these attitudes as threats and reacted against any concept of parity, creating a power struggle of the most classic sort.

The polarization between those who advocated a behaviorist model for bringing about educational reform and the exponents of the freer developmental, open model was similar but less clear cut. The behaviorist model was pushed most vigorously by two educational theorists, one a psychologist and the other a philosopher. Neither public schools nor Teachers College personnel enthusiastically supported such a model, and community and liberal arts people tended to oppose it because they feared it could be used as a tool for manipulation at a time when manipulation was to be feared. They supported, instead, an open classroom model resembling the British Infant School. This polarization, which took the form of an ideological difference, never really became political. These differences rendered progress toward the project goals slow, difficult, and indecisive during the 1970-71 academic year, when tension still ran rather high on compus and in the community in the wake of the Cambodian invasion, general racial unrest, and campus disturbances of May 1970.

As for the directors, Paul Olson, a liberal arts-oriented person, was a controversial figure. Erwin Goldenstein, on the other hand, was a member of the Teachers College faculty, and he was closely identified with the education Establishment. He also enjoyed at least a modicum of respect among liberal arts scholars as a result of his scholarship and his considerable activity in university-wide political activities, and he was slowly earning a measure of credibility with minority teachers. Because relations were so tenuous, Goldenstein made a conscientious effort to maintain close liaison with all task forces. This effort provided him with new perspectives, which he sometimes articulated with vigor and feeling, but it also roused the suspicion of many of his colleagues that he had modified his allegiance to the teacher education program. While his own colleagues began to feel that he had sold out, other groups perceived him as moving too slowly, perhaps indecisively, toward project goals. What Goldenstein was actually trying to do was to convince the people concerned with Teachers College that alternative models of teacher preparation were needed. Even though the model they were using had enjoyed some notable successes earlier, it was becoming the object of considerable criticism as new social and educational forces developed.

The strategy of opening questions, backing away, and then creating new structures did have some measurable effect, but it is difficult to separate what the project created from what it contributed, both financially and by engaging the energies of people across the university. It is best to look at the goals from the perspective of change *created* or *possibly created.*

Goal I: *Field work and earlier induction of prospective teachers into the field and field-teaching experience.*

Perhaps the most notable example of this kind of work is the work of the NUSTEP project, which affects 65-70 percent of the students entering secondary education and involves the departments of secondary education, educational psychology, mathematics, health, business, and English, as well as several other departments, in a joint field-based clinical competency-based program. This program, part of the behavioristic thrust at Nebraska that developed concurrent with TTT, advanced secondary education field experience and prestudent teaching experience in the schools at least a year in the professional sequence. (A somewhat similar advance of the introduction to field experience was also developed by the elementary education department and expanded with TTT funds.) Though the NUSTEP system was begun by the department of secondary education over a year prior to its receiving TTT support, it was moving parallel to TTT effort along several lines. TTT monies were the first monies from outside regular departmental allocations given to NUSTEP, and the additional funds enabled the program to include a number of pre-dominantly minority practicum sites, to develop arts and sciences components, and to refine several learning modules. The program is still imperfect in its evaluation and feedback aspects. There is not yet a full inclusion of arts and sciences in the scheme, and there are other difficulties to be resolved. At the same time it is clearly the dominant secondary reform mode. The creation of a "behavioristic" alternative model has led, incidentally, to moves to create a humanistic model, a notion that the project had gambled on early. If the logjam broke, it was anticipated that it would break in several directions.

Goal II: *Early and thorough introduction of teaching candidates to outsiders' communities.*

Aside from the work that has been done by NUSTEP, some of the best education work introducing teaching candidates to outside committees has been:

- For native Americans—TONIC (Tutors of Nebraska Indian Children), a TTT-organized course of study involving teaching Winnebago and Lincoln Indian children was offered through the English and philosophy of education departments and supported by both institutional and volunteer agency funds.
- For Chicanos—The Chicano Awareness Centers were organized and initially supported by TTT and loosely affiliated with the University of Nebraska at Lincoln, where teacher education practicum work may be done and where "Action" students have their internships.
- For all ethnic groups—The recently developed Institute of Ethnic Studies was jointly sponsored and staffed by the Teachers College and the College of Arts and Sciences in whose creation TTT played a major role.
- For ethnic minorities and lower-middle-income whites—The development of the Lincoln Cooperative Schools project will become, at the level of elementary education, what NUSTEP has become at the secondary level, a major institutionalized teacher education alternative.

Probably the most significant internal institutional change attributable to the Nebraska TTT project was the creation of the Cooperative

Schools project, an alternative school-based teacher education program involving the University of Nebraska at Lincoln and the Lincoln public schools. Some of the TTT's funded small proposals, especially those dealing with early practicum experiences and the education of low-income and ethnic minority group education, coupled with the direction taken by the TTT Institute (the program for fellows), seemed to lead almost inevitably to the development of an alternative program. Earnest planning for such a program had its genesis in the deliberations of the planning committee charged, in the fall of 1971, with the responsibility of preparing the draft for the 1972-73 proposal. This idea, transcending to a considerable degree both the differences and the power struggles that had plagued earlier TTT efforts, was readily accepted by the planners and later approved by the steering committee and university and public school authorities for transmission to OE, where funding was secured. Thus, the TTT project merged into the Cooperative Schools project. This apparent metamorphosis relieved the project of some of the most bitter controversies of earlier years, but it by no means transformed it into the utopian education program that has been sought from the beginning and that continued to elude everyone's grasp.

After considerable backing and filling in the effort to find a proper clinical school site, two schools that expressed considerable interest in the project were eventually selected: one had the second highest percentage of minorities enrolled among the city's elementary schools and had been nominated by the superintendent of schools; the other, a "blue-collar" and "professional" school, was nominated by its own faculty and principal who were quite enthusiastic about the project. The two sites were selected rather than one upon the recommendation of Lincoln's Superintendent John Prasch, based on the feeling that parents in a given school would be less likely to object to "experimenting" on their youngsters if another school were involved as well. While this was regarded as something of a complicating factor, the project staff raised no serious objections, and the steering committee approved the arrangement.

The Cooperative Schools project produced some organizational changes. The old TTT steering committee that had watched over the effort to institutionalize for some years was retained as the policymaking body, while more specific planning was made the responsibility of a newly created planning council that drew its membership from public school, Teachers College, liberal arts, and local community representation. In addition, community advisory committees for each school were created on the recommendation of the TTT's community task force. Support for, and advice concerning, the project were given by all four TTT task forces. The TTT project coordinator became the director of the Cooperative Schools project, and Joe Aguilar, a Chicano educator and scholar who had been a 1971-72 TTT fellow, was named assistant director, giving part of his time to the project while completing his doctoral studies and assuming the directorship at the beginning of the 1973-74 school year.

The school-based teacher education program was relatively unplanned during 1972-73 and 1973-74. The process brought to the schools, the faculty selected from Teachers College and the college of arts and sciences, and the communities served were based on open cooperative decision making rather than sophisticated, easily definable educational ideologies. The closest approximation to the process that evolved that is available in print is a summary of the one operating at Johnston College, University of the Redlands, that appears in its accreditation report (available from the Johnston College chancellor's office).

One feature of the first year of Cooperative Schools' operation was a series of in-service seminars involving teachers in the two schools, administrators, Teachers College and arts and sciences faculty members, fellows, and graduate students. These seminars dealt with such subjects as cultural awareness, the creative uses of media, language development, Piagetian theory, and creative drama. In the seminars the distinction between teacher and taught was often deliberately blurred. At the same time ten fellows, all experienced elementary school teachers, and ten project staff with expertise in such areas as psychology, science, media, minority cultures, and reading, as well as part-time university faculty members from such disciplines as geography, political science, philosophy, and educational psychology, supplemented the efforts of regularly assigned classroom teachers to enhance the educational experiences provided for youngsters in the two schools. Undergraduate psychology and teacher education students were involved, by virtue of the fact that instructors of several sections of child psychology, educational psychology, elementary school mathematics, elementary school art, and history and philosophy of education already had their students involved in prestudent teaching practicum experiences at both schools. Relationships among the various groups and individuals thus involved were permitted to develop naturally, with a virtual absence of administrative pressure. For all of its apparent lack of structure, the blending of seminars with direct work with elementary school pupils, teachers, and parents exemplified the continuing effort to wed theory and practice begun in the project in 1967-68. Furthermore, this arrangement represented a confluence of the two streams of endeavor previously identified as project and institute.

A clearly defined alternative model of teacher education did not evolve as rapidly as had been hoped. In the first year new and meaningful relations among university and public school faculties and students, along with some parents, were established, and an atmosphere of trust gradually grew. Community advisory committees at each school, however, did not function as well as had been anticipated. They had difficulty defining their functions and establishing appropriate relationships with the executive boards of the PTA's. Apathy on the part of some members, aggressiveness on the part of others, and a feeling of impotence on the part of still others resulted in a minimum of meaningful input from community representatives. Parental involvement in media seminars at one school did result in the creation of positive community concern in that school. Community organizers employed by both schools created some significant pockets of community interest but not on any substantial or continuing basis. The history of community participation has been sufficiently marked by discouragement, lack of clear definition, and slow responsiveness to community reaction. Clear and continuous lines of community input and management systems have not yet been created, to the detriment of the orderly conduct of affairs.

Plans for the 1973-74 school year reflected a continuation and further development of activities begun the previous year. Joe Aguilar, who was eminently familiar with TTT and Cooperative Schools endeavors, assumed direction of the project. He had become a member of the state-wide community task force in 1969, had served as principal of the only elementary school in the state that enrolled a majority of Chicano students, had been a TTT fellow in 1971-72, and had been assistant project director in 1972-73. With the strong support of the steering committee, especially its cochairmen, the new director moved the project in the direction of a genuine school-based teacher education model. Buoyed by his elementary school experience, his rank in the department of elementary education, and especially his consummate tact, he was able to bring a diverse group of people—teachers, administrators, parents, university faculty members, and professional evaluators—together in support of a cooperatively developed, rather clearly defined alternative teacher education model. He was especially effective in eliciting the vital support of the department of elementary education despite some key pockets of resistance based on unhappy memories of previous years. This was accomplished while activities at the schools reflected the 1972-73 pattern. One significant modification, however, was the creation, in each school, of a Research and Development room. (R&D is something of a misnomer. Competent, independent, creative teachers provide all interested pupils with special activities in such areas as art, mathematics, and creative writing that may not be available in the regular classrooms.)

Loss of TTT Funds

The most significant development of the 1973-74 and 1974-75 work is the fact that the local funding from the University of Nebraska at Lincoln and the Lincoln public schools had replaced federal TTT funding. Of all the institutional changes that may be attributed to the TTT investment in the Nebraska project, the Cooperative Schools are undeniably the direct consequence of that investment. The new local start is small. The project functioned in 1974-75 with ten undergraduate teacher education students enrolled at each school. Two on-site professors, one from the University of Nebraska at Lincoln faculty in elementary education and one from the staff of the public schools, were appointed for the two schools. Each coordinated and participated in the teacher education activities in the school. Thirteen semester credit hours of educational experience were provided at the two sites during each semester and were furnished by faculty members in educational psychology, elementary education, English, the history and philosophy of education, sociology, and philosophy. These experiences centered chiefly in the areas of general child development, the development of logical thought in children, children's literature, and community study. While the success of the program is by no means assured, the university has completed the first year of an alternative school-based teacher education program in 1974-75, and it was a definite outgrowth of the TTT project. Plans for 1975-76, in their final stages, represent some modification of earlier efforts. In short, a federally supported development has become a locally supported program. Whereas the NUSTEP program was only fostered by TTT, this internal program emerged from it.

Goal III: *To plan joint arts and sciences-education work particularly germane to the education of teachers.*

In this area a most important outcome of the activity of TTT personnel was the creation of a new "Purposes of the University" document and a related management system for the total university. This system requires that the university take cognizance of specific state-community manpower needs, phase out unneeded programs, and develop a fusion of theoretical and practical education in all areas of state need that require using arts and sciences theory as part of a coherent program rather than depending on technical education to accomplish tasks that are more than technical. The position of the document develops, for the whole university, a parity-planning procedure similar to that used in TTT. This policy statement is now being implemented in all segments of the university through administrative, faculty, and community action and through a management system keyed to the statement. The document applies to education in its relation to arts and sciences and the community as well as to other professional sequences and promises a fusion not possible before.[5]

If the "Purposes of the University" document is the most general product of TTT arts and sciences-education activity, the most specific and concrete are the TTT special project sequences in arts and sciences that have been institutionalized—in children's literature, linguistics and reading, adults' and children's fantasy, and in geography, mathematics, philosophy, and biological science. The small TTT projects that contributed most to these arts and sciences changes include: a joint workshop in elementary school mathematics conducted by the departments of elementary education and mathematics; the support for a teaching-learning center that has developed into a significant agency for improving instruction all across the university campus, but especially in arts and sciences and in education; several arts and sciences-education workshops in minority group education that have developed into regular offerings; and the offerings in philosophy and education dealing with Piaget and children's learning. Both colleges have also been affected by TTT's role in the creation of the Institute for Ethnic Studies, by the creation of a Mexican-American advisory committee to the chancellor, by the TTT project's insistence on the recruitment of ethnic minority students at the graduate and undergraduate levels, and by the establishment of a chancellor's Minority Roundtable. In addition, Teachers College has in some sense reacted to Bigelow's admonition to "capture the graduate college" by introducing a much more flexible program of doctoral studies in education. The university, which has not been notably aggressive in its hiring of minority employees, has hired at least three minority persons who were TTT fellows or staff on its arts and sciences-education and academic-administrative staff.

Goals IV

and V: *To plan clinical schools and systematic training through discussions of NUSTEP and the Cooperative School projects.*

One further feature of "systematic training" deserves discussion. The original emphasis on English linguistics and literature and the follow-up emphasis on related arts and sciences disciplines in the early stages of the project may make it appear somewhat "airy" and unconcerned, for all its community emphasis, with the day-to-day issues of what jobs people can get, what technical skills are demanded in the local labor market, and whether young people are emerging from school not only with civic capabilities but also with "work tools" necessary for survival in the community.

Vocational education was thoroughly discussed by the community task force at meetings in 1971 and 1972. Participants at these meetings, in addition to regular task force membership, were representatives of industry and labor, presidents of vocational-technical colleges, staff people from the state's department of education; faculty members from the university's Teachers College, college of agriculture, college of arts and sciences, and college of engineering. Concern at these meetings centered around the tendency of high schools to stress college preparatory education at the expense of occupational education, a lack of adequate programs to train teachers for postsecondary vocational schools, and a tendency to demean the dignity of work on the part of even parents and high school counselors. At one meeting the community task force passed a resolution urging the University of Nebraska to create a coordinating agency for vocational education in order to make more meaningful the attempts to meet this need in discrete colleges divided according to the economic contours of the state.

It would be folly to claim that the TTT project was the single, or even the chief, factor impelling the progress that has been made in coordinating vocational education at the University of Nebraska at Lincoln. And the progress achieved so far undoubtedly falls short of what many task force members had hoped. Nevertheless, the university has created a post of coordinator of vocational education and employed in this position Dr. Hazel Crain, whose authority extends over programs preparing teachers for agricultural education, home economics, business education, distributive education, industrial education, and health occupations education. A master's degree program in vocational education, along with more flexible doctoral studies in education, was approved by the Board of Regents in the spring of 1974. The effort of the new, coordinated programs to reach into the community allows for forty semester hours of skill work for industrial education teachers, and these may be taken at one of Nebraska's vocational-technical colleges. (A second link with vocational education is being established with a newly developed community education program at Teachers College that received initial impetus from a Mott Foundation grant. This development is not claimed as a TTT success, but it is "in the direction" envisaged by the Nebraska TTT project in 1970 and 1971. TTT might have had an easier time with the "community parity" concept and rural reform had it represented its efforts as continuous with efforts in community education made by Vaughn Phelps, Dale Hayes, and Walt Beggs in the 1950's.[6] Hindsight is easy. The point is that too often TTT did not build on congenial indigenous radical reform traditions of a populist sort that would have provided a sense of regional identity and continuity with a historical tradition.)

Goal VI: *To relate the whole process of education to the demands which citizens of all racial groups are making for better teachers.*

It became clear that parents of minority children would be able to affect the university only if clear channels of access and tools were provided. The early TTT efforts to give parents power in the schools through giving them a clearer picture of their rights in Title I and in the use of the Johnson O'Malley funds led to more structured efforts to give minorities a voice in higher education also. TTT Project community people (Leonard Springer, Robert Mackey) and the TTT director (Paul Olson) wrote the statute that made the Nebraska State Indian Commission into a statutory all-Indian body empowered to review state and federal programs for native Americans (much of that body's review has been directed at the University of Nebraska). A similar Mexican-American effort at a TTT workshop led to the creation of the chancellor's Mexican-American advisory committee for the University of Nebraska, a group intended to have similar functions. A black who worked closely with the TTT, Ernest Chambers, now sits in the state legislature (earlier he was widely regarded in white circles as an "unrepresentative self-appointed spokesman"). He ran for governor in 1975 and picked up more votes than people expected. He has had a significant effect on university minority policy. Another black who was a TTT staff member is now head of the University of Nebraska's Department of Minority Affairs, a minority student support agency.

A result of the TTT minority-low-income effort and of the decline of higher education enrollments in the state has been that increasing segments of the university have become committed to a genuine open admissions policy so that no student will be kept from the university by lack of money. Studies and legislative efforts to support such a policy are going ahead now. The University of Nebraska at Lincoln had 265 minority freshmen in the fall of 1974-75. The number of students in residence (300-400) falls far short of the 1,000 students which it should have, even taking cognizance of high school dropouts, but it is certainly more than the fewer than 50 of 1967. (The University of Nebraska at Omaha, the new branch, had about 800 minority students.)

The University of Nebraska still is not delivering the services that it ought to deliver to minority and low-income people. In one case, Indian students at Lincoln have recently asked that federal funds be taken away from the university for its failure to do a good job. Even though a process has been initiated that has brought some educational change to a large, complex organization that operated in an austere financial and political environment, too many things that should have happened did not.

One area in which the TTT project failed to achieve any significant impact is that of sensitizing school administrators to the needs of ethnic minority youngsters. A few administrators from various schools in the state did attend some community task force-sponsored regional meetings throughout the state in 1969-70, and former participants and staff have conducted a few workshops dealing with this issue at several locations in the state. But the impact of such activities has been minimal at best, and certainly no dramatic change in administrative attitudes can be claimed. The greatest hope in this area lies in the activities of Joe Aguilar, former participant and now director of the Cooperative Schools project. He provides a minority education component in a required aspect of programs leading to the master's degree and the six-year certificate in educational administration, as well as conducting a special workshop on minority education during a summer session in 1975. Yet, it is hard to claim that the important citadels of educational power have been scaled when one of the most visible has hardly been touched. Wherever change was produced, it was not linear change amenable to linear management evaluations. No one in the leadership of the project believed in linear management. No single new structure encompassing all of teacher education such as North Dakota's Center for Teaching and Learning emerged. The ideological tensions between developmentalists and behaviorists, centralizers and decentralizers, professionals and community still exist. As alternatives have developed, however, the tensions and mutual criticisms have assumed more direction and produced more reasoned educational change. Many of the most powerful structures that emerged were not located within the university at all; they were structures through which neglected communities could articulate their sense of what would constitute good educational practice and develop the talent to secure it for themselves. The change produced within the university occurred among pockets of students and in an informal network of faculty, through the creation of partial structures and an incomplete realizations of goals sought.

We have plenty of "dolphin's muck and mire" to worry about. Were we to begin again, we might begin with a longer planning period, a more rational and specific assessment of needs by the community, a clearer commitment from the powerful to respond to need, and a full consultation with all planning authorities at all levels, including the state legislature. We might seek a more adequate local commitment to reform prior to the release of federal monies.

Certainly no federal money ought to be granted that places the project director under discretionary obligation, but places the recipient institution under no obligation. Money ought to be let by competitive contract alone. School systems and universities should be compelled to treat the contracted money as hard money used to create permanent institutional structures, to hire permanent faculty, and to create permanent change. It is not clear whether the University of Nebraska would have been willing to commit itself to such a course in 1967 or to the changes that actually resulted as a consequence of TTT's more disorderly way of channeling money. It is clear that many powerful forces in the state would not have committed themselves to such change in 1967. It may be that it would have been more fruitful, in such circumstances, to have used the money spent on the University of Nebraska on other structures, as, for example, the Fund for Improvement of Post-Secondary Education, which spent its money creating new higher education structures sponsored by oppressed groups and designed to serve their needs. One such small, local, culture-specific school, the Winnebago-Santee-Omaha College, which was supported by the fund, exists in Nebraska. At the same time, higher education's intractable large institutions are hard to ignore. Some changes did occur at Nebraska as a result of TTT money. More might have occurred had the national strategy included an assault on conventional accrediting, licensing, and management structures—a perception reached late and arrived at with difficulty. In any case, a university that was about as complacently conventional as any could be in 1967 now has alternative projects—from the five-million-dollar State University of Nebraska (SUN) project dedicated to nontraditional learning, to voluntary open learning projects in the Teacher College, to cluster colleges and field-learning settings of all sorts (Centennial College and University Studies, for example). Although this was not altogether TTT's doing, it did play a role. It is not easy to say in clear, unequivocal terms that education or teacher education are better for the Nebraska project. They are at least more interesting.

OTHER PERSPECTIVES

Focus on TTT's

One target of this goal was the gatekeepers of education—university deans, administrators, and professors in major disciplines—for they determined the success or failure of the entire program. Herbert W. Wey, director of the TTT project at Appalachian State University and later chancellor of the university, wrote of the gatekeepers' roles at his university:

Our successes came about for a number of reasons. First, the Project had the active support and influence of the Chancellor of the University. Administered from his office, the Project had prestige and respect from all quarters on the campus. Next in importance was the high quality of persons elected as program participants. These persons were selected by deans and department chairpersons with the stipulation that only the strongest faculty members were to be nominated—that is, those faculty members who were open to new ideas and who were influential in their departments. These participating faculty members have now become the change agents within their own departments and colleges. In sum, the quality of persons selected for participation was extremely high and represented the very best and most outstanding professors in the University. An additional component to the success of the program was ensured by allowing the persons selected to have the major input into the planning of the training program and its operation. . . .

The residual benefits of the Triple T program may be seen in the joint appointees which now function within the College of Education from 17 academic departments. These 23 persons serve as bridges between the components of the teacher education program and between the University and the public schools. The Triple T Project made the joint appointee program possible by creating a climate suitable to its initiation by providing travel, supplies, and equipment, and consultant monies. Further residual benefits have occurred and are occurring in improved instruction in departments which had professors participate in the Triple T program.[7]

The interdisciplinary cooperation Herbert Wey wrote about was achieved to a greater extent at Clark University than anywhere else, but it placed a great amount of pressure on the TTT-Ph.D candidates. In the summer of 1974 Richard Ford looked back on the problems this pressure created:

Pressures for "immediate action," or for some type of specific and tangible changes in the schools, at that time, became so overwhelming that we could not limit ourselves only to graduate instruction. Some on our faculty regarded this move as the destruction of the program. From my own perspective, I am glad it worked out that way. I think it brought a sense of vitality and involvement rarely experienced within a graduate program, especially in the context of the disciplines of geography, history, and economics. However, there was a cost. And I think the cost was largely absorbed by the graduate students. What it amounted to was that the Ph.D candidates completed the existing requirements (not the regular Ph.D. requirements but those set by the departments as the special TTT sequence—but organized before the pressures for "immediacy" evolved). So most of those who finished did a Ph.D. with an additional dimension of action-based endeavors. One can rationalize that because the stipends were considerably larger than those of regular graduate students, and because they had support for summers as well (regular graduate students had no summer support), that the additional work was not onerous. On the other hand, a degree is a degree, and graduate institutions should try to maintain some equity in expectations of graduate students. The TTT fellows did not necessarily serve two masters. But they were subjected to time demands which were, I think, above and beyond what the regular graduate students did.[8]

Parity

Richard Ford also addressed himself to this second national goal and cited lack of trust as contributing to lack of achievement:

I think the issue of trust was uppermost in our shortcomings. University or school personnel have a rather bad track record in community endeavors. And to find ourselves suddenly expected to be active and visible in dozens of community actions was more than we could manage with our limited staff. So, in some cases, our graduate students could not, or did not, follow through. In other cases, because of incredibly rapid change within community leadership and community identity, the ground rules shifted to the point where we could not move. But in most of these situations it evolved back to a matter of trust. And in those community activities which succeeded—and some succeeded quite well—it was because our personnel could follow through and deliver on what was expected.

Where trust existed, however, a number of linkages outside the university still exist, according to Ford, but he also pointed out that such linkages "have very little to do with university policy and much more to do with personal relationships":

For example, I think of [Irving] Schwartz and his contact with dozens and dozens of teachers in the Worcester schools. In my own situation, I have worked actively in a number of community settings and assume that that role will continue. I have also stayed close to the Worcester schools. In the case of Duane Knos, he, too, is closely involved with a number of teachers and school projects. And as several new projects begin to develop here at Clark, I find that linkages with local industry, nearby social action agencies, and local funding groups are much more available, I think largely because of the TTT experience. And that was not necessarily one of our objectives back in 1968.[9]

When trust was lacking, Ford wrote, the project failed:

In the case of dealings with Burncoat Senior High School, or Chandler Junior High School, although we continue to work well with teachers and students within those buildings, we missed the boat with, in both cases, one key administrator (a department chairman in one case and a building principal in another). And in failing to establish trusting relationships there, we failed.[10]

New Educational Methods

Under the leadership of John Jarolomik, TTT's director at the University of Washington, the project brought about a nation-wide change in the teaching of social studies. Jarolomik, also a noted social studies professor, utilized TTT's funding and ideology to attract talented graduate students and able consultants to the university:

What the program intended to do, and indeed did succeed in doing [Jarolomik wrote in his final report], was to pump into the bloodstream of social studies education of this nation a cadre of highly competent individuals who were capable of moving into positions of leadership in teacher education, and who would bring to those positions the vision and the fundamental notions that were embodied in the concept of the Tri-University Project and the TTT Program. . . .

The project provided opportunities for intensive study in substantive fields of the social sciences and related disciplines, in curriculum and instruction, in the psychology of learning, and coordinated all of those experiences with related laboratory-type experiences with teachers and with elementary school pupils. A basic concept that flowed through the project from start to finish was the notion that improved teacher preparation comes about when teacher-training programs provide a well-balanced combination of work in substantive fields, in professional education, and in practical field experiences, all of which are soundly based on current research and theory of curriculum, instruction, and the psychology of human learning. As a general principle, the project provided participants with training experiences that directly paralleled those that . . . would be required . . . when they returned to their regular positions.[11]

Participants in the program have served as chairmen on national committees concerned with social studies, and have written textbooks for use in schools and colleges. The University of Washington is recognized, according to Jarolomik, "as one of the leading institutions in the United States in the preparation of social studies educators at the graduate level." Jarolomik attributes this entirely to the TTT project there.

Graduates of the University of Washington's doctoral program in social studies teach in universities throughout the country, and the demand for more such teachers continues. "In spite of the large number of doctorates produced in social studies education in recent years both here and elsewhere," Jarolomik wrote, "this university continues to get more requests for doctoral placements than it can supply."

Institutionalization

The Center for Teaching and Learning at the University of North Dakota epitomizes the realization of this fourth goal. The Center had its roots in the New School, a project started in the spring of 1968 to upgrade teachers without degrees who were teaching in the public school system in North Dakota, and to explore the possibilities of open classrooms. While teachers without degrees studied at the New School to obtain them, Ph.D. candidates in education took over their classrooms and developed the open classroom idea. When the TTT Program came into being, the politically astute dean of the New School, Vito Perrone, adapted the New School program to meet TTT standards, thereby qualifying for TTT funds.

"TTT's influence can hardly be minimized," Perrone wrote in his final report. He went on to say that "its advocacy of an educational reform process which included *all* parties having a stake in education was consonant with the dialogue occurring within North Dakota. And TTT's moral as well as fiscal support was critical to the New School's ultimate success in moving from intellectual assent to affirmation in practice."[12]

The New School and the school of education at North Dakota University merged to become the Center for Teaching and Learning. The center expanded activities to include OE's Follow Through programs, which were aimed at helping disadvantaged youth, and the Future Indian Teachers program.

Multiplier Effect

Probably no better example of the multiplier effect exists than the TTT project at Michigan State University, which is one of the largest teacher-training institutions in the country. The TTT project at Michigan State represented a microcosm of the entire TTT Program in its attempt to achieve all of TTT's national goals. Leaders of the project believed in the TTT dream—that American education can be changed—and implemented their belief in a practical way. The basic purpose of the Michigan State University TTT project, according to Leland W. Dean and Joseph T. Vellanti, its codirectors, was:

To bring about the type of institutional change at the University that would provide the greatest promise of redesigned teacher education programs more relevant to the real world of local school and community. One of the basic assumptions of the project was that local school people should make significant contributions to the design of teacher education programs. It meant that a climate and setting should be created in which discipline professors, education professors, local school personnel, and community persons work in cooperative, mutually contributory concert. It was planned and expected that each step in the development and implementation of the project would proceed on the parity basis of equally shared responsibility in making decisions on planning committees, clinic teams, operations board, and the advisory board.

The specific *need* to which this basic purpose was addressed was the production of teachers who were more competent, and whose discipline knowledge and teaching behavior were more relevant to the real world of the school, the community which surrounds and supports it, and the students who populate it. This was at the heart of the TTT national movement.[13]

The first two years of the program were devoted to getting liberal arts and education professors, and their graduate students, involved in the problems of the secondary school. By the third year the directors had extended the program to the elementary level. "The major thrust of the TTT elementary component," the directors explained in their final report, "was aimed at developing a new kind of elementary schoolteacher who was basically well educated, engaged in teaching as clinical practice, was an effective student of the capacities and environmental characteristics of human learning, and functioned as a responsible agent of social change."

These objectives involved new roles for the university professor. At Michigan State these roles consisted of planning and coordinating activities with TTT, university, and community persons; teaching methods classes; being involved in the community through activities with teacher candidates and the community coordinator. There were also visits to pupils' homes and various field activities. "The inherent benefits of participation," the codirectors concluded, "greatly enriched the competencies of the university professor for today's ultimate concept of teacher education."

In the public schools a new educational method was introduced in which TTT schools acted as centers for a cluster of other schools.

Vellanti and Dean also reported that the Science and Mathematics Teaching Center operation, which involved professorial fellows, was focusing on:

[institutionalizing] gains from earlier TTT experiences. The endeavor attempted to speak of these identified concerns related to teacher education in the chemistry, physics, earth science, and mathematics departments:

1. to designate a person part-time in each discipline area to be a teacher education liaison, to advise candidates and peers on teaching as a career;
2. to have these individuals teach sections of ED 327 Teaching Methods, on a partial basis;
3. to have these individuals offer ED 450 class sections or other teaching-oriented seminars for the departments' preservice teachers;
4. to have these individuals encourage preeducation activities for prospective candidates, recruiting of new freshmen, program revisions as needed, inservice involvement, and, especially, first-year teaching follow-up.

The codirectors and the coordinator, who were in daily contact with all aspects of the program, reached some major conclusions about the TTT and future programs:

1. Communications among the faculty members of several university departments engaged in teacher education improved. The extent is difficult to measure, but it can be reported that professors from eight university departments participated in the activities of the elementary component and thirty departments in the secondary component's endeavors. Further, the collaboration of faculty continued at the close of TTT, with plans to intensify interfacing relationships in the future.

2. The preparation of teachers must be a cooperative effort between schools, universities, and the communities they serve. In the past, the responsibility for training teachers has been left solely to the university, where the atmosphere is excessively theoretical. The schools where teachers teach have a large responsibility for training teachers, and, because they are actually engaged in the practice of teaching children, they can add a dimension of reality to teacher preparation. In addition, schools serve the community, and the community pays the bills for the schools. The community, therefore, should have a voice in deciding what kinds of teachers should be in the schools and how those teachers should be prepared.

Vellanti and Dean concluded that American education has existed in separate boxes, but, they reported, if American education is to improve, "it is essential that the schools, the universities, and communities collaborate on projects, pool their knowledge, share ideas, and get to know and respect one another."[14]

6

SITE VISITORS

A team of experts made several trips to each TTT site. They observed activities, discussed projects, and interviewed individual participants. They also studied pertinent documents and reports compiled by ERC evaluators. This distinguished group of educators included: Egon G. Guba, professor of education, Indiana University; A. Harry Passow, Jacob H. Schiff Professor of Education and chairman of the department of curriculum and teaching, Teachers College, Columbia University; Francis S. Chase, professor emeritus of education, University of Chicago; Harry N. Rivlin, dean, school of education, Fordham University; Robert B. Silvers, managing editor, *New York Review of Books;* Ralph W. Tyler, senior consultant, Science Research Associates, Chicago; Robert Kibbee, chancellor, City University of New York; Robert Cross, professor emeritus, college of arts and sciences, University of Virginia; and John J. Callahan, assistant professor, department of city planning and education, University of Virginia.

CLARK UNIVERSITY

It was clear from the site visitors' reports that the success of the TTT program at Clark University could be attributed to strong leadership from such dynamic people as Richard Ford and Irving Schwartz. Harry Passow reported, after a visit in 1972, that:

Dick Ford and Irv Schwartz are probably two important causal factors. Ford appears to be an incredibly well-organized, hard-working, persistent, committed, eye-on-the-goal individual who has provided leadership in the most positive sense to the mixed bag of individuals involved in TTT and the Training Complex. . . . Schwartz is Mr. Charisma of the team—creative, articulate, manipulative, and knowledgeable. The Autobiography Group and all of its spin-offs are Schwartz's. His interpersonal relationships with people at the university, in schools, in the community, and among students are close. . . . In the time we were at Clark, Schwartz and Ford seem involved. . . . In their quite different ways, they are the Clark TTT Program.[1]

All site visitors agreed that the first goal, the training of TTT's, for which Clark serves as an example, had been reached, with the qualification that it seemed to place additional burdens on both the doctoral candidates and the liberal arts professors involved.

It was generally agreed that the second goal, parity, had not been reached, but there was wholehearted agreement that the third goal, instituting innovative educational practices, had been reached. Although the visitors questioned whether institutionalization, the fourth goal, had actually been attained, they did agree that there had been a multiplier effect, which was the fifth goal. Ralph Tyler reported: "My analysis leads me to the view that the dynamic qualities of half a dozen Clark staff members, the small size of the university, and its reputation for excellence furnish important components for the success of its TTT Program."[2]

HUNTER COLLEGE AND CITY UNIVERSITY OF NEW YORK

In these reports, the site visitors again both agreed and disagreed. With reference to the first goal, they agreed that there was good leadership at both places, but no TTT's were recruited or trained in the program. They also agreed that there was not much parity (goal two) at the executive committee level. At a committee meeting R. B. Silvers wrote: "two of the directors made forceful presentations about their needs for more funds . . . , but I would stress that at no point were any of the others present asked for their views on the redistribution of funds, nor did they volunteer their views. Neither the student and faculty representatives from Hunter and City Colleges, nor the various representatives of citywide organizations, had anything concrete or specific to say about the requests by the program directors."[3]

Egon Guba felt that the "executive committee is hardly representative of the community, however, [since it consists] mainly of university faculty and students, with only four members drawn from community elements (and these being formal agency representatives). . . . If the definition of parity is extended to mean inclusion of the point of view of wider reference groups, including, for example, the cooperating teachers, liberal arts college representatives, other teacher education groups in or out of the CUNY system, or trainees, we must conclude that their representation is either nonexistent or very limited."[4]

On the other hand, Francis Chase saw great evidence of parity. "Parity goes beyond representation on the advisory committee," he reported, "and permeates every part of the program so that it becomes a cooperative enterprise in which the community, the public schools, and the college are engaged for the improvement of education. Under this arrangement, all teach and all learn; college professors learn from parents and children as well as from school personnel; college instructors instruct elementary school children as they try out their theories and provide models for teachers and teacher trainees; the contribution of children, parents, school personnel, liberal arts and education faculties are accorded mutual respect." Chase gives two reasons for the success of parity: first, all the participants "exhibited pride in the program and a sense of being important contributors to it. Second, the stimulation arising from exchanging ideas and sharing work with persons outside their usual circle of familiars . . . helps them sense they may be learning as much as they are teaching."[5]

There was also agreement that, through the extensive use of open classrooms, the third goal, instituting innovative educational methods, had been achieved. "The predominant innovation is, of course, moving the training programs out of the university and into the public school setting," Guba reported. "Apparently, too, instruction is based very little on conventional didactic approaches; instead, there is heavy reliance on problem analysis and on the use of supporting instructional materials which are brought in from the university. . . . The prevailing organizational feature is that of a teaching-learning team in which everyone is both teacher and learner (even the children are aware of their role in contributing to the training of teachers, for example)."[6]

It was agreed by some, too, that CUNY was moving toward institutionalization (goal four) and would probably spread the idea of field-based training throughout the system. Here, again, the experts disagreed. And, since institutionalization had a direct effect on attaining the multiplier effect (goal five), there was disagreement there, too.

MICHIGAN STATE UNIVERSITY

This is the institution about which Harry Passow reported that all of the goals were reached, "probably more so than at some of the other institutions visited."[7] In examining the degree of parity, both Egon Guba and Passow mentioned that the role of the public schools was very strong. "In many ways," Guba reported, "the public schools are pushing harder than is the university to make the program a success."[8] Passow cited Lansing's school superintendent, Carl Candoli, as saying, "TTT has forced MSU personnel to take a continuing look at education in the public schools, to take a hand in dealing with the problems, and to accept responsibility."[9] This was an unusual aspect of the MSU project. In most projects, initiative for TTT activity stemmed from the universities.

The site visitors reported that there was a move toward the third goal of instituting new educational methods. As for the fourth and fifth goals, institutionalization and the multiplier effect, the visitors reported that the cluster program (TTT schools as a center for other schools to relate to) was in existence, and that there were plans for projects that would involve many more people. Francis Chase reported on the achievement of the multiplier effect:

The TTT goal of multiplier effects is also in process of being achieved chiefly through the efforts of Dean William B. Hawley in the university and Superintendent Carl Candoli of the Lansing Public Schools. For example, Superintendent Candoli is planning to involve other Michigan universities in arrangements similar to that developed with MSU through TTT. Multiplier effects are also being achieved through faculty and student interaction in the university. Through the work of the community consultants, ideas generated through TTT are also being extended to other schools and organizations in Lansing.[10]

UNIVERSITY OF NEBRASKA

Reports were mixed at the University of Nebraska. One expert reported all goals achieved; two reported only parity had been achieved; one stated that none had been achieved. All experts cited a lack of planning or focus and a lack of clearly defined goals. Harry Rivlin did, however, see some progress toward the attainment of the TTT goals and cited the following accomplishments as evidence: university faculty visited and worked in the school; teachers became aware of different cultural patterns; teachers became more sensitive to the need for educational change; the Nebraska University Secondary Teacher Education Program (NUSTEP) relaxed its structure to permit students to plan the activities they needed in order to become more effective; the establishment of an Ethnic Studies Institute at the university was facilitated; and the first master's degree presented to an American Indian at the university came through the TTT Program.[11]

APPALACHIAN STATE UNIVERSITY

Robert Cross, formerly president of Hunter College, found Appalachian State to be a "kind of rural Hunter College; a long tradition of teacher training on which a more general university set of functions is uneasily grafted; a student clientele, mostly first generation, in college; a cohort of parents who think of collegiate education as a vehicle of economic but not really cultural mobility; an economic ambiance which stresses conformity to perceived, immediate economic needs; a faculty rather divided between the old-timers understandably content with what they have wrought, and skeptical about change, and a youthful group willing to think about (and perhaps act on) the unthinkable."

At Appalachian State a separate residential freshman college was started by three TTT members. It was called Watauga College, and Cross found it to be "a living-learning enterprise, with the general education requirement of the university being team taught, and a generally more relaxed intellectual atmosphere prevailing."

But Cross doubted that the experiment would be extended to sophomores and questioned whether there were enough students to sustain it. His general feeling about TTT at Appalachian State was "that a nucleus of strong leaders, including necessarily the president, have been able to make discernible changes for the better at ASU. And I think a number of them are likely to be continued—perhaps even improved on—when TTT funding ends."[12]

NORTHWESTERN UNIVERSITY

The experts saw this institution as a traditional one, moving slowly from a suburban midwestern outlook to a more metropolitan one. It did recruit TTT's from minority groups, and they intended to return to the inner city to teach. Parity, the evaluators agreed, was not reached, and movement toward educational change was slow. One interesting change did, however, occur in the doctoral program. Egon Guba reported on this: "Students assert it is increasingly difficult to tell the difference between the TTT doctoral program and other doctoral programs, especially that in school administration, because the conventional programs have changed by taking on the characteristics of the TTT Program."[13] None of the site visitors saw much evidence of either institutionalization or the multiplier effect.

In addition to addressing themselves to specific questions, the site visitors made three pertinent observations. Although these were expressed in diverse ways, there seemed to be agreement that the success of TTT at any given site depended on whether a place was ready for change and whether there was strong leadership that welcomed community participation. The visitors also agreed that there was a lack of parity. Where it was present at all, parity existed only to a token extent. Most advisory boards, the visitors reported, tended to be dominated by university professors and public administrators, with few or no effective spokesmen for parents or community.

After completing their reports, the site visitors compiled a list of criteria for program success. This list was based on conditions that usually existed in successful projects. According to the visitors, the TTT projects were successful where several (or all) of the following criteria were met:

- where the project's goals coincided with, or reinforced, local priorities and interests and the institutions involved were not only ready for change but were glad to serve as partners in change;
- where projects used preexisting institutional mechanisms and the culture of the surrounding community and did not try to force the use of new methods and standards;
- where project goals and methods were flexible, allowing continual

modification through trial and error and creating constructive tensions among the major groups involved rather than irresolvable conflicts;

— where there was sufficient steady funding not only to permit realistic long-range planning but also to fit the project into the existing reward system of the university;

— where project leadership coincided with institutional leadership (especially the college presidents, deans, department chairpeople, and senior professors), but also included dynamic individuals able to work with and motivate participants;

— where the administrations involved, and expecially the university administration, provided help to the greatest extent possible, which usually did not occur at large and prestigious institutions where TTT was just one more federal project among many but did occur at lesser-known schools where TTT was visible and had relatively high status;

— where the project staff at all levels consisted of people who believed in what they were doing, felt the endeavor meshed with their own values and ideas, received multiple and simultaneous benefits from their work, and developed personally satisfying new roles and relationships;

— where most participants were volunteers (people who selected the project out of some real interest in improving education rather than vice versa) and thus tended to remain more flexible and to keep up their interest longer;

— where formal and informal training of participants was an integral part of the project's program and where program participants were unobtrusively used to train one another, moving out slowly to embrace new members;

— where there was some ineffable combination of luck, talent, vision, and energy.

Obviously, these criteria were not met at every single project or even, altogether, at many projects; the remarkable thing is that they *were* met at so many sites and that, with hindsight, the TTT participants were able to perceive these as the needed elements for success.

7

ERC EVALUATORS

PERSPECTIVE ON ATTAINMENT OF GOALS

Goal 1: The Focus on Training TTT's

Something of the scope of TTT is revealed in the number of TTT's involved in various activities at different sites. There were 545 non-education faculty and 460 school administrators involved in training almost 4,000 prospective classroom teachers as well as TT's and TTT's.

Liberal arts colleges, too, played a leading role in achieving TTT's first goal. It has been estimated that 85 percent of the instruction of a prospective teacher comes not from his education school professors but from the liberal arts teachers. This point, vital for any understanding of teacher training, was raised by Donald Bigelow early in the development of the program:

Most people assume that in the education of teachers the salient problem will be found in the professional sector, but I believe the biggest single problem lies in the liberal arts sector, in the preparation the prospective teachers get in their own teaching fields and in general education. . . .

TTT, therefore, emphasized the inclusion of liberal arts professors, and as many as twenty-one of the full-time projects succeeded in involving them one way or another. In some cases they participated in consultations on education school curricula; in others they worked with school system officials; in still others they had firsthand experiences in the classrooms.

Interest in an interdisciplinary approach to teacher training was already alive at City College in 1969. Under the direction of Vivian Windley (see Chapter 4), the TTT Program actively drew liberal arts people not only into curriculum planning but right into the public school classrooms. The City College program has sought to bring about an interdisciplinary merger of the liberal arts and sciences and education faculties to bridge their professional estrangement. For example, nine liberal arts professors—an anthropologist, a sociologist, a geographer, a political scientist, a historian, a speech and theater professor, and two English professors—from seven departments were involved for the first time in the in-service training of teachers.

At San Fernando Valley State College, TTT established a new Bilingual-Bicultural Component that was, in effect, a new major for those education students especially interested in minorities. A third of the courses were in liberal arts subjects, a departure for that school, which meant that liberal arts professors were directly involved in the preparation of prospective teachers. The Center for Teaching and Learning at the University of North Dakota and the thirty faculty members from ten different departments at Hunter College who took time off to plan a whole new teaching curriculum joining education and liberal arts perspectives serve as additional examples. At Fordham University two physics professors who became TTT fellows for a semester found their involvement in teacher education and classroom work so exhilarating that they volunteered to continue the work for another semester—without pay.

Andrew Timnick, a professor of chemistry at Michigan State University who spent the fall of 1970 in the secondary schools of Lansing, Michigan, under the TTT Program, wrote:

Through the seminars, workshops, team discussions, discussions with community coordinators, visits to classrooms at different junior and senior high schools, discussions with student teachers as well as experienced teachers, participating in teaching and supervision of laboratory classes, I became aware of the many factors which are involved in determining how successful and effective a teacher can be.

. . . While being involved in secondary chemistry and biology classes, it became apparent to me that these courses have become more rigorous. Perhaps our department alone, or in collaboration with faculty from education, should examine our offerings with a view toward possible modifications in the existing program to include some opportunity for the prospective teachers, and teachers who have been away from formal training for some time, to gain experience in science courses as they will be taught in the secondary schools. As a first step I propose to arrange a meeting in our department between interested and available secondary chemistry teachers and members of our department to discuss such a modification in the teacher-training program as well as using the opportunity to brief them on the current content in our introductory chemistry courses. . . .

As a result of the participation in the TTT project, I believe that I will be a more effective adviser for prospective secondary teachers and will be better qualified to participate in assessing the effectiveness of our teacher program.

Such programs did not always move smoothly, given academic jealousies. At Appalachian State University, for example, one professor remarked that, at the start, liberal arts participants "took a lot of ribbing . . . some of them even wept because they felt they had compromised their integrity in relation to their own disciplines. It took them a year to feel comfortable." And, even after a highly successful course in education had been established at a university that combined a regular liberal arts history curriculum with the teaching of history, and students rejoiced, according to one interested professor, the history department took a dim view of the enterprise and refused to promote a junior member who was involved in it. The autonomy of the liberal arts professor, however, had been cultivated over a period of almost a thousand years and had historical precedence in liberal arts colleges. No matter how much liberal arts deans wanted to help train teachers, they first had to contend with their own professors. Of course, TTT was designed so that only willing and courageous faculty were plunged into a new group experience, but how did that benefit the liberal arts college? If there had been as strong a sense of need for reform as there was in teacher education departments and in school districts, then an incentive for continued participation might have existed. Even as late as 1973, however, the dean in a college of liberal arts said, "If the world of our students is changing, we have an even greater responsibility to hold on to the best of our Western heritage." In other words, the college existed to serve societies yet to come—not the present one.

TTT involved hundreds of liberal arts professors, but it is doubtful that the high walls between education departments and the academic disciplines have come down. Even in the most egalitarian of institutions, where academic distinctions and status were never terribly important, there was little institutional basis for continuing, functional relationships after TTT funds were cut off.

The deeply rooted tradition of specialized knowledge as the basis for professional identification and of narrowly focused research as the basis for academic advancement could not easily be refaced by a few years of experimentation, no matter how stimulating personal experiences were for some, unless there were clearly defined institutional mechanisms to maintain the functional value of interdisciplinary effort. The lesson was clear. Professors would not put aside their academic capes unless such behavior was functional in terms of rewards bestowed by their institutions.

Goal 2: Parity

The original parity concept, as it emerged from the U.S. Office of Education in the 1960's, centered around a movement to have liberal arts and education professors share in the preparation of teachers. The public schools were to be involved strictly as educational consumers. The concept was based on a very practical rationale. University recipients of TTT funds had been left with the problem of finding ways to encourage the participation of other groups on a lasting basis, while at the same time meeting annual project costs. The notion of sharing resources to increase resources proved viable here. In effect, the institutions responsible for teacher training said to the public schools and to the community: "We have a training job to do, and extra funds to do it, but we need your help. We will share our resources if you share yours." As a result, new institutions and people were asked to help, and their contributions were, in turn, to enliven and sharpen the reform strategies being planned.

The term "parity" was not used initially. When it was coined, it signified a three-way interaction, but it was still far from the definition that finally came to be: "an equal sharing in *both the production and consumption* of educational goods." The community was not explicitly involved at this earlier stage, primarily because many people at OE (including Donald Bigelow) felt that the inclusion of public school representatives would itself ensure community involvement. When it was later discovered that community people had been playing nowhere near the role in public education that had been imagined, the community was explicitly included as a fourth parity level. Indeed, the term parity eventually became synonymous with the involvement of community persons, simply because they were the most obvious example of persons never before involved.

Although it was a worthwhile notion and fully consistent with the nation's democratic values, parity irritated all participants. It was the product of turbulent times in both the academic community and the nation. It was never adequately defined, and its essential theme—that all members of the educational world, including the least advantaged, should participate in the learning process—was in direct conflict with what had been an earlier TTT fundamental principle—that change would be brought about by the concerted efforts of the most adventuresome and enlightened members of the scholarly world. On the one hand, therefore, TTT insisted that the program should involve the tradition-bound and conventional poor minorities of America; on the other hand, it demanded that the most reform-minded and innovative segments of powerful, elite universities be involved. This contradiction could be resolved in only a few places, and many projects were crippled by it.

Giving the community an equal voice seemed reasonable enough, or at least politically prudent, in theory and even on paper. Very few TTT academicians, however, ever really envisioned actually *sharing* power with uneducated or ill-educated blacks and Chicanos who had their own problems. At Hunter College, despite a verbal commitment to "community control," it was never assumed that a local mother and a university president would have an equal influence on decision making. In spite of the fact that it was university people who first insisted on parity, many academicians undoubtedly regarded the whole thing as an unpleasant invention of Washington bureaucrats, one more requirement that had to be given pro forma recognition but was too impractical to be implemented. Even projects that applauded the parity idea in theory and intended to try to make it operational found that actually establishing parity, in addition to all the other pressures of a new project, was either too difficult or too time consuming.

From an overview of the TTT experience, it seems clear that, with only a few exceptions, both national and local TTT administrators tried, at some level, to involve community people in both the planning and the operation of the programs. It seems equally clear, however, that all of these attempts fell short of granting true equality to the communities as envisioned in the original parity design.

Concern for parity appeared to diminish as projects went along, which led to a kind of slow disenfranchisement that might be labeled the "TTT shuffle." City College phased out a special training program after the first year of operation and cut back on a system of giving salaries and credits toward special degrees, to the disappointment of many participants (see Chapter 4).

Though part of the problem was clearly an unwillingness on the part of TTT educators to share their power, other considerations further complicated the relationship between the community and the university. One consideration that created complications was the sharp difference in values and attitudes between, for example, white, well-educated, middle-class males and primarily black, working-class females; another was the frequently formal, professional manner of educators in contrast to the often gregarious and informal manner of certain community leaders. This was certainly true for the TTT project in Memphis, where some of the academics struck the community people as being archetypical "honkies" incapable of operating in a ghetto school.

It is also apparent that educators underestimated the extent of community resistance to federal programs such as TTT. At Temple University one community representative who acted as liaison between town and gown maintained that much of her time was spent reassuring urban residents that TTT was a legitimate and workable way to improve education, not some bureaucratic scheme to "rip them off."

For school and college to cooperate with community to the point of interdependence meant they would have to "give" and expect to "get." They had resources, money, skills, knowledge, and facilities that they were willing to give, but what could they get? They could get considerable talent, acumen, and enthusiasm from individuals, but these could be purchased. What, as an institution, could they receive that was within the domain of another institution to give? In some cases, residue funds, staff, and activities from the Model Cities program, OEO's Community Action program, or other HEW, Justice Department, or Labor Department programs were available. But communities do not usually control such resources, and they are not organized to provide them. The only thing they had to give was the enormous potential of their solidified support, and, to most schools and colleges, it appeared unlikely that the communities would give even that. With nothing to offer at the parity bargaining table but the independent contributions of isolated individuals, the community, it appeared, could never be an equal partner in TTT. Despite some expressions of good intentions in Washington and the best of intentions at a few project sites, parity appeared unattainable, as all parties—community, school, college—eventually acknowledged.

The most usual means of establishing parity was to use a member of the school community as a so-called "resource person" in the classroom or in seminars with undergraduate and graduate trainees. The twenty major projects that tried this approach usually reported success. At the University of Pittsburgh, for example, various representatives of the inner city became members of the TTT teaching team, visited high school classes and served as informal tutors, organized and ran university seminars to acquaint future teachers with the realities of the ghettos, and participated in overall evaluations of TTT projects and personnel. At San Jose State College there were 114 volunteers, mostly community people without university educations, who were trained as teacher aides and worked as paraprofessionals in the San Jose school system. Fourteen of them went on to the college for further training, some of whom may even have earned their teaching certificates. At the University of South Florida, in Tampa, a number of community people were selected as TTT aides to meet with TTT undergraduates and ground them in the social, economic, and cultural dimensions of both the black and Spanish communities where, eventually, they would be working. The grounding even included a variety of visits, with the aides serving as liaisons, to heretofore unknown sections of the inner city.

Another approach to parity—the selection of members of minority groups as education undergraduates in TTT projects—was tried at several other sites, often in cities with some previous commitment to minority enrollment. City University of New York, as well as Southeastern State College in Durant, Oklahoma, made a special point of recruiting TTT trainees from low-income groups, half of them from the black community.

There was also an ambitious effort to involve community people in a number of projects by placing nonacademic representatives on official TTT committees organized to oversee entire projects. Hunter and Southeastern State did this, and both reported positive results from community input at this level. Dr. Milton Gold, head of the Hunter project, reported, for example, that "prior to TTT, members of the community had little influence over the schools" but that, thanks to parity, they could now "voice their opinions in ways that the school policy makers could not ignore." A similar compliment came from the Temple University project. A member of the community who participated in the project reported that care taken to involve all sorts of local participants in policy decisions (even members of the Black Panther party when it was still active) enabled "a program truly representative of the community's educational needs" to develop.

All that said—and many more such examples could be cited—it must be acknowledged that the working out of a radical concept of parity was much less successful than its most ardent proponents had hoped. Still, the parity experiments cannot be dismissed as either liberal pipedreams or bureaucratic fandangos. Granted, there were no miracles, but there were local successes. What proved totally unworkable at some places provided the opening wedge for needed reforms at others. At all times parity served the dual function of beacon and conscience, pointing toward what *might* be, reminding of what *should* be. And as long as one poor black woman, in this case a Ms. Frankie King, community representative at the Auburn University project, could say, "My involvement in TTT has been one of the most rewarding experiences in my life," then the parity program was worthwhile.

Goal 3: New Educational Methods

One thing those involved with TTT learned very quickly: there was no real shortage of ideas about what should be done in American schools, only a shortage of money, people, and enthusiasm to carry them out. When TTT supplied the money, the projects supplied the people, and the people supplied the enthusiasm, a host of innovations quickly took shape. At least twenty-three TTT projects sponsored formal changes of one kind or another in classrooms within school districts, and sometimes a single project experienced everything from new learning laboratories to open classroom techniques. This focus on innovation was central to TTT. Innovation is, after all, the single most important component of any experiment and the core of its existence.

Some of the TTT projects established their innovations in separate classes or schools adjacent to the regular school, so as to provide a fresh new atmosphere. There were eight teaching centers and nine resource centers focusing on media, bilingual education, and history. One of the most ambitious of these centers was an outgrowth of Harvard University's project. It was an experimental three-year secondary institution called the Pilot School, which was formally set up within the Cambridge school system but, in practice, operated separately. Four of eleven teachers were supplied by the public school system; the remaining seven were doctoral students on TTT fellowships at Harvard. It is not surprising that the range of innovation was broad, including:

— a so-called "modular" schedule, dividing the school day into twenty-four fluid parts;

— homogeneous classes, with members of all three grades in each room;

— experimental courses, including Afro-American Studies and an environmental program carried out in conjunction with the Cape Cod National Seashore Administration;

— parental participation in classroom work, staff hiring, and curriculum development;

— student power, not only regarding such informalities as having students on a first-name basis with teachers, but also giving them a strong voice in curriculum development, classroom procedures, discipline, and extracurricular activities, including a student government.

The goal of all this, as set forth by the people themselves, was quite clear:

It is important to make clear that these projects are not undertaken as academic exercises nor uses of a community setting as a convenient specimen to examine from a perspective of neutrality and remoteness from the lives of the participants. Nor are they undertaken simply in order to do some immediate social good for this one particular school. Rather, they are being conducted as far more complex and demanding tasks. First, they are undertaken in response to specific requests for help by Pilot School staff—help with real problems that might benefit from our joint efforts to understand the forces that shape the school. Second, the joint effort is undertaken self-consciously with a three-part goal: (1) to set an example of socially responsible, useful, and theoretic daily fruitful clinical training and research as a model for educators and social scientists of all kinds; (2) to help the participants improve this school as a model for other public schools; and (3) to contribute to more general knowledge.

Each participant had his personal estimate of how successfully this goal was reached, but none doubted the value of such an experimental school in exploring them.

Another similar school established under TTT was the Adjunct School, located near the regular Worcester North High School and an outgrowth of the Clark University project (see Chapter 3). The school, despite some problems of attendance, proved to be a worthwhile addition to the system. In the words of one local administrator, it exemplified the "excitement, thoughtful reflection, interest, and energy" of TTT.

Other schoolroom innovations brought about under TTT auspices were not quite so ambitious. At times new techniques or subjects were introduced into existing classrooms. City College and the University of Nebraska made extensive use of the open classroom idea, and at the University of Illinois, where a similar experimental attitude prevailed, classes made use of such techniques as creative drama, simulation games, computerized instruction, and so-called "nondirected teaching," another form of classroom liberation. Broad use of team teaching at New York University and at Syracuse University gave a group of teachers responsibility for several classes and cross-class projects. At San Francisco State College a Mathematics System Laboratory, a full-scale learning laboratory, was installed. There were daylong sessions in the local high school so that interested students (and teachers wanting to learn the techniques for other classes) could study the most sophisticated computer methods and the newest mathematical tools under the direction of a full-time, TTT-hired specialist.

Of all the classroom changes brought about through TTT efforts, perhaps none has been as widely influential as the so-called "practicum" or "student teaching." Graduate and undergraduate trainees were given an opportunity to become acquainted with their ultimate audience, schoolchildren.

Michigan State University was most imaginative in its use of "student-teaching clusters." Groups of eight or nine undergraduates were assigned to a single school for a term, observed various classes for awhile, taught those they felt most comfortable with, participated in team-teaching projects with the regular teachers, and then worked with their colleagues to present a single science or social studies unit to another class of a different age group. Temple University added another dimension by having their student teachers not only work with regularly scheduled classes, but also hold demonstration classes for other students. Interested teachers then held give-and-take seminars attended by program participants and interested members of the school's faculty and administration. Hunter College (see Chapter 4) began its field experience in the freshman year, so that, as Elaine Block said, "by the time they graduate they are experienced teachers." San Jose State College preferred to concentrate most of its practicum into a fifth year of study for those working toward teaching credentials or postgraduate degrees, but it provided tutoring, small-group instruction, videotape lessons, seminars, and home visits to staff members as part of an intense practicum year. In many teachers colleges and in more than a third of all TTT-involved colleges, students are evaluated on their classroom performance, and only those with recognized ability to teach are certified.

Another major innovation was bringing university professors, from liberal arts or education faculties, into the classroom. Two City College professors reported that, after initial trepidation, they found the whole adventure "to be among the most exhilarating of their professional life."

This element of the TTT Program was so new that not every institution was willing to try it, and only the more innovative projects did so. Yet, at the fourteen sites where it was tried, the outcome was as favorable as it was at City College. Both the project and the individuals profited. At the University of Miami one professor, who happened to be the education editor of the Miami *Herald*, used his newspaper in local classrooms as a kind of up-to-the-minute textbook, an instant learning tool for sociology, history, political science, and much else. At the University of Illinois two English professors signed up for a full year of teaching sophomore English to "low-ability" high school students, an experience that benefited a number of TTT undergraduate students as well. The reaction of the professors to this classroom experience was almost uniformly favorable.

One of the finest testaments came from Dr. Robert Nikin, a TTT participant at Appalachian State University, where the TTT faculty was actively involved in working in the rural schools of North Carolina's Watauga County. The director of the project there reported that at first Nikin did not know what to expect from TTT:

He was not particularly interested in the public schools, not believing that what we do and they do is in any way truly related. . . . This fall Bob has gotten into the schools, and he has taken some science demonstrations there. He has also gone out and worked with the physics teachers in the high schools, assisting them in the use of the equipment that they didn't know how to use. . . . Now he has come back and written a letter to me stating that he has become convinced that we have to completely change our physics course for high school teachers.

Another professor at Michigan State's school of education added: "By working with many people in community agencies I have broadened my own perspective on their needs and concerns and am able to see how greater advantage can be taken of their ideas."

It should not be thought, of course, that all of the interaction in the schools was successful; nor should such a utopian eventuality really have been expected. At some schools the university professor would come in "wearing his title," in the words of one critical New York school principal, and, from that lofty position, would proceed to alienate not only the students but classroom teachers and administrators as well. Some academicians, moreover, inevitably chose to regard the TTT grants as found money and the TTT opportunity as a free ride. They tended simply to go through the motions and put in time as passive and not very helpful observers. At times no attempt was made to involve community people—especially in ghetto areas where the white professor was faced with predominantly black students—so normal societal hostilities were never broken down, despite attempts by interested faculty members. Then, too, at elementary schools where no genuine interest existed in the first place or where preexisting faculty or administrative rivalries exacerbated suspicion of any outsiders, no amount of good will on the part of university personnel could create an effective program. This was especially true in the case of certain Memphis schools where a TTT team attempted to operate for a while.

Still, where the teachers-in-the-schools experiment was attempted with drive, understanding, and preparation, it seems to have been one of the most memorable parts of the TTT Program. This report by an outsider observing the Hunter College experience is perhaps the best summary of the possibilities and the degree of success:

There is little doubt that those Hunter College faculty members from the education department and the liberal arts faculty who are working in the schools are themselves being changed while they are changing the instructional programs of the few schools involved. Specifically, the elementary science education team (a professor of science education, a physics department professor, and the school science coordinator) were developing what seemed to be a more relevant science program and more relevant science-teaching experiences. If one wishes to call this a "clinical experience," it was clinical for the instructors, students, and teachers.

Goal 4: Institutionalization

The ultimate measure of TTT will be determined by how many specific programs and general ideas were incorporated into the public schools, surrounding communities, and teacher-training institutions. From the vantage point of the present, it is possible to report on those parts of TTT that seem to have achieved permanence.

Perhaps the most wide-ranging institutionalization that came about as a result of TTT is in the area of new courses and other curricular changes at the university level. Virtually all of the universities that stayed with the TTT Program for more than a year incorporated some of its principles into their graduate and undergraduate instruction. Most often this meant a stronger emphasis upon actual teaching experience in the field and required changes in college courses to accommodate the change in emphasis. There were also many instances where special courses or programs were established (Indian or black studies, bilingual workshops), where undergraduate programs were adjusted to permit individualized schedules, where new doctoral programs were established to cover various aspects of teacher training, and where teaching methods were altered to allow for community-resource people, extensive seminars, student-led classes, computerized techniques, and other innovations. Fordham University, under TTT guidance, installed a new division of urban education within its school of education; Auburn University introduced a new elementary education program; San Jose State College created a professional development center that coordinated professional activities for the local school system; Appalachian State University had an entirely new college, created by TTT participants, that housed 120 people in a coeducational dormitory and offered them an experimental learning environment. Instances of curriculum changes are far too numerous to detail. Scarcely any curriculum went untouched. Perhaps something of the scope of TTT influence is suggested by changes at the University of Wisconsin, where TTT participants developed five entirely new courses that became a regular part of the graduate curriculum: Teaching Public Issues, Learning in the Community, History and Social Science in the Curriculum, Values and Valuing in Schools, and Independent Fieldwork.

Institutionalization in an even more official way—by sanction of the state government—was also provided in at least three states where TTT's path-breaking work sufficiently impressed the local legislators. State education systems in Texas, Washington, and Rhode Island formally adopted certain of the TTT principles and emphasized such elements as classroom training for undergraduate students, periodic reeducation of professors of education, and greater cooperation between school systems and universities. Other states seem likely to follow these leads by requiring practicum work and a careful evaluation of it (the so-called Performance-Based Evaluation Certificate) for teaching licenses.

At a higher level—that of the federal government—TTT still has an effect. After the program's demise, some of the hard-learned lessons were transferred into Project Open, another OE attempt to strengthen teaching, but one that shunned rigid requirements and laid very little stress on funding at all. Instead, such ideas as broad community involvement, continual interaction among educational groups, and the spreading of innovative ideas through communications networks were stressed. Out of this, in turn, came a still-growing Superintendents' Network, which was started in 1972 as a means of establishing close communication among small groups of school superintendents, applying the principles of "systems theory" to city-wide school problems, and then trying to convey the lessons learned to a broad range of school administrators. Who knows what other shoots may yet spring from the TTT kernel?

There remains another level of institutionalization that may prove more profound than any yet mentioned, and that is the effect on primary and secondary schools, where teacher training reaches fruition. Since so many schools were involved, and within those schools so many classes, no one has a record of just how many new programs caught hold and took permanent shape. All it is possible to say is that some TTT-initiated program became part of the curriculum in every single school where it operated. In most cases this has meant not only the adoption of new techniques like the open classroom, but also the growth of new ideas about how students should learn and teachers should teach. Beyond that, it is impossible to say what effect the young people who went through TTT as T's or TT's and are now at work either in primary schools or education colleges will have.

One thing we *do* know: in more than a dozen of the primary schools where the teachers themselves were drawn into TTT and where they had an opportunity to work with university professors and attend college seminars, this sort of in-service training has become part of the curriculum, usually under the auspices of the school or the school system. Once TTT showed how valuable this continued exposure could be, administrators and teachers perpetuated it.

The schools near Southeastern State College, for example, continue to send superior classroom teachers to the college's Experienced Teacher Fellowship Program, where they can earn doctoral degrees under professorial supervision. The Los Angeles schools near San Fernando Valley State College, to take another example, became so dependent upon the college's TTT-developed Learning Center and Bilingual-Bicultural Teacher-Training Program that they found funds to continue both efforts, and the projects have become completely intertwined with the school system. More than seventy school teachers are enrolled every term. Similar in-service training programs have been, or are being, institutionalized at the State University of New York at Buffalo, the University of Pittsburgh, Harvard University, Appalachian State University, the University of Miami, Michigan State University, the University of Nebraska, San Jose State College, and the University of Washington, a pretty significant geographical sweep.

Goal 5: A Multiplier Effect

We also know that TTT influenced the curricula of many primary and secondary schools. Again, any attempt to measure this effect, given the enormous number of classrooms, was impossible, and yet there have been indications from enough separate sites to suggest that the total effect may be large. Team teaching, for example, was instituted under TTT auspices at New York University, Syracuse University, and Texas Southern University; individualized science instruction was adopted at Appalachian State University and the University of Buffalo; intensive "learning laboratories" for the classroom were installed at City University of New York, Clark University,

Harvard University, Michigan State University, San Fernando Valley State College, and Temple University—again, an impressive geographical cross section. Most elements remain intact. New courses developed under TTT found a home, apparently permanent, at virtually every place where they were tried: San Fernando Valley State College started computer-programming courses at San Fernando High School that had to turn away applicants; Wisconsin TTT participants developed a community-study course requiring a considerable amount of individual fieldwork that was successful enough to be adopted by two Madison high schools.

We will probably never know the extent of TTT's institutionalization, its long-range settlement into the schools, its alteration of university curricula, its influence on classroom teachers, its cumulative effect on succeeding generations. It suffices to know that the first stone makes ever-increasing ripples, and a pebble the size of a pea has been scientifically measured to be capable of making no fewer than 287 ripples in a large-sized pond.

TTT, as must be evident by now, has unquestionably been a catalyst for beneficial change; an exhilarating experiment in a gloomy laboratory; a chance for at least a few individuals, in some cases whole institutions, to break out of the past. Where some saw a lack of direction in TTT, others saw flexibility and profited; where a few took advantage of federal largesse to have an easy year, others were eager to try something new and different and learned; where some institutions merely adapted new concepts to old practices, others slowly altered and grew.

CONCLUSION

What, then, are we finally to make of TTT, this experiment in American education? We have seen its beginnings and its promises; we have examined the setting and the working out of its goals; we have tasted the sweet and the bitter. Now, having had time to assimilate the experience, what will draw together the past and provide a service for the future?

To understand the outcomes of the TTT Program, I have used every source of information available to observe and deduce in as natural a way as possible the sequence of events that occurred at each site. No attempt has been made to test theory or to determine the significance of observed events relative to each other through statistical procedures. The lack of control over thousands of events that are the natural antecedents of observed outcomes and the inability to isolate the effect of one or a few of these events in the real world makes such a procedure methodologically unsound. Instead, observation of the course of certain events over a certain period of time under certain conditions is the basis for generalizing. This method is not a historical one since we are a part of the data; nor is it an ethnographic one since we have not immersed ourselves for a long period of time in the events we are trying to understand. It is the "field method," wherein extended observations of groups across activities and settings provide tentative formulations.

To extract what can be learned from TTT, we have followed a carefully planned procedure throughout this book. First, we reconstructed what the program was intended to be and to deliver.

Then, we collected various forms of evidence as to what the program was and, in fact, produced. Now, perhaps it is possible to extract the lessons TTT has to teach regarding the nature of the experiment.

THE DARK AND LIGHT SIDES

Probably the major difficulty with TTT was in its formulation; something was wrong from the very start. The ideas were clear, and the intentions were good, but, in the hard world of national education, that was not enough.

To begin with, TTT, in spite of a long period of gestation, was rushed to birth. When federal money finally became available in 1967, TTT seemed to be the most logical funnel through which funds could be channeled. It was unfortunate that clear programmatic goals had not been set; nor had the education community determined the best use of federal levers to improve local education. The bureaucratic confusion that resulted has already been indicated.

Without clear-cut goals, money was spent more on the basis of hope than of certainty. This aspect of TTT was in keeping with the philosophy of Donald Bigelow, that, if you got enough good people involved in innovative schemes, they would somehow come up with positive new ideas and education would inevitably be enriched. No doubt such an approach would have worked, too, had there been enough money for enough time, had the federal trough stayed as open and as full as in years past. But the Nixon administration intervened. Don Davies, Bigelow's boss, and other powerful critics insisted upon immediate and tangible results, and TTT suddenly had to become a sharp-cutting diamond instead of a wide-furrowing plow. Vagueness that might have produced unanticipated benefits over a long period of time appeared clumsy and inefficient when faced with demands for immediate results. Wide-ranging experiments that would have been tolerated under other federal programs, and unstructured project designs that might have paid off in other years, were inevitably curtailed.

Most of the projects ultimately funded by TTT had been established on the basis of the project director's personality and ambience rather than on the specifics of any design. Donald Bigelow had, after all, been in this business for a number of years. He knew the kind of people who were interested in change and were willing to put in extra hours on innovations, and he preferred to give money to them.

Along with the deception that often accompanies federally funded programs, there was the messianic fervor that attends much proposal writing, and there were clear expressions of commitment from people and agencies that never materialized. TTT welcomed men willing to try to shake the earth, and some grandiose plans resulted. Plans for new centers for urban studies, ethnic understanding, or social research were drawn up, but never developed or were merely hollow shells. Sometimes existing centers or established programs were given new names or assigned new responsibilities, but permitted to continue what they had been doing all along. Some of TTT's most successful projects capitalized on such momentum, but other projects suffered.

Without organizing principles, the hodgepodge of local activities put together to satisfy national TTT guidelines soon lost direction. In many cases liberal arts professors did what they had always done, except that they did it in public school buildings, but with no awareness of the dynamics of their new setting. School building administrators, although they admitted such new methods as open classrooms, did not provide the sustained support and organizational climate required.

This failure to establish an underlying rationale and the lack of unifying principles resulted in autonomous behavior that was more self-serving than socially constructive. Without a common purpose, participants often pursued personal and narrow interests, further fragmenting local projects. The most common symptom of project malaise was faulty program design. The poetry of proposal writing could mask incongruities and inconsistencies in project *plans*, but *designs* demanded systematic structural analyses of project elements. More often, when processes or activities for achieving outcomes were unavailable, there was no indication as to how they could be created or what resources and project conditions would be needed to carry out necessary research and development work. The inability of planners to distinguish between the resources and processes they would use to provide training service and those needed to do research and development work was sometimes fatal. When, for example, services such as parent clinics, personal tutoring, and alternative school management proved to be well received, it was not clear how the graduate student providing them could continue. A national program spawning local experiments could hardly prepare for all contingencies, but there should have been some reserves for dealing with the unexpected. Too often, TTT projects also suffered from a lack of cooperation between establishment personnel and parity boards struggling to control resources for new purposes.

The role of leadership was clear, but not its workings. Some leaders challenged staff or community opposition; others retreated before stubbornness and strength when born of conviction. A few great directors seemed to let go the reins of control, freeing others to act decisively. Some strong leaders were weak while those who appeared weak were strong. Highly emotional men lost followers while controlled personalities gained converts. Of those who promised the most, some delivered, but others did not; of those who promised little, some brought forth much. The riddle of leadership is truly a "puzzlement." The presence of bedrock support for local project directors, however, appears to have been critical.

Institutional support of TTT projects ultimately appeared as a determining factor in success or failure. Time and again failure of TTT projects can be traced to lack of resources to satisfy plans, purposes, and ideals that had little or nothing to do with the program. Some real but hidden designs on TTT funds were: to advance individual careers by gaining prestige through securing federal grants; to acquire and support additional graduate students and create jobs; to enlarge spheres of control; or, where purposes were incompatible with TTT goals, to make minor adjustments of publicly stated intents to serve covert purposes.

TTT had little effect on the reward system of universities. Until new institutional incentives and structures are brought into existence and maintained, it is unlikely that there will be much more cooperation between those who teach and those who teach teachers.

Finally, TTT suffered from the most fatal of contradictions: The guards were asked to reform the prisons. Despite all the talk about parity and encouraging the participation of various segments of the educational community, the role of education schools remained dominant throughout. Most of the initial planning came from professors at education schools; most of the project directors and overseers came from education schools; most of the individual projects were designed by professional educators; all of the money was given over to education schools, to be administered as they saw fit. He who not only pays the piper but thinks him up in the first place, advertises for him, gets him into town, and then plans his whole performance is likely to call the tune—not to mention the whole symphony. Yes, TTT wanted to change the training of teachers, but for the most part it ultimately put that job in the laps of the people who had been training teachers all along and not doing a terribly successful job of it: colleges and graduate schools of education.

This, then, is the dark side of the slate, with just enough light applied so that we can see what went wrong and possibly what to improve upon the next time. But there is also a bright side of the slate—one that has been indicated often and should not be forgotten now.

TTT, where it worked best, established a local mood that was, perhaps more than anything else, a spirit of enthusiasm for change and experimentation. And the experiments were daring ones that might reform society as well as improve teacher training. Where TTT flourished, new and functional interinstitutional relationships were established. The most impressive indicators of success—innovative curricula at all levels and new kinds of trainers and trainees in new roles—seemed to stem largely from the collaborative relationship achieved between public schools and colleges. Although this worked to only a small degree in parity and interdisciplinary cooperation, even in these areas it meant that there was activity where earlier none had existed.

LESSONS LEARNED

Two factors, innovative individuals and emergent institutions, made TTT an efficient vehicle for the changes it sought to foster. It represented the application of a universal principle that has enormous potential for social reform in America today: the power to act stems from the free man's power to choose.

Innovative Individuals

Freedom of choice. The importance of freeing individuals to choose between viable options seemed central to much of TTT's success. At the university level, when grants were first announced, most interested parties had real freedom of choice as to how they would define the training program, what corrective course they would pursue, and with whom they would work. Professors who were most effectively involved in project work were those who defined their own roles, made their own jobs, and improved their course work by considering corrective alternatives. When school administrators, teachers, and lay people were free to participate in or ignore the project, to redefine their roles and step aside when inclined without the stigma of failure, school, community, and university relationships were most rewarding and enduring. Perhaps the most obvious successes that attended freedom of choice were at the classroom level, where many students of all ages were genuinely free to pursue alternative learning strategies or to help devise new ones.

Creativity. Clearly, the opportunity to create was closely aligned with the freedom to choose. Often freedom of choice stimulated the ability to create, which in turn increased the number of options available. Where participants faced problems squarely, aware that their efforts alone would make for success or failure, they were generally creative and persistent. The conditions required for effective problem solving are often not present in institutions that support educational practitioners. Time, that most precious of commodities for the educator, always seems insufficient to the task. Under TTT, time was generally bought and allocated like any other commodity. When used to foster creative problem solving, the relationship of dollar costs to established benefits seemed favorable.

Decision making. Another emerging realization was that, owing to sufficient time and institutional continuity, decision making on an incremental basis was possible. Long-range plans could easily be modified on the basis of cumulative experience; short-term planning could be used to test ideas, revise them, and test them again. The use of the experimental approach to decision making was as important a part of TTT as its experimental approach to instructions. Decisions made by organizations, teams, and individuals were retained or dropped as their interest, ability, and commitment varied. Decisions were never final, and decision makers were never isolated individuals wielding power vested by authority.

Obviously, the initial climate of those organizations that changed the most and gained the most under TTT auspices may have been determinant. In other words, where there was an institutional ability to involve staff in making decisions and in creating viable alternatives from which they could then choose, success was likely. Where TTT staff, time, and money could be used to involve more experienced people who could take more time to make more careful decisions, projects showed dramatic results.

Synergism. The flood of human energy that attends any joint endeavor that is freely chosen and shaped by participants is probably greater than the sum of individual contributions. Where TTT projects realized this potential, participants gave freely to each other and realized more than they gave. In the conduct of human affairs there exists a remarkable contradiction of the law of conservation of energy that applies so relentlessly in physics.

The Emergent Institution

While synergism was the result of freeing individuals to do their own thing, a whole set of principles emerged from the conditions that make for a successful, changing institution:

— The small task force or goal-oriented team is essential; all the benefits that accrue to task-oriented teams are present, and the institution facilitates their existence.

— Leaders at all levels within such an organization expect failure as well as success, and, although success is rewarded, failure is not penalized.

— Institutional and societal goals at the highest level of formulation may be questioned, and this appears to be a continuing, though not a compulsively extended, activity.

— The values of "others" are given serious consideration and the resultant ambiguity of purpose and uncertainty of procedure are tolerated and cultivated.

— Communication in small groups and in the larger organization itself is informal, open, and direct. A high level of trust permits most communication to be visible to people within the group; feelings of security negate the need for confidentiality where those outside the small group or the institution are concerned.

— One's status in such a group is defined largely by functions rather than title, and graduate or even undergraduate students are valued as highly for their contributions as professors or administrators.

— The freedom of individuals to choose within the kind of "open" university is legitimized by mechanisms that permit withdrawal from the task force without stigma. When a professor withdraws from a school-based activity, it is with the belief that his peers and mentors recognize that he has chosen something else equally relevant. Students, too, must exercise such options as essential learning experiences in self-determination.

— The institution is an organism that requires nurturing and protection. The healthy organization is one that takes just enough, but no more, of the resources of its members and clients to meet its own needs. It contributes to the maintenance of an environment that helps to provide it with essential sustenance and serves as a buffer against incursions or the temporary absence of nutrients. The essential institutional condition of an easy interdependent relationship with a larger society may be hard to realize. But the size and the purpose of an institution may determine this relationship. Where colleges are relatively small and serve well-defined communities, their institutional health and contextual compatibility may be good. The present state of junior colleges in this country may be a case in point.

— The interests of institutions must differ, and some institutional conflict in a pluralistic society must be expected. It is how conflict is managed that is all-important. Some institutions have been about the positive business of open negotiations for a long time; others sealed themselves away from such crass business long ago. Some institutions have learned that only by trading with others that which is your best to give are you likely to receive what you probably need most. Those who have learned this lesson through experience are most likely to continue to practice it and to benefit from it.

— And, finally, TTT has taught how to bring about change in others and ourselves; how to express strongly held beliefs clearly and forcefully so they can be understood by all; how to listen and to invite strong rebuttal so that friction may produce sparks of understanding otherwise denied us. Some institutions understand the importance of revealing value conflicts and of finding ways to deal with them openly in the heat of debate. Part of the art of resolving value conflicts is to tolerate them long enough to submit them to experimental test and analysis. Institutions that practice action research aimed at uncovering or refuting values represent the cutting edge of social reform. The products of such research are never large or definitive; instead, bit by bit, experiment by experiment, knowledge about which beliefs are verifiable and which are not is accumulated. Perhaps it would be better to call these experiments planned interventions, or socially engineered programs, because they serve as well as inform.

Changing schools through social engineering. Changing schools requires a special kind of engineering that goes beyond the given axioms and theories of any mathematical or scientific system. To change a school, you must question a value. And to engineer a change in a school, you must establish conditions under which values can be questioned and modified. The existence of institutions compatible with such conditions is no doubt rare, but we know some existed. They cultivated restless men prone to try experiments that question assumption, eager to assume leadership in the testing of their ideas.

For such leaders, TTT was a splendid challenge as well as a grand experiment. They welcomed the opportunity to extend social research while at the same time contributing to immediate social need. For them, schools and educational practice can be changed just as rivers can be dammed and crop yields can be tripled. And for them, new values can be translated into action only through the creation of new institutions or through the substantial modification of those that already exist.

There need be nothing elitist about this notion of institutional leadership. Its presence may have little to do with charismatic qualities or the ability to attract money, though these attributes may mask it. Rather, such leaders are generally surrounded by innovative people, free to think and move with little concern for personal or institutional survival. Many of the resources drawn by such leadership are gratuitous or obscure, somehow drawn from sources designed to serve other purposes or people. Large amounts of human energy are created in a milieu that often defies description and the laws of nature—or at least the laws of mechanics. This miraculous violation of the law of quantum mechanics is what makes social engineering so attractive and should reduce the fears of those free spirits who see in it mechanistic forms of control.

Given these assumptions, schools exist to deal with social ills. They are empowered to shape children who will in turn reconstruct society. Schoolteachers, therefore, require training in the art and science of social engineering, and teacher-training programs should be based on known principles of social engineering.

Identifying future sites. Given the importance of social engineering, it may be possible to identify future sites that have a potential for maximizing the benefits of funds intended to produce institutional reform. Have foundations or federal agencies with such ends in mind ever systematically tried to identify such investment opportunities? If not, can it be said that federal social intervention strategies have ever been adequately planned? If most innovative school programs have failed after vast sums of federal money have been pumped into experimental programs, may it not be that the larger institutional context of the projects and the organizational characteristics have been largely ignored both as conditions for obtaining funds and as criteria for evaluating success?

The purpose here is not to criticize federal programs but to extract from the TTT experience what may be of value for future federal efforts. It is not unreasonable to suggest that a number of conditions associated with TTT success could now be used as selection criteria for future programs resembling TTT. A list of indicators of positive institutional attributes, prepared as an exercise in clarifying ERC generalizations that derived from evaluation of TTT, forms an addendum to this chapter. It stands not as a monument to our success or as a reminder of the difficulty of our task, but as an expression of our honest effort to learn from the experimental experience in which we shared. We no longer claim objectivity, only dedication to a common task and a higher purpose that stretches before us. If new conditions with predictive power can be verified and used to select sites for further institutional reform efforts, the grand experiment should be performed again. To do less would be to continue to permit formal education to ignore the real needs of our changing society.

SELECTION CRITERIA FOR FUTURE PROGRAMS

Indicators of positive institutional attributes, given a federally planned, programmatic intervention are:
- Is the new program compatible with existing programs in the institution, especially in regard to resource demands and values served?
- Is the institution's leadership explicitly committed to the goals of the new program?
- Are other leaders (and staff) committed to the goals of the new program?

— To what extent can existing institutional units be used to support the new program? (Will the institution's established institutional and community linkage support the new program, or will new units and linkages have to be created?)

— Is there ability to create new structures, particularly small, task-oriented groups within the institution, to execute the program, or is there a possibility of creating new interinstitutional relationships in support of the program?

— If the program seeks to change institutional behavior, can it reach and influence the institution's gatekeepers?

— Will the institution change its reward system to support new employee behaviors required by the new program?

— Will the local design of the new program be planned and assessed by staff members instrumental to the operation of the new program?

— Will all major functional organizational units within the institution be:
   a. meaningfully involved?
   b. available as a resource?
   c. at least knowledgeable about and supportive of the effort?

— To what extent will existing funds and new funds be used to free personnel and acquire new resources to carry out program research and development activity?

— Will the institution require extrinsic rewards from the program to advance larger institutional interests? (If so, would these rewards be overhead funds, increased public support, or recognition of key personnel, and what are the larger institutional interests to be served?)

— Where new strategies to achieve program goals must be devised,
   a. is there an awareness within the organization of this need?
   b. is there evidence of project familiarity with relevant literature?
   c. have special resources been organized to meet this need?
   d. have problem-solving processes been used in the organization in the past, and to what effect?
   e. is there a problem-solving or evaluation and research capability within the institution to meet this?
   f. will small experiments be run using samples of the population that are as independent as possible of major service programs already the responsibility of the local agency?
   g. will staff training be an intrinsic part of the project work?

      h. will staff training be valued for its contribution to individuals as well as for its solution of problems?

— If functional, task-oriented groups are created and used within the organization,

      a. are task-oriented groups created with a sense of participatory ownership?

      b. have members clearly defined responsibilities?

      c. are members' roles functional and compatible with abilities?

      d. are members personally committed to their role in the group?

      e. are interpersonal relations within the group supportive?

      f. is the institution committed to the member's new role contribution?

      g. are there intrinsic group rewards and institutional rewards for the member?

      h. is a method of member removal from the group by self or by management available in a manner that attempts to protect the member's status and self-respect?

— If both clients and general public are involved in the program, will a careful distinction be made between joint planning responsibility (design work) and staff action responsibility (operations work)?

— Will a public evaluation system be used?

— Will the institution remain sensitive to and responsible toward the changing needs of the community for service? (Will the community be represented by all of its interest groups, and will the mechanisms that exist to resolve differences between these groups be independent of program activity while remaining within the scope of program work?)

— Will sound management principles be followed with regard to business accounting, purchasing of goods, distribution of goods, and personnel practices?

— Does staff authority go with staff responsibility, and will principles of accountability prevail?

— Will contingency planning be in effect and, where such plans do not cover events as they occur, will a policy or design board be available to make unexpected decisions quickly?

— Will staff feel ownership and will it feel comfortable with a decision-making role in the program?

— Does leadership include:

a. the charismatic leader (noninstitutional) for new value-oriented programs?

b. the low-profile leader for well-institutionalized efforts?

c. the person-oriented leader for service and dissemination programs?

d. the product-oriented leader for model-building programs?

— Should the new program design:

a. come from field initiative where possible?

b. provide for varying levels of goal attainment and effort, depending on contingency conditions in the field?

c. be developmental, dependent on incremental experience—that is, not exclude the possibility of new resources, processes, or goals that may be discovered experientially?

d. permit and expect that design changes will be made while the program is in operation, and that no ultimate authority should exist to restrict design change? (And, after a design change has been made on rational and formal grounds, should administrative control procedures be used to operationalize the change?)

e. require that the test of design functionality always be applied?

f. provide for benefits to participants at each level of the institution or organization through which program sources must flow to achieve ultimate goals? (For example, should all regional, state, local community, school, classroom and individual students derive benefits from a federally funded reading program, and should these benefits be primarily intrinsic satisfactions associated with participants' roles in the program effort, or may they be extrinsic and of tangible worth to institutions and individuals?)

g. provide for the cultivation of new and enlarged human resources from within the institutions and target communities involved?

— Would closer cooperation between independently funded institutions have a greater impact on the same population or allow interdependence for essential services or personnel? (As such institutions often find themselves in competition for funds, personnel, and even clients, how can cooperation be achieved under such competitive conditions?)

— Have project personnel stimulated serendipitous spin-offs through personal and informal activity?

ABBREVIATIONS

AACTE	American Association of Colleges of Teacher Education
ANOV	Analysis of Variance
BEPD	Bureau of Educational Personnel Development
BESE	Bureau of Elementary and Secondary Education
CBTE	Competency Based Teacher Education
CIRCE	Center for Instructional Research and Curriculum Evaluation
DAC	Division of Assessment and Coordination
DEM	Discrepancy Evaluation Model
DEPT	Division of Educational Personnel Training
DPA	Division of Program Administration
DPR	Division of Program Resources
EPDA	Education Professions Development Act
ERC	Evaluation Research Center
ESEA	Elementary and Secondary Education Act
HEW	Department of Health, Education, and Welfare
K-R 20	Kuder-Richardson Formula 20
LTI	Leadership Training Institute
NDEA	National Defense Education Act
NEA	National Education Association
NUSTEP	Nebraska University Secondary Teacher Education Project
OE	United States Office of Education
OEO	Office of Economic Opportunity
OPPE	Office of Program Planning and Evaluation
PSSC	Physical Sciences Study Committee
T, TT, TTT	Teachers, Teacher Trainers, Trainers of Teacher Trainers
TEPS	Teacher Education and Professional Standards

NOTES

Notes to Chapter 1

1. James Bryant Conant, *The Education of American Teachers* (New York: McGraw-Hill Publishing Company, 1963).

2. "Rationale for a New Examination of Secondary Education," *Education Digest*, 39 (February 1974), 3.

3. R. J. Havighurst *et al.*, *Growing Up in River City* (New York: John Wiley and Sons, 1962), pp. 46, 64.

4. Mario D. Fantini, *Alternatives for Urban School Reform* (New York: Ford Foundation, n.d., p. 2; reprinted from *Harvard Educational Review*, 38 [No. 1, 1968]).

5. John Holt, *How Children Fail*, Delta Books (New York: Dell Publications, 1964).

6. Bertram B. Masia and P. David Mitchell, "Evaluating a National Program: The Training of Teachers of Teachers," in *Proceedings of the 1968 Invitational Conference on Testing Problems* (Princeton, N. J.: Educational Testing Service, 1969), pp. 72-78.

7. John G. G. Merrow, II, "A Case Study of the Bureau of Educational Personnel Development: Decision Making in the U.S. Office of Education" [hereafter cited as Merrow, "Case Study of BEPD"], unpublished qualifying paper, Harvard Graduate School of Education, February 1972. The portions included here are largely verbatim, although some modifications have been made. The final chapter of Merrow's dissertation tells the story of BEPD's disappearance. It appeared as "The Politics of Educational Policy Making: The Case of Renewal," in *Teachers College Record*, 76 (No. 1, 1974), 19-38.

8. Samuel Halperin, major author of EPDA, personal interview.

9. Interviews, July 1971.

10. Again, perhaps not all the possibilities; the three objectives for the first meeting of Wood's group did not include the question of administrative structure. Memo, Russell Wood to EPDA "Think Group," August 18, 1967.

11. Russell Wood, interview of July 1971. Also, Wood wrote Allen on August 31, 1967: "Holding the National Conference gives us more flexibility in the composition of the Planning Coordination Committee. Many of the organizations and concerns that should for one reason or another be reflected in planning can be included in that conference."

12. "A Report to the U.S. Commissioner of Education Planning the Development of the Education Professions by the Planning Coordination Committee for EPDA [known as the Allen Report]." The report begins with a "basic recommendation," to be a "unifying theme underlying subsequent recommendations."

13. "Administrative Plans for the Education Professions Development Act" [hereafter called the Wood Report], December 1967, xerox, p. 1.

14. Merrow, "Case Study of BEPD."

15. *Ibid.*

16. Donald N. Bigelow, speech before the Fifth Annual Conference of Directors of Training Programs supported by the Office of Education, entitled "The Fourth Revolution" and published in *The Liberal Arts and Teacher Education* (Lincoln: University of Nebraska Press, 1971), p. xxix.

17. B. Othanel Smith, Saul Cohen, and Arthur Pearl, *Teachers for the Real World* (Washington, D. C.: American Association of Colleges for Teacher Education, 1969).

18. Don Davies, "The Relevance of Accountability," address before Dean's Conference on Teacher Education, sponsored by College of Education, University of Minnesota, Radisson Hotel, Minneapolis, December 4, 1969.

19. Merrow, "Case Study of BEPD."

20. B. Othanel Smith, *On the Preparation of the Teachers of Teachers* (Washington, D. C.: U.S. Government Printing Office for the Office of Education, U.S. Department of Health, Education, and Welfare, 1968).

21. J. Lloyd Trump, "The Experiments We Need," unpublished manuscript written in the early 1960's.

22. Roy Edelfelt, "The Reform of Teacher Education," *Journal of Teacher Education,* 23 (No. 2, 1972), 117-125.

23. Masia and Mitchell, *Evaluating a National Program.*

24. Mary Jane Smalley, Chief, Site Planning and Development Branch, Northeast Division, BEPD, "Pluralism and Cultural Pluralism in the Training the Teacher Trainers Program," in *Cultural Pluralism in Education,* ed. William R. Hazard and Harry N. Rivlin (New York: Meredith Publishing Company, 1971), p. 145.

Notes to Chapter 2

1. *The Role of Evaluation in the Trainers of Teacher Trainers Program* (Cambridge, Mass.: Center for Educational Policy Research, 1971), p. 212.

2. Walter H. Crockett, "Report on TTT Site Visits Conducted in November and December, 1969," p. 4.

3. *The 1969 LTI-TTT Site Visitation Procedure* (Urbana: Center for Instructional Research and Curriculum Evaluation, University of Illinois, 1970), p. 29.

4. Bertram B. Masia and P. David Mitchell, "Evaluating a National Program: The Training of Teachers of Teachers," in *Proceedings of the 1968 Invitational Conference on Testing Problems* (Princeton, N. J.: Educational Testing Service, 1969), p. 82.

5. *Aperiodic Report: Trainers of Teachers' Trainers (TTT) Evaluation 71* (Urbana: Center for Instructional Research and Curriculum Evaluation, University of Illinois, 1969), p. 10.

6. Donald Bigelow, interview of July 20, 1971.

7. Malcolm M. Provus, *Discrepancy Evaluation Model* (Berkeley, Calif.: McCutchan Publishing Corporation, 1971).

8. Diane Kyker Yavorsky, *Introduction to Discrepancy Evaluation Model*, Occasional Paper 110 (Charlottesville: Evaluation Research Center, University of Virginia, 1974).

9. Appendix A, Table A.2.

10. *Ibid.*, Table A.1.

11. Michigan State University, Final Report.

12. *Ibid.*

13. Appendix A.

14. *Ibid.*, Table A.3.

15. Appendix A.

16. *Ibid.*, Table A.4.

17. *Ibid.*, Table A.5.

18. *Ibid.*, Table A.6.

19. *Ibid.*, Table A.7.

20. See the last paragraph in Chapter 1.

21. Impact Measurement Instrument, Appendix B.

22. Appendix D.

23. Appendix C.

24. See Chapter 5, note 8.

25. Appendix D, Table D.1.

Notes to Chapter 3

1. Subject B. C., a senior at Clark who student taught at Tahanto High School, interview reported by S. Bernstein, March 21, 1972.

2. E. Fenton, A. N. Penna, and M. Schultz, *Comparative Political Systems: An Inquiry Approach* (New York: Holt, Rinehart, and Winston, 1967).

3. Vincent Keane, a teacher at Tahanto High School, interview reported by S. Bernstein, February 16, 1972.

4. Robert George, "A New Approach to High School Psychology," *Social Studies*, 64 (No. 1, 1973), 20-25.

5. Subject E. M., sophomore in Training Complex, interview reported by S. Bernstein, April 6, 1972.

6. Subject P. P., senior in Training Complex, interview reported by S. Bernstein, February 9, 1972.

7. Subject B. M., interview reported by S. Bernstein, May 4, 1972.

8. Robert Morrill, interview reported by S. Bernstein, May 4, 1972.

9. Ralph Tyler, report of field visit to Clark University, May 1, 1973.

Notes to Chapter 4

1. CUNY-TTT, Funding Proposal, 1972-73, p. 1.

2. Milton Gold, acting project director and dean of teacher education, Hunter College, interview of April 12, 1973.

3. Charles Coleman, assistant TTT director, Hunter College, interview of November 20, 1972.

4. James Borrero, interview of November 20, 1972.

5. Lorri Lippman, interview of February 7, 1973.

6. Gold, interview of April 12, 1973.

7. Site visit, team report, 1971.

8. Mae Gamble, interview of February 7, 1973.

9. Gold, interview of April 17, 1973.

10. Julie Wood, interview of May 1, 1973.

11. Sidney Schwager, interview of May 3, 1973.

12. Artie Galaskewicz, interview of November 20, 1972.

13. Borrero, interview of November 20, 1972.

14. Vivian Windley, "Training Teachers of Teachers," brochure prepared for parents of pupils at Public School 192 with TTT funds in 1972, p. 1.

15. CUNY-TTT, Funding Proposal, 1972-73, p. 13.

16. Borrero, interview of November 20, 1972.

17. Vivian Windley, "A New Look at Teacher Education," *Urban Review*, 5 (No. 4, 1972), 5.

18. CUNY-TTT, Funding Proposal, 1971-72, p. 52.

19. Vivian Windley, interview of May 21, 1973.

20. *Ibid.*

21. CUNY-TTT, Funding Proposal, 1972-73, p. 13.

22. Windley, interview of April 13, 1973.

23. Windley, interview of February 8, 1973.

24. CUNY-TTT, Funding Proposal, 1972-73, pp. 11-12.

25. Benjamin Rosner, dean of teacher education, CUNY, interview of May 1973.

Notes to Chapter 5

1. See the report of this first conference in *Craft of Teaching and Schooling of Teachers* (Lincoln: Curriculum Development Center, University of Nebraska, 1967).

2. One suspects that the project was less effective than it might have been in community participation areas because it lacked a firm legal analysis of community rights. See Lawrence Freeman, "Legal Barriers to Possible Improvements of Teachers' Education Programs," *Study Commission Newsletter on Legal Rights* (Spring 1974).

3. For details, see letters and statements written by Vivian Robinson, Gerald Walton, and Max Larsen in the Nebraska TTT files.

4. See Frederick Edelstein, "The Politics of Ethnic Studies in Higher Education," unpublished dissertation, University of Nebraska, 1973.

5. "Purposes of the University," adopted by the University of Nebraska Faculty Senate and Board of Regents, 1974.

6. See Kenneth Haskins' remarks before Walter Mondale's Select Committee on Equal Opportunity, which contrast the early Community Education models with those being sought from 1967 to 1970 by blacks in Intermediate School 201, Adams-Morgan, Woodlawn, and New York City decentralization. Haskins' statement is contained in "Hearings before the Select Committee on Equal Opportunity of the U.S. Senate, 92nd Congress," pt. 13, pp. 5858-90.

7. Letter to author, August 1974.

8. *Ibid.*

9. *Ibid.*

10. *Ibid.*

11. University of Washington, Final Report, 1973. Information concerning this report is available through John Jarolomik at the university.

12. University of North Dakota, Final Report, presented to the National Advisory Council on Education Professions, May 17, 1973. Information concerning this report is available through Vito Perrone at the university.

13. Michigan State University, Final Report, 1973. Information concerning this report is available through Leland Dean at the university.

14. *Ibid.*

Notes to Chapter 6

1. A. Harry Passow, site visit report, April 24, 1972, p. 4.

2. Ralph W. Tyler, site visit report, May 1, 1973, p. 7.

3. Robert B. Silvers, site visit report, April 27-28, 1972, p. 2.

4. Egon G. Guba, site visit report, May 1, 1972, p. 3.

5. Francis S. Chase, site visit report, April 27-28, 1972, pp. 8-9.

6. Guba, site visit report, May 1, 1972, p. 4.

7. Passow, site visit report, June 10, 1972, p. 3.

8. Guba, site visit report, May 31, 1972, p. 2.

9. Passow, site visit report, June 10, 1972, pp. 2-3.

10. Chase, site visit report, June 2, 1972, p. 3.

11. Harry N. Rivlin, site visit report, May 15, 1972, p. 1.

12. Robert Cross, site visit report, May 7, 1972, pp. 3, 4.

13. Guba, site visit report, May 8, 1972, p. 4.

APPENDIXES

APPENDIX A. Installation Measurement Instruments

INSTRUMENT 1

February 16, 1971

Dr. John Doe
Associate Professor of Counselor Education
University of _____

_____

Dear Dr. Doe:

We are currently involved in processing your project design information for intensive analysis via computer. Procedures for updating information about project activities are also being prepared and will be sent to you before March 10th, along with a computer printout of your design. As the activities go ahead, we are also ready to move into our second evaluation phase, which focuses on the installation of project activities.

The basic objective of this second evaluation phase is to determine project capabilities for carrying out intended activities. Impact evaluation will be conducted in May and June. The focus here is only on activities that had been planned for the time period of September 1970 to February 1971. It may be that some activities intended for the time period of September 1970 to February 1971 were not able to be carried out, that more or less of various types of people were involved in the activity, or that the activity was substantially changed.

167

As it is clearly impossible to analyze each of the major project activities of every project, two of your activities have been selected with the assistance of the Office of Education TTT staff. The primary bases for selection of these activities are that they are usually practicums, that they involved a broad range of types of individuals, and that they are consistent with other program priorities.

This phase of our evaluation will consist of two stages. The first stage consists of questions one through four that are attached to this letter. It focuses on general information about the project as a whole and specific information about two of your project activities and the identification of the individuals who are involved in these activities. The second stage will focus on further specific information both from you and from the individuals involved in the two activities. The two activities of your project that we are particularly interested in are (element number and name) and (element number and name). An individual taxonomy (see *Individual Taxonomy for Use in Installation Measurement*) for your use in responding to this instrument follows.

We would like to receive the completed questionnaire from you by February 22nd. A self-addressed envelope is enclosed for your convenience. If you have any problems or questions, please feel free to call us.

We hope your project is doing well. Thanks for your cooperation.

Sincerely yours,

Individual Taxonomy (for use in installation measurement)

TTT-level
  Actual
    School district superintendents
    Graduate faculty in education
    Other graduate faculty
    Public school supervisors of cooperating teachers
    Institute of higher education administration
    Other (specify)
  Potential
    Graduate students in education preparing to teach in graduate school
    Other graduate students preparing to teach in graduate school
    Other (specify)
  Other (specify)
TT-level
  Actual
    Student teacher supervisors in the University
    Cooperating teachers who supervise student teachers
    Public school principals
    Local education agency department chairmen

Local education agency curriculum supervisors
Leaders of teacher teams
Resource colleague (i.e., a person who is trained to provide expertise in a
    specific area to his colleagues)
Undergraduate faculty in education
Other undergraduate faculty
Other (specify)
  Potential
Graduate students in education preparing to teach undergraduates
Other graduate students preparing to teach undergraduates
Graduate students preparing for supervisory roles in the public schools
Teachers preparing on a part-time basis for supervisory roles
Other (specify)
Other (specify)
T-level
  Actual
Classroom teachers
Paraprofessionals in fixed positions
Public school counselors
Other
  Potential
Undergraduates in education
Other undergraduates
In-service paraprofessionals in a career ladder
Preservice paraprofessionals in a career ladder
Graduate students preparing to teach in public schools
Other (specify)
Other (specify)
Ultimate consumer
  Students
  Adult trainees
  Other (specify)
Community level
  Community leaders
Public officials
Community organization leaders
Community agency personnel
Other (specify)
  Private citizens
Parents of public school students
Representatives of minority groups
Other (specify)
  Outside resources
Evaluation staff
Government agency staff
State department of education staff
Other (specify)
Other (specify)

QUESTIONNAIRE

1. Are there any project activities (elements) that you had intended to have underway by this time (September 1970-February 1971) that were not begun as planned? If there are, please give the names your project had assigned to them below. We are only interested here in elements, not in subelements.

_____
_____
_____

2. Projects may have undergone a number of changes by this time. For your total project, please give the number of each type of person that you expected to be involved at the present time. This information is *not* to be supplied element by element but only for the project as a whole. Space has been provided below for the information. In the first column give the category from the Individual Taxonomy (see attached *Individual Taxonomy for Use in Installation Measurement*); in column two give the number of persons of that category expected when you completed your project design, and in column three give the actual number of persons of that category who are presently involved in the project. For example, if you had intended in September to have ten graduate professors from education involved in the project and now have eleven, put 2. 1. 1. 2 in column one, ten in column two, and eleven in column three.

(1) Individual taxonomy category*	(2) Expected number at design time	(3) Actual number involved at present

*See *Individual Taxonomy for Use in Installation Measurement*. If no category is appropriate, please attach a footnote describing the type of individual.

3. We are particularly interested in the elements in your project that are mentioned in the accompanying letter. Please give the following information about each element. If more space is needed, continue the list on an attached sheet of paper. We are particularly interested here in the people you had identified on design form one (Elements Form) as "individuals involved" in the element.

First Element
a. Project name for activity _____
b. Date when the activity began (1970-71) month _____ , day _____
c. Date when you expect the activity to be completed (1970-71) month ___ , day _____
d. Name of staff person responsible for the activity _____
e. The information called for on the attached forms [see Figure A.1] for each of the individuals involved in the activity

4. Repeat item 3, above, for the second element.

FIGURE A.1—FORM USED FOR EACH ELEMENT IN A PROJECT

Individual taxonomy category*	Name of person	Address				Sex	Race or cultural group	Approximate age
		Street	City	State	Zip code			

*See *Individual Taxonomy for Use in Installation Measurement.* If no category is appropriate, please attach a footnote describing the type of individual.

TABLE A.1—ELEMENTS INVOLVED IN PROJECTS AND NUMBER OF TIMES MENTIONED AS ACTIVITIES BY PARTICIPANTS

Element	Times mentioned
Planning	8
TTT program component	37
Needs of community	13
Needs of schools	9
General	8
Course work	1
Formal university courses (i.e., in college catalog)	2
Education courses (unspecified)	1
Education courses (specified)	29
Liberal arts courses (unspecified)	0
Liberal arts courses (specified)	11
Special courses (designed for TTT or other experimental programs)	8
Education courses (unspecified)	1
Education courses (specified)	49
Liberal arts courses (unspecified)	0
Liberal arts courses (specified)	48
Academic seminar work	3
History and systems of education	0
Research methods	1
Area surveys (unspecified)	0
Area surveys (specified)	10
Curriculum	2
Curriculum (specified)	7
Supervision	2
Supervision (specified)	1
Evaluation and assessment	3
Community and contemporary problems	4
Community problems (specified)	19
Methods of instruction	4
Teacher training	7
Individualized course work	20
General	1
Practicum	11
Personal learning experience (i.e., the participant is to enter this experience without his "title," and let the situation affect him *as a person*)	2
Residence in a neighborhood composed of a particular ethnic or disadvantaged group	5
Interaction with the agencies of the community as a person (i.e., try to get welfare, treatment at a clinic, a ride on the bus, etc.)	2

TABLE A.1—*continued.*

Element	Times mentioned
Clinic experience (i.e., the participant keeps his title and interacts with the situation)	9
Clinical experience in the schools	11
Observation	5
Observation (specified)	25
Participation	7
Participation (specified)	58
Observation	1
Participation	6
Clinical experience in the community-at-large	19
Individualized clinical program	4
Seminar-based research (i.e., research conducted and presented before a group of participants)	4
Dissertation	4
Instructional methodology	4
Individualized instruction	2
Microteaching and videotape recording	3
Computer-aided instruction	1
Other	4
Curriculum construction	11
Selection	1
Adaptation	1
Development	11
Group dynamics	6
Role-playing techniques	2
Encounter group-sensitivity training	3
Brainstorming	2
Unstructured ("rap") sessions	6
General	11
Staffing arrangements	3
Experiments in joint appointments	4
Interdisciplinary within the Institute of Higher Education	4
Among such institutes	3
Between such institutes and public schools	5
Between such institutes and community	4
Between public school and community	1
Experiments in supervision	1
Team of participants supervises preservice training	5
Team of participants supervises in-service training	2
Experiments in staffing in the classroom	4
Team teaching (peer team)	4

TABLE A.1—*continued.*

Element	Times mentioned
Team teaching (team made up of different ranks)	3
Instruction with availability of consultant team	3
Experiments in joint problem solving	21
Experiments with facilities	4
Teaching field centers (i.e., places where Institute of Higher Education, Local Education Agency, and community people may interact)	8
Resource centers (i.e., places where hard-to-get materials and media may be obtained, studied and demonstrated)	9
General	3
Management and coordination of TTT	9
Directing board arrangements	6
Parity board which directs	15
Parity board which has advisory powers only	11
Other directing body	14
Coordinating all inter- and intraagency cooperation	13
Responsiveness to outside agency controls	1
Maintaining adequate support system arrangements	6
Identification, recruitment, placement	14
General	9
Evaluation and assessment	29

TABLE A.2—PERSONS INVOLVED IN THE TTT PROGRAM IN NOVEMBER
1970 AND MARCH 1971

Taxonomy	Number involved		Difference in number
	November 1970	March 1971	
TTT-level	10	10	0
TTT-level, actual	10	9	−1
School district superintendents	78	72	−6
Graduate faculty in education	460	405	−55
Other graduate faculty	438	371	−67
Public school supervisors of cooperating teachers	89	92	+3
Higher education administrators	138	131	−7
Other TTT-level, actual	174	148	−26
TTT-level, potential	0	0	0
Graduate students in education preparing to teach in graduate school	245	258	+13
Other graduate students preparing to teach in graduate school	230	183	−47
Other TTT-level, potential	31	31	0
Other TTT-level	88	61	−27
TT-level	21	20	−1
TT-level, actual	0	0	0
Student teacher supervisors in the university	70	83	+13
Cooperating teachers who supervise student teachers	701	766	+65
Public school principals	244	318	+74
Local education agency department chairmen	82	104	+22
Local education agency curriculum supervisors	52	62	+10
Leaders of teacher teams	61	64	+3
Resource colleagues	63	86	+23
Undergraduate faculty in education	149	156	+7
Other undergraduate faculty	106	135	+29
Other TT-level, actual	99	95	−4
TT-level, potential	0	0	0
Graduate students in education preparing to teach undergraduates	81	109	+28
Other graduate students preparing to teach undergraduates	27	35	+8

TABLE A.2—*continued.*

Taxonomy	Number involved		Difference in number
	November 1970	March 1971	
Graduate students preparing for supervisory roles in public schools	107	112	+5
Teachers preparing on a part-time basis for supervisory roles	26	27	+1
Other TT-level, potential	21	21	0
Other TT-level	88	84	−4
T-level	0	0	0
T-level, actual	0	0	0
Classroom teachers	2,132	2,538	+406
Paraprofessionals in fixed positions	142	149	+7
Public school counselors	80	93	+13
Other T-level, actual	12	13	+1
T-level, potential	0	0	0
Undergraduates in education	2,285	2,568	+283
Other undergraduates	284	335	+51
In-service paraprofessionals in a career ladder	30	28	−2
Preservice paraprofessionals in a career ladder	2	71	+69
Graduate students preparing to teach in public schools	375	302	−73
Other T-level, potential	68	91	+23
Other T-level	30	41	+11
Ultimate consumer	0	0	0
Students	10,957	11,060	+103
Adult trainees	0	0	0
Other ultimate consumer	20	0	−20
Community level	80	75	−5
Community leaders	94	120	+26
Public officials	40	41	+1
Community organization leaders	115	136	+21
Community agency personnel	81	78	−3
Other community leaders	33	14	−19
Private citizens	13	14	+1
Parents of public school students	5,020	5,205	+185
Representatives of minority groups	159	212	+53

TABLE A.2—*continued.*

| | Number involved | | Difference in |
Taxonomy	November 1970	March 1971	number
Other private citizens, community level	43	56	+13
Outside resources	7	7	0
Evaluation staff	23	27	+4
Government agency staff	21	8	−13
State department of education staff	17	17	0
Other outside resources, community level	43	26	−17
Other community level	40	40	0

TABLE A.3—RACIAL-ETHNIC AND SEX CHARACTERISTICS OF PERSONS FROM A SAMPLE OF PROGRAM ACTIVITIES

Racial-ethnic group	Male	Female	TOTAL
Black	225	489	714
White	1,243	1,479	2,722
Mexican-American	47	50	97
American-Indian	10	18	28
Puerto Rican	15	27	42
Oriental	8	18	26
Undesignated	213	539	752
TOTAL	1,761	2,620	4,381

INSTRUMENT 2

March, 1971

Dear Colleague:

We have been asked by the Office of Education to help evaluate the Teacher Training Program at (name of school). To do this job well, we need information concerning your involvement, aspirations, and insights into certain aspects of the program.

Enclosed is a questionnaire to provide us with some of your responses to one of the specific activities in the program. This activity is carefully described in the enclosed questionnaire.

Experience shows that the average person takes about thirty minutes to complete the form. Would you please help us make your voice heard by returning the forms to us by (eight days after mailing date). A self-addressed envelope is enclosed for your convenience.

Sincerely yours,

QUESTIONNAIRE

We are interested in what you do in connection with a particular part of the Teacher Training Program (TTT) run by (name of university). We want you to tell us about your participation in (description of the activity).

This activity has been formally called (name given the activity by project staff). It will be called "the activity" throughout this questionnaire.

Now, complete the questions to the best of your ability.

Section I: General information

1. Name of project_____
2. Name of "the activity" _____
3. On the average how many times per month are you involved in the activity?   _____
4. On the average, how many days per week are you involved in the activity?   _____
5. On the average, how many hours per week are you involved in the activity?   _____
6. Of the hours per week devoted to the activity, how much time is spent working in a group with the other participants rather than with a particular individual?   _____

7. Of the time spent with individuals, how many hours per week are
    spent in individual conferences or work with the following
    types of people:
    a. university professors in education   _____
    b. university professors in arts and sciences   _____
    c. graduate students   _____
    d. supervisory school personnel   _____
    e. school teachers   _____
    f. community persons   _____
    g. school administrators   _____
    h. university administrators   _____
    i. school children   _____
    j. others (describe) _____   _____

8. What are the major things this activity is supposed to accomplish?
    1. _____
    2. _____
    3. _____
    4. _____
    _____
    _____

9. What are the major things done to accomplish the purposes listed above?
    1. _____
    2. _____
    3. _____
    4. _____
    _____

10. When did the activity begin during 1970-71? Please give the month, day,
    and year.   _____

11. Will the activity end before September 1971? If yes, please give the
    month, day, and year.   _____

Section II: People involved in the activity

This set of questions focuses on various types of people who may be involved in
the activity. The questions are intended to get *your* impressions of the activity
and the people involved in the activity. If any question is not applicable to the
activity in which you are involved, simply write in "not applicable."

1. How many university professors of education are participating in the
    activity? _____

2. What one major effect do you think the involvement of university professors
    of education in the activity will have on:
    a. what they teach: _____
    _____
    _____
    b. their teaching methods: _____
    _____
    _____

c. their relations with students: _____
_____
_____

d. their relations with school people: _____
_____
_____

e. their relations with community people:_____
_____
_____

f. their relations with professors from arts and sciences: _____
_____
_____

3. How many of each of the following types of persons are involved in
   the activity:
   a. university professors in education   _____
   b. university professors in arts and sciences   _____
   c. graduate students   _____
   d. supervisory school personnel   _____
   e. school teachers   _____
   f. community persons   _____
   g. school administrators   _____
   h. university administrators   _____
   i. others (describe) _____   _____

4. If there are school persons involved in the activity, do you feel that they:

	Yes	No	Not applicable
a. are adequately represented (numbers)?	_____	_____	_____
b. have equal voice in discussions?	_____	_____	_____
c. have equal voice in decisions about the content and direction of the activity?	_____	_____	_____
d. have equal voice in evaluation of the activity?	_____	_____	_____

5. If there are university persons in education involved in the activity, do you
   feel that they:

	Yes	No	Not applicable
a. are adequately represented (numbers)?	_____	_____	_____
b. have equal voice in discussions?	_____	_____	_____
c. have equal voice in decisions about the content and direction of the activity?	_____	_____	_____
d. have equal voice in evaluation of the activity?	_____	_____	_____

6. If there are university persons from the arts and sciences involved in
   "the activity" do you feel that they:

	Yes	No	Not applicable
a. are adequately represented (numbers)?			
b. have equal voice in discussions?			
c. have equal voice in decisions about the content and direction of the activity?			
d. have equal voice in evaluation of the activity?			

7. If there are community persons involved in the activity, do they:

	Yes	No	Not applicable
a. have adequate representation (numbers)?			
b. have equal voice in discussions?			
c. have equal voice in decisions about the content and direction of the activity?			
d. have equal voice in evaluation of the activity?			

8. Do you think that the activity is intended to affect the following persons?

	Yes	No	Not applicable
a. university professors in education			
b. university professors in arts and sciences			
c. graduate students			
d. supervisory school personnel			
e. school teachers			
f. community persons			
g. school administrators			
h. university administrators			
i. school children			
j. others (describe) _____			

9. What do you think will be *one* major change in each of the following types of persons as a result of the activity? If one of the categories is not appropriate for your activity simply mark "not appropriate."

a. University professors in education: _____
_____
_____

b. University professors in arts and sciences: _____
_____
_____

c. Graduate students in education: _____
_____
_____

d. Supervisory school personnel: _____
_____
_____

e. School teachers: _____
_____

f. Community persons: _____
_____

g. School administrators: _____
_____

h. University administrators: _____
_____

i. School children: _____
_____

j. Others: _____
_____

Section III: Institutions involved in the activity

In a number of the TTT projects various types of institutions are thought of as being involved or represented in an activity. At the end of this questionnaire you will find a list of institutions to use in identifying those that you feel are involved in this activity.

1. List the institutions that you feel are involved or represented in the activity.
    _____
    _____

2. Do you think that the activity is intended to change the following institutions?

	Yes	No	Not applicable
College(s)	____	____	_____
Graduate school(s)	____	____	_____
Public schools or school districts	____	____	_____
Community	____	____	_____
State education agencies	____	____	_____
Parity boards	____	____	_____
Teacher organizations	____	____	_____

3. Do you think that as a result of the activity you will be able to change your own institution (e.g., school, university, community, etc.)?
    Yes _____ No _____

4. If yes, name the institution you intend to change.
    _____

5. If yes, indicate the changes you intend to make in this institution.
    1. _____
    2. _____

6. How could the activity be changed to have greater influence on this institution?

_____

_____

_____

7. Please indicate what you think will be *one* major change, as a result of the activity, in each of the following institutions?

   a. College(s): _____

   _____

   b. Graduate school(s): _____

   _____

   c. Public school(s) or school district(s): _____

   _____

   d. Community: _____

   _____

   e. State education agencies: _____

   _____

   f. Parity boards: _____

   _____

   g. Teacher organizations: _____

   _____

8. List *one* or *two* major ways that you think you will change as a result of the activity.

   1. _____

   _____

   2. _____

9. Are you involved in other activities in the program beside the activity described on the first page of this questionnaire?   Yes ____ No ____

10. If yes, please describe each of these other activities on a single line below.

   1. _____

   2. _____

   3. _____

   4. _____

Note: Please provide any general comments you care to make about:
The activity:

_____

_____

_____

_____

The program, in general:

_____

_____

_____

_____

List of Institutions (for use in responding to questionnaire)

Graduate institution (undergraduate and graduate degrees granted)
  Education department or school
  Arts and sciences department or school
  Administrative unit of university (specify)
  University board or other formal public support base
  Special structures (specify)
Four-year college (no graduate degrees granted)
  Educational department or school
  Arts and sciences department or school
  Administrative unit of institution (specify)
  College board or other formal public support base
  Special structures (specify)
Two-year institution (degree-granting or nondegree-granting)
Local education agency (preschool through high school)
  Preschool
  Elementary school
  Secondary school
  Adult education
  Administrative unit of school system (specify)
  School board or other formal public support base
  Teacher organizations
Community
  Formal structures (specify)
  Informal structures (specify)
State
  Department of instruction
  Board, governor, and public support base
Regional education agencies
TTT project staff
Parity board
Federal agency (specify)
Congress and public support base

TABLE A.4—PARTICIPANTS' PERCEPTIONS OF THE TYPES OF INSTITU-
TIONS INVOLVED

Type of institution	Number of participants who said the institution was involved
1. GRADUATE INSTITUTION (unspecified)	282
2. Education department or school	235
3. Arts and sciences department or school	116
4. Administrative unit of university	19
5. University board or other formal public support base	3
6. Special structures	5
7. FOUR-YEAR COLLEGE (unspecified)	102
8. Education department or school	40
9. Arts and sciences department or school	23
10. Administrative unit of institution	4
11. College board or other formal public support base	3
12. Special structures	4
13. TWO-YEAR INSTITUTION	10
14. LOCAL EDUCATION AGENCY (unspecified)	258
15. Preschool	19
16. Elementary school	180
17. Secondary school	114
18. Adult education	3
19. Administrative unit of school system	22
20. School board or other formal public support base	47
21. COMMUNITY (unspecified)	147
22. Formal structures	63
23. Informal structures	56
24. STATE (unspecified)	12
25. Department of instruction	18
26. Board, governor, and public support base	
27. REGIONAL EDUCATION AGENCIES	5
28. TTT PROJECT STAFF	98
29. FEDERAL AGENCY	27
30. CONGRESS AND PUBLIC SUPPORT BASE	2
31. PARITY BOARD	22
32. TEACHER ORGANIZATIONS	6

TABLE A.5—PERSONS INVOLVED IN THE TTT PROGRAM IN NOVEMBER 1970 AND MARCH 1971, BY REFERENCE GROUP

Reference group	November 1970		March 1971		Difference in number
	Number	Percent	Number	Percent	
Education professors	1,268	4	1,051	3	−217
Other professors	545	3	506	1½	−39
Trainees (TTT, TT, T)	3,900	15	4,255	15	+355
School administrators	460	2	521	1½	+61
School staff	3,383	14	3,944	14	+561
Community	5,698*	21	5,991**	22	+293
Public school students	10,957	41	11,060	44	+103
TOTAL	26,211		27,338		+1,117

*Includes 5,020 parents of public school students.
**Includes 5,205 parents of public school students.

TABLE A.6—RESPONDENTS' PERCEPTIONS OF THE INTENDED EFFECT OF THE ACTIVITIES ON VARIOUS PERSONS, BY REFERENCE GROUP

Reference group	Responses			Total number responding
	Yes	No	Not applicable	
University professors in education	449	72	213	734
University professors in arts and sciences	299	91	344	734
Graduate students	422	59	253	734
Supervisory school personnel	344	78	312	734
School teachers	511	45	178	734
Community persons	311	87	336	734
School administrators	361	77	296	734
University administrators	260	101	373	734
School children	458	49	227	734

TABLE A.7—RESPONDENTS' PERCEPTIONS OF THE INTENDED EFFECT
OF THE ACTIVITIES ON VARIOUS INSTITUTIONS

Type of institutions affected	Responses			Total number responding
	Yes	No	Not applicable	
Colleges	413	73	248	734
Graduate schools	401	81	252	734
Public schools or school districts	475	58	201	734
Community	333	103	298	734
State education agencies	138	138	458	734
Parity boards	85	117	532	734
Teacher organizations	125	138	471	734

APPENDIX B. Impact Measurement Instrument

May 14, 1971

Dear TTT Participant:

It is the desire of the Office of Education to evaluate and improve the TTT Program (Teacher Training) with which you have been associated this past year. The success of this effort depends largely on your careful reply to the enclosed questionnaire.

Often we hear it said that the federal government should be more responsive to "the people." Here is a very real instance in which the government will use your views and opinions as a basis for making policy decisions affecting a program.

Please help us by returning this form in the self-addressed envelope as soon as possible. On the average, a little over one hour of your time is needed. We recognize that this questionnaire will take some of your valuable time, but only your time and advice can make federal programs like this more useful to American teachers and students.

If you have in no way been connected with the program, please return the questionnaire with a brief note scribbled across the face. Otherwise, please respond fully.

Sincerely yours,

QUESTIONNAIRE

Section I

Many TTT projects are focusing on a specific subject area (e.g., language, mathematics, social studies). This section is addressed to the preparation given in such specific areas.

1. Did the TTT project that you are associated with prepare you in a specific subject area?   ( ) yes   ( ) no

2. If your answer to (1) above was YES, what particular area was this training in? _____

3. If your answer to (1) above was YES, how would you rate its quality relative to other training that you have had?

   ( )   ( )   ( )   ( )   ( )
   poor   excellent

4. Do you believe that the training that you received included the most current findings in the field?

   ( )   ( )   ( )   ( )   ( )
   stone age   predominance
                                                              of current material

5. Do you think that the TTT project was successful in motivating its participants (in general) to the point that they will "swim upstream" to implement the knowledge that they have gained from the project?

   ( )   ( )   ( )   ( )   ( )
   no   high
   success   success

6. How would you rate the relative importance of university course work to actual field experiences?

   ( )   ( )   ( )   ( )   ( )
   course work   field experience
   most important   most important

Section II

Below and on the following pages is a list of topics covered by TTT projects across the country. We are interested in your opinion of the preparation which you received (if any) on each topic and your estimate of how much use this preparation will be when you are on the job. Please use this procedure:

(1)   Read through the items and decide if the project intended to cover each topic. Write NA (not applicable) in front of the topics that the project *did not* cover. If the project covered the topic, complete (2) and (3):

(2)   *Satisfaction:* In column "A" rate your satisfaction with the preparation that the project gave you in each topic using this scale:

1   2   3   4   5
did not   most questions
learn a thing   answered

(3)   *Utility:* In column "B" rate how much you think you will use the knowledge that you have gained from the topic using this scale:

1	2	3	4	5
never use it				knowledge essential to job

Use one of the numbers 1 to 5 to respond to each item.

Topic	A Satisfaction	B Utility
1. Individualized instruction		
2. Problems of novice teachers		
3. Different approaches to teacher preparation		
4. Curriculum development		
5. Problems in graduate education		
6. Contemporary student attitudes toward the educational system		
7. Values held by teachers		
8. Skills in making decisions in educational contexts		
9. Models for teacher certification		
10. How to run a school system		
11. Interaction analysis		
12. Media and materials		
13. Problems involved in institutional change		
14. Theories of learning		
15. Child development, language acquisition		
16. Child development, cognitive development		
17. Child development, socialization		
18. Behavior modification		
19. Group dynamics		
20. Techniques in problem solving		
21. Effective interpersonal relations		
22. Effects of economic deprivation		
23. Ethnic differences in lifestyles		
24. Community factors in educational needs		
25. Learning styles of economically deprived youth		
26. Adaptation of instruction to meet the needs of the student population		
27. Availability of educational resources		
28. Attitudes and aspirations of parents		
29. Formal and informal power structures in the target community		
30. Research findings on cultural differences		
31. Contributions and problems of the business sector		
32. Curriculum design		
33. Research methodology		
34. Computer techniques in instruction		

Section III

This section addresses skills in which many TTT projects are training participants. Please give us your opinions about this training if you believe that the
question is relevant to your own project. If you believe that the question is not
related to your experience with TTT, please mark it NA (not applicable).

1. What is your opinion of this statement: "Teaching is an art; it cannot be
    objectively evaluated."

    ( )   ( )   ( )   ( )   ( )
    disagree   agree
    very much   very much

2. Who is this TTT project primarily intended to serve?_____

3. Are classroom children involved in your project?   ( ) yes   ( ) no

4. If yes, describe the characteristics of these children._____

5. While associated with the TTT project did you receive training in the
    evaluation and assessment of teaching behavior?   ( ) yes   ( ) no

6. How confident would you feel about conducting an evaluation of a teacher
    in a classroom setting?

    ( )   ( )   ( )   ( )   ( )
    not at all   very
    confident   confident

7. How much credence do you think a "typical" teacher would give to the
    results of an evaluation of his teaching conducted by a "typical"
    participant in your own TTT project?

    ( )   ( )   ( )   ( )   ( )
    no   very much
    credence   credence

8. What is your opinion of this statement: "A teacher ought to adjust his
    behavior to the needs expressed by his students"?

    ( )   ( )   ( )   ( )   ( )
    disagree   agree

9. What is your opinion of this statement: "In this TTT project, a professor
    learns as much as his students."

    ( )   ( )   ( )   ( )   ( )
    disagree   agree

10. Rate the extent to which the training you received from the TTT project
    has increased your knowledge of the needs of minority groups along these
    dimensions.

	no new knowledge				very much new knowledge
Economic needs	( )	( )	( )	( )	( )
Psychological needs	( )	( )	( )	( )	( )
Educational needs	( )	( )	( )	( )	( )
Other (specify) _____	( )	( )	( )	( )	( )

11. Rate the extent to which the training *you* received from the TTT project has increased your knowledge of educational opportunities in these areas.

	no new knowledge				very much new knowledge
Individualized instruction programs	( )	( )	( )	( )	( )
Media and support programs	( )	( )	( )	( )	( )
Counseling programs	( )	( )	( )	( )	( )
New curricula	( )	( )	( )	( )	( )
Paraprofessional training programs	( )	( )	( )	( )	( )
Other (specify) _____	( )	( )	( )	( )	( )

12. On the basis of this knowledge do you feel that you have been prepared to integrate the needs of the target population with existing educational opportunities?

( )   ( )   ( )   ( )   ( )
not   very well
prepared   prepared

13. Do you feel that you have been prepared in the mechanics of creating *new* educational opportunities to meet educational needs (proposal writing, curriculum design, etc.)?

( )   ( )   ( )   ( )   ( )
not   very well
prepared   prepared

14. Which one of these changes would have resulted in the most improvement in your ability to apply knowledge to a practical situation?
( )   More course work
( )   Extended practicum
( )   Closer cooperation with professors and school personnel
( )   Changes in school or university policy (specify) _____

_____

( )   Other (specify) _____

15. Do you feel that the project has prepared you to evaluate the merits and impact of educational programs?

( )   ( )   ( )   ( )   ( )
no   thorough
preparation   preparation

16. Do you feel that the project has prepared you to use research methodology in the evaluation of educational programs?

( )   ( )   ( )   ( )   ( )
no   thorough
preparation   preparation

17. Do you feel that the project prepared you as a teacher to deal with the underlying determinants of the life-styles of minority groups?

( )   ( )   ( )   ( )   ( )
not much   very much

18. Did you receive any *direct* training in how to adapt what you learned to the place where you will be employed when you leave the TTT project?
( ) yes   ( ) no

19. Here is a sample of topics that are being treated by TTT projects across the country. We are interested in how confident you would feel serving as an expert on each topic.

	no confidence				very confident
Individualized instruction	( )	( )	( )	( )	( )
School-community relations	( )	( )	( )	( )	( )
Evaluation and accountability	( )	( )	( )	( )	( )
New instructional program	( )	( )	( )	( )	( )
Group dynamics	( )	( )	( )	( )	( )
Interdisciplinary programs	( )	( )	( )	( )	( )

20. Did you receive direct training in the *design* of curricula while you were associated with the TTT project?   ( ) yes   ( ) no

21. If your answer to (20) above was NO, do you think that your association with TTT has *indirectly* given you enough skills to design a curriculum? ( ) yes   ( ) no

22. Did you receive direct training in the *evaluation* of curricula while you were associated with the TTT project?   ( ) yes   ( ) no

23. If your answer to (22) above was NO, do you think that your association with TTT has *indirectly* given you enough skills to evaluate a curriculum? ( ) yes   ( ) no

24. Has TTT given you practical experience in the design, modification, or evaluation of curricula in your own subject or teaching area?

	your own subject area	another subject area
Design	( ) yes ( ) no	( ) yes ( ) no
Modification	( ) yes ( ) no	( ) yes ( ) no
Evaluation	( ) yes ( ) no	( ) yes ( ) no

25. On the basis of your experience with TTT, how confident would you feel about discussing curriculum alternatives *in your own field* with a recognized expert?

( )   ( )   ( )   ( )   ( )
not at all   very
confident   confident

26. On the basis of your association with TTT, do you feel motivated to modify, implement, or design a curriculum?

( )   ( )   ( )   ( )   ( )
not at all   very
motivated   motivated

Section IV

A large number of TTT projects have components which involve training in classroom management skills. This section addresses itself to these components; please read each of these items and decide if your project intended to prepare you in the skill described. If it *did not* intend to prepare you in this skill, write NA (not applicable) in the space provided. If the project did give you preparation in the skill, rate the quality of this preparation using this scale:

1	2	3	4	5
poor preparation				excellent preparation

Skill	Quality of preparation
1. Instructional skills in minority group settings	_____
2. Skills in supervising student teachers	_____
3. Ability to use feedback from students in teaching	_____
4. Skill in using expository mode of instruction	_____
5. Skill in using inquiry mode of instruction	_____
6. Skill in producing an individualized program of study	_____
7. Skill in defining staff roles and responsibilities	_____
8. Skill in using videotape as a diagnostic technique	_____
9. Preparing undergraduates for meaningful interaction with different ethnic groups	_____

Section V

Some TTT projects are involved in training participants in research methodology in one form or another. Often, this is done in a graduate-training program. The first part of this section deals with these programs.

Part A:

1. If you are in a degree program, did you complete the requirements for the academic degree toward which you are working?
   ( ) NA   ( ) yes   ( ) no   Which degree? _____
2. Have you been successful in finding employment for next year?
   ( ) yes   ( ) no
3. If the answer to (2) above is YES, rate the extent to which your training in TTT will be used in your job.
   ( )   ( )   ( )   ( )   ( )
   not at all   extensively
4. Do you feel that you will be able to influence an institution which would employ you to change in accordance with the goals of TTT?
   ( )   ( )   ( )   ( )   ( )
   not at all   much change

Answer this if your answer to (1) above was NO.

5. Check the item which best reflects the reason that you have not completed your degree requirements:
   ( )   not scheduled to this year
   ( )   withdrawn from program; explain _____
   ( )   Other _____
   _____

Part B: This section asks about research opportunities in your TTT project.

1. Did you have the opportunity to conduct research while you were associated with the TTT project?   ( ) yes   ( ) no

Answer these if your answer was YES.

2. Did you have the necessary resources to conduct your study?
   ( ) yes ( ) no
3. What part of the resources for your research came from the TTT project?
   ( )   ( )   ( )   ( )   ( )
   none   about half   all

4. Did you complete your research while associated with the TTT program?
( ) yes   ( ) no
5. What were the sources of your data?
( ) Experiment performed in a laboratory situation
( ) Students at a university or college
( ) Faculty at a university or college
( ) Students at a secondary/elementary school
( ) Faculty at a secondary/elementary school
( ) Administrators at a secondary/elementary school
( ) Parents of public school students
( ) Individuals from the community
( ) Other (specify)_____
6. What is your opinion of this statement: "Most techniques of research are sterile. They cannot be used to answer questions about the real world."
( )   ( )   ( )   ( )   ( )
strongly   strongly
disagree   agree
7. What is your opinion of this statement: "Current research is not conducted in accord with social concerns."
( )   ( )   ( )   ( )   ( )
strongly   strongly
disagree   agree
8. Estimate how your research prepared you to do the following:
a. gain a better knowledge of the problems of inner-city schools.
( )   ( )   ( )   ( )   ( )
no   excellent
preparation   preparation
b. interpret research data and apply it to a specific problem.
( )   ( )   ( )   ( )   ( )
no   excellent
preparation   preparation
c. turn professional problems into researchable questions.
( )   ( )   ( )   ( )   ( )
no   excellent
preparation   preparation

Section VI

Most TTT projects view themselves as forces for change. This section addresses itself to the extent to which you perceive the TTT project effecting changes in other institutions. Please read each item and rate the extent to which you believe the TTT project has achieved each of the following changes. Use the scale shown below. Write in one number on each line.

1   2   3   4   5
little   very much
achieved   achieved

Achievement

1. Disseminating the goals and objectives of the TTT project _____
2. Bringing about effective interdisciplinary relationships _____
3. Making clinical experience a formal part of graduate programs _____
4. Establishing new relationships (formal and informal) with groups outside the university for developing and implementing new programs _____
5. Involving liberal arts departments in educational issues _____
6. Bringing about effective relations with minority groups _____
7. Making educational methods courses more relevant to contemporary educational problems _____
8. Developing a sense of responsibility for effecting change in the public schools _____
9. Developing cooperative relationships between schools, colleges, and community _____
10. Promoting increased personal contacts between people from schools, colleges, and the community _____
11. Developing formal and informal contact between school personnel and parent groups _____
12. Changing entrance requirements for university degree programs _____
13. Changing personnel hiring practices. _____
14. Changing state certification policies _____
15. Other (specify) _____ _____

Section VII

One of the aims of TTT projects is to train participants to react to situations with a diversity of solutions. This section deals with the ability to make decisions under constraints: a hypothetical situation is presented in which you are to play a role in several structured decision-making problems. This is not a "test," in that there are no "right or "wrong" answers.

Problem situation

The school of education of a large university decided to revise its entire program of *clinical experiences for undergraduates in education.* This school did an unusual thing: they entrusted absolute control over this project to *one man.* This man did some work on the project, but was forced to leave because of ill health; the school of education liked what he had accomplished so far, so they hired *you to complete his work.*

You may assume the following:

(1) The university is located in the central core of a large city, and is directly adjacent to a concentration of low-income minority groups.

(2) The university has 15,000 students and grants both undergraduate and graduate degrees.

(3) The school of education is well funded; you may take this to mean that the project will be given adequate resources.

(4) The faculty of the school of education is enthusiastic about the project

and a number of faculty members from other departments have also expressed interest. You may take this to mean that the project has been developed in a positive emotional climate.

(5) You may assume that the project is to be implemented in the 1972-73 academic year, so you are not under any time pressure.

Among other things, here are some problems which must be solved to complete the project. (Remember you must work within the constraints of the situation.)

Problem 1: A maximum of 100 hours of consultant time has been allocated to help you plan the project. Further, the following people are to be involved; it is your problem to decide how *much* of each person's time to use in planning the project. Disregarding rate of pay, please estimate how you would distribute the time over these people.

Time   *People*

_____ a. Dr. Smith, the chairman of the school of education at a noted university

_____ b. Mr. Jones, the leader of an action group in the neighboring community

_____ c. Dr. Newton, a specialist in the field of media and materials

_____ d. Mrs. Clifford, the chairman of the city school board

_____ e. Dr. Bell, a specialist in evaluation

_____ f. Dr. Green, an assistant professor in the school of arts and sciences who has worked closely with undergraduates in education

_____ g. Mr. Cook, the principal of a school in the disadvantaged community

_____ h. Mr. Gray, a school teacher in the disadvantaged community

_____ i. Miss Johnson, an undergraduate student in the school of education

_____ j. Bobby Honda, a student in the local school

_____

100 TOTAL (Your total must be 100 hours)

Problem 2: It was decided that the program should publish a list of desired characteristics of good teachers. A list of suggestions was solicited from a wide variety of people. They are presented below, and it is your job to select *five* of them for publication. Please check your *five* choices in the space provided.

_____ 1. A teacher's first duty is to his students.

_____ 2. Appropriate student behavior should be promptly rewarded.

_____ 3. A teacher should be aware of many approaches to the classroom situation.

_____ 4. A teacher should ensure that every student goes as far and as fast as he can.

_____ 5. The Socratic method produces the best teaching.

_____ 6. A good teacher can teach any material well regardless of his personal attitudes toward the material.

_____ 7. A teacher should be involved in school and community politics as well as his classroom.

_____ 8. A good teacher should be able to motivate his students so that they will be receptive to learning.

———   9. A good teacher should understand the psychological and social determinants of his students' behavior.

——— 10. A good teacher realizes that his personal values can at times interfere with the effectiveness of his teaching.

Problem 3: It was also decided to have a special program of course work to prepare the students for their clinical experiences. In conjunction with the school of arts and sciences, a list of course topics was prepared. The topics listed below were the result of these deliberations; further, it was decided that *twenty* semester hours of classroom work would be used for this preparation. The problem is: how would you distribute class time over these topics? Please indicate the number of hours you would allocate to each one. If you believe that something should not be covered, write "0."

Hours   *Topic*

———   1. Learning theory

———   2. Structural linguistics

———   3. Behavior modification

———   4. Media and materials

———   5. Research methodology

———   6. Curriculum design

———   7. Computer programming

———   8. Sociology of the inner city

———   9. Child development

——— 10. Power and values in contemporary society

——— 11. History of the public school system

——— 12. Organizational patterns in the public schools

—————

20 hours TOTAL

Problem 4: It was also decided that the students and their critic teachers would benefit by a program of "occasional lectures." Funds were earmarked for *five* lectures by authorities in various fields. Your job is to select *five* lectures from among these suggested topics. Place a check mark before your *five* choices in the space provided.

———   1. "Maintaining student self-confidence"

———   2. "Building student skills with educational TV"

———   3. "Proven methods of classroom management"

———   4. "The role and performance of a public school administrator"

———   5. "Techniques of interaction analysis"

———   6. "Strengthening verbal skill with classical languages"

———   7. "Practical problems of managing institutional change"

———   8. "Attitudes and aspirations of public school parents"

———   9. "Informal power structures in the inner city"

——— 10. "The role of the business community in education"

——— 11. "Structural linguistics in the classroom"

Comment:

Problem 5: It was decided that students involved in the project should have experiences in the inner-city community *in addition to* their teaching duties. A committee composed of faculty, students, and community people proposed the following list of experiences; your job is to select *three* of them that will best prepare participants to deal with the environment in which they are teaching. Please place a check by your *three* choices in the space provided.

_____ 1. A bus tour through the economically disadvantaged area of the city

_____ 2. A program in which the student lives in the neighborhood where he is receiving his clinical teaching experiences

_____ 3. A program in which the student spends a few evenings riding in a police patrol car

_____ 4. A program in which the student attends classes at a trade school in the disadvantaged area

_____ 5. A laboratory simulation of various roles in the economically disadvantaged community

_____ 6. An encounter group situation with various people from the community

_____ 7. The student attempts to play the role of prospective client with community agencies (welfare, unemployment, health care, etc.)

Problem 6: Who do you anticipate will derive *training benefits* from this program? Below is a list of possible recipients. Place a check mark beside all of those that you feel will derive training benefits as a direct result of this hypothetical project.

_____ 1. Children in school

_____ 2. Classroom teachers

_____ 3. Undergraduate students at a university

_____ 4. Graduate students at a university

_____ 5. Education personnel from the state

_____ 6. Undergraduate faculty at a university

_____ 7. Graduate faculty at a university

_____ 8. Community people

Section VIII

This section addresses itself to broad attitudes toward the TTT program.

1. Do you think that the things that you learned while you were associated with the TTT project will be useful to you when you leave the program?

( )   ( )   ( )   ( )   ( )
not at all   extremely
useful   useful

2. Do you think that your own TTT project is trying to disseminate its goals and values to other educational institutions?

( )   ( )   ( )   ( )   ( )
little   trying
effort   extremely hard

3. Do you think that other educational institutions will eventually come to accept the goals and values of the TTT program and put them into practice?

( )   ( )   ( )   ( )   ( )
no   most
institutions   institutions

4. How important to good teacher training is cooperation between education and liberal arts faculties in colleges and universities?

( )   ( )   ( )   ( )   ( )

not at all   of paramount
worthwhile   importance

5. How important is community participation in teacher training?

( )   ( )   ( )   ( )   ( )

causes more   of paramount
problems than   importance
it solves

6. Assume for the moment that you have the power to change one thing about the project. What would you change? _____

_____

7. What do you think the major results of TTT will be?

_____

_____

8. Please make any additional comments that you wish.

_____

_____

TABLE B.1—CONTINGENCY ANALYSIS BETWEEN RESPONSE TO THE IMPACT QUESTIONNAIRE AND T-LEVEL*

| T-level | Response category | | | TOTAL |
	Non-respondent	Not involved	Respondent	
No T-level identified	76.68** / 80	4.26 / 4	55.38 / 58	142
TTT	244.08 / 197	27.12 / 26	76.28 / 229	452
TT	311.04 / 272	34.56 / 36	224.64 / 268	576
T	303.48 / 364	33.72 / 42	219.18 / 156	562
Community	102.60 / 137	11.40 / 13	74.10 / 40	590
TOTAL	1,050	121	751	1,922

*X^2 = 98.20, d.f. = 8, p. < .01
**Expected frequency

TABLE B.2–CONTINGENCY ANALYSIS BETWEEN RESPONSE TO THE IMPACT QUESTIONNAIRE AND SEX*

| Sex | Response category | | | TOTAL |
	Non-respondent	Not involved	Respondent	
Male	483.38** 462	53.70 59	349.05 374	895
Female	549.72 583	61.08 62	397.02 373	1,018
TOTAL	1,045	121	747	1,913

*X^2 = 6. 70, d.f. = 2, p. < .05
**Expected frequency

TABLE B.3–DESCRIPTIVE STATISTICS FOR RESPONDENT ATTITUDE TOWARD TRAINING IN CURRICULUM DESIGN, DEVELOPMENT, AND IMPLEMENTATION

| Reference groups | Statistics | | |
	Sample size	Mean	Variance
Trainees	241	2.66	1.79
Faculty	216	2.47	1.78
Overall	457	2.57	1.79

TABLE B.4–DESCRIPTIVE STATISTICS FOR RESPONDENT ATTITUDE TOWARD TRAINING IN SKILLS OF SUPERVISION

| Reference groups | Statistics | | |
	Sample size	Mean	Variance
Trainees	237	7.31	9.02
Faculty	214	7.64	8.36
Overall	451	7.47	8.72

TABLE B.5—DESCRIPTIVE STATISTICS FOR RESPONDENT ATTITUDE TOWARD TRAINING IN THE EVALUATION OF EDUCATIONAL PROGRAMS

Reference groups	Statistics		
	Sample size	Mean	Variance
Trainees	236	3.89	2.39
Faculty	212	3.68	2.76
Overall	448	3.79	2.57

TABLE B.6—DESCRIPTIVE STATISTICS FOR PARTICIPANT SATISFACTION WITH TRAINING IN SKILLS THAT MAXIMIZE THE PRODUCER-CONSUMER RELATIONSHIP

Reference groups	Statistics		
	Sample size	Mean	Variance
Trainees	234	4.38	5.29
Faculty	212	3.80	6.28
Overall	446	4.10	5.83

TABLE B.7—DESCRIPTIVE STATISTICS FOR PARTICIPANT SATISFACTION WITH TRAINING IN THE INTEGRATION OF EDUCATIONAL NEEDS AND OPPORTUNITIES

Reference groups	Statistics		
	Sample size	Mean	Variance
Trainees	234	6.27	9.07
Faculty	211	5.76	12.32
Overall	445	6.03	10.65

TABLE B.8—DESCRIPTIVE STATISTICS FOR PARTICIPANT ATTITUDE TOWARD CLINICAL EXPERIENCES (PRACTICUM)

Reference groups	Statistics		
	Sample size	Mean	Variance
Trainees	233	3.65	3.20
Faculty	211	3.54	3.36
Overall	444	3.60	3.27

TABLE B.9—SUMMARY OF THE ANALYSIS OF VARIANCE (METHOD OF UNWEIGHTED MEANS) FOR REFERENCE GROUP BY QUALITY OF TRAINING IN KNOWLEDGE OF STUDENT FACTORS

Source	d.f.	Sum of squares	Mean square	F
(1) Reference group	1	2.72	2.72	1.04ns
(2) Quality of training	1	13.99	13.99	5.36*
(1) by (2)	1	.89	.89	1.00
Within	889	2,324.81	2.62	—
TOTAL	892	2,342.41	—	—

*p $<$ .05, d.f. = 1,889

TABLE B.10—DESCRIPTIVE STATISTICS FOR COMPARISON OF FACULTY AND TRAINEES IN AREA OF KNOWLEDGE OF COMMUNITY FACTORS

Reference groups	Knowledge of community factors					
	Satisfaction			Utility		
	Sample size	Mean	Variance	Sample size	Mean	Variance
Trainees	234	5.33	10.63	233	6.06	10.81
Faculty	212	5.93	10.36	211	8.66	10.06

TABLE B.11—SUMMARY OF THE ANALYSIS OF VARIANCE (METHOD OF UNWEIGHTED MEANS) FOR REFERENCE GROUP BY QUALITY OF TRAINING IN KNOWLEDGE OF THE COMMUNITY

Source	d.f.	Sum of squares	Mean square	F
(1) Reference group	1	80.00	80.00	7.72*
(2) Quality of training	1	118.67	118.67	11.45*
(1) by (2)	1	0.00	0.00	1.00
Within	896	9,283.27	10.36	—
TOTAL	899	9,481.94	—	—

*p $<$ .01

TABLE B.12—DESCRIPTIVE STATISTICS FOR COMPARISON OF FACULTY AND TRAINEES IN THE AREA OF KNOWLEDGE OF INSTRUCTIONAL METHODS

Reference groups	Knowledge of instructional methods					
	Satisfaction			Utility		
	Sample size	Mean	Variance	Sample size	Mean	Variance
Trainees	234	2.90	2.31	233	3.09	2.20
Faculty	212	3.08	2.31	211	3.26	2.37

TABLE B.13—SUMMARY OF THE ANALYSIS OF VARIANCE (METHOD OF UNWEIGHTED MEANS) FOR REFERENCE GROUP BY QUALITY OF TRAINING IN KNOWLEDGE OF INSTRUCTIONAL METHODS

Source	d.f.	Sum of squares	Mean square	F
(1) Reference group	1	6.48	6.48	2.04 ns
(2) Quality of training	1	8.09	8.09	3.54 ns
(1) by (2)	1	.09	.09	1.00
Within	889	2,033.74	2.29	—
TOTAL	892	2,048.40	—	—

TABLE B.14—DESCRIPTIVE STATISTICS FOR RESPONDENT ATTITUDE TOWARD BALANCE BETWEEN PARITY SECTORS

Reference groups	Statistics		
	Sample size	Mean	Variance
Faculty	211	4.00	2.03
Trainees	233	3.88	2.05
School administration	70	3.81	2.30
School staff	184	3.35	2.44
Community	39	1.13	1.17

TABLE B.15—SUMMARY OF THE ANALYSIS OF VARIANCE FOR REFERENCE GROUPS ON "BALANCE BETWEEN PARITY SECTORS"

Source	d.f.	Sum of squares	Mean square	F
Reference group	4	292.68	73.17	34.53*
Within	732	1,551.58	2.12	—
TOTAL	736	1,844.26	—	—

*p $<$ .01, d.f. = 4,732, $F_{.99}$ = 3.32

TABLE B.16—DESCRIPTIVE STATISTICS FOR RESPONDENT ATTITUDE TOWARD INSTITUTIONAL CLIMATE

Reference groups	Statistics		
	Sample size	Mean	Variance
Faculty	211	4.73	2.47
Trainees	233	4.52	3.24
School administrators	70	4.34	3.56
School staff	184	3.95	4.04
Community	39	2.13	1.69

TABLE B.17—SUMMARY OF THE ANALYSIS OF VARIANCE FOR REFERENCE GROUPS ON "CHANGES IN INSTITUTIONAL CLIMATE"

Source	d.f.	Sum of squares	Mean square	F
Reference group	4	256.56	64.14	20.48*
Within	732	2,295.03	3.14	—
Total	736	2,251.59	—	—

*p $<$ .01

TABLE B.18—SUMMARY OF THE ANALYSIS OF VARIANCE FOR REFERENCE GROUPS BY ATTITUDE TOWARD CHANGES IN SPECIFIC INSTITUTIONAL POLICIES

Source	d.f.	Sum of squares	Mean square	F
Between	4	18.92	4.73	3.31 ns
Error	732	1,051.33	1.43	—
TOTAL	736	1,070.25	—	—

TABLE B.19—DESCRIPTIVE STATISTICS FOR RESPONDENT ATTITUDE TOWARD CHANGE IN SPECIFIC INSTITUTIONAL POLICIES

Reference groups	Statistics		
	Sample size	Mean	Variance
Faculty	210	1.31	1.66
Trainees	233	1.14	1.46
School administrators	70	1.14	1.25
School staff	184	.89	1.28
Community	39	1.38	1.61

APPENDIX C. Institutional Objectives for the TTT Program

Objectives:

1. Approval of project components by the management board.
2. Recruitment and selection of trainees.
3. Operation of project decision-making structure according to plan.
4. Use of TTT resources and personnel by schools and by other units of the university.
5. Use of community resources and personnel by the schools, the university, and the TTT project.
6. Communication about TTT with other projects.
7. Focus on needs of disadvantaged children in the training of T's, TT's, and TTT's.
8. Necessary staff changes and rearrangements to allow the TTT project to function in the schools and in the university.
9. Improve morale and internal communication of project participants.
10. Continuous evaluation of project with modification as a result of feedback from the evaluation.
11. Improve relations between schools, the university, and the community.
12. Improve relations between education and arts and sciences departments, resulting in direct participation of arts and sciences faculty in education and interdisciplinary training environment for TTT's and TT's.
13. New or revised doctoral program.
14. New or revised masters program.
15. New or revised bachelors program.
16. New or revised courses.
17. Provision of practicum for TTT participants (i.e., paraprofessional through doctorate).
18. In-service training program for school personnel.
19. New or revised curriculum for the schools.

20. Changes in admissions or hiring criteria and procedures.
21. Provision for resource centers to support instructional activities.
22. Design of data-gathering structures relevant to evaluation.
23. Formal procedures for dissemination of TTT results.

TABLE C.1—INSTITUTIONAL OBJECTIVES BY PROJECT

Institution	Variable (institutional objectives*)																						
	1	2	3	4	5	6	7	8	9	10	11	12	13	14	15	16	17	18	19	20	21	22	23
Appalachian State University	X	X	X						X	X						X			X				X
Auburn University											X												
Berkeley Unified School District			X			X					X						X	X					
City University of New York	X		X	X	X	X	X	X	X	X	X	X	X	X	X	X	X	X	X	X		X	X
Clark University				X	X					X	X								X				
Columbia University		X							X							X			X		X		
Fordham University		X							X							X			X				
George Peabody College for Teachers	X															X	X	X	X				
Harvard University								X			X												
Indiana University	X			X	X			X	X		X					X		X	X		X		X
Michigan State University	X						X		X	X	X					X			X		X		
New York University											X												
Northwestern University			X				X		X		X		X			X			X		X		X
Portland State University											X	X											
San Fernando State College	X		X	X	X	X	X	X	X	X	X	X	X			X	X	X	X		X		
San Jose State College			X	X		X			X		X	X				X	X		X				
Southeastern State College		X							X	X	X					X	X	X	X				X
State University of New York (Buffalo)		X	X	X						X	X					X	X	X	X				
Syracuse University			X	X														X	X	X			
Temple University		X	X	X		X		X	X	X	X	X	X			X		X	X	X	X		
Texas Southern University		X	X	X	X	X		X	X		X	X	X	X		X	X	X	X	X	X	X	X
University of Chicago		X	X	X	X	X		X	X		X	X	X	X		X	X	X	X	X	X	X	
University of Illinois				X	X						X	X				X	X	X			X	X	X
University of Miami	X	X			X													X			X	X	X
University of Minnesota	X		X				X	X	X	X	X						X		X		X	X	
University of Nebraska										X	X									X			
University of North Dakota			X	X					X		X		X	X	X	X	X	X	X	X	X	X	
University of Pittsburgh	X	X	X	X		X		X	X		X	X		X		X	X	X	X		X	X	
University of South Florida																					X		X
University of Washington																							
University of Wisconsin (Madison)										X	X	X	X		X	X			X				
Washington University	X	X	X	X		X	X	X	X	X	X	X	X	X	X	X	X	X	X		X	X	
Wayne State University			X			X	X	X	X		X	X	X			X		X					

*To identify the variables, see list preceding table.

APPENDIX D. Individual Change Variables within TTT Projects

Variables:

A. Knowledge
 1. Knowledge of educational practice
    a. Teaching
       (1) individualized instruction
       (2) microteaching
       (3) maintaining student self-confidence
       (4) accessibility to instruction
       (5) difference between expository and inquiry modes of instruction
       (6) properties of conceptually based lessons
       (7) new teaching methods that can be used in class and nonclass settings
       (8) methods for relating theory and practice
    b. Teaching preparation
       (1) factors associated with novice teachers
       (2) paraprofessional training
       (3) models for teacher preparation
       (4) cultural variation in teacher preparation
       (5) curriculum development and its relation to teacher training
       (6) gaps in teacher preparation
       (7) identified problems in graduate education
       (8) student attitudes toward teachers
       (9) values held by teachers
    c. Administration and supervision
       (1) decision-making procedures
       (2) relations between students and faculty

      (3)   models for certification
      (4)   process knowledge of school-system operation
      (5)   role and performance of public school supervisors
   d. Counseling
      (1)   techniques of interaction analysis
   e. Media and materials
      (1)   knowledge of variety and availability
   f. Institutions
      (1)   relationship between graduate school of education and related disciplines
      (2)   cross-disciplinary issues
      (3)   practical and theoretical problems involved in institutional change
2. Knowledge of psychological factors
   a. Learning theory
      (1)   field theory (Lewin and others)
      (2)   behaviorist theory
      (3)   awareness of characteristics that facilitate or prevent learning
   b. Child development
      (1)   development of ethics
      (2)   acquisition of language
      (3)   maturational factors
      (4)   cognitive processes
   c. Behavior modification
      (1)   nature of change and role of change agent
      (2)   theories of intervention and evaluation
   d. Attitude theory
   e. Group dynamics
      (1)   awareness of barriers to effective interpersonal relations
   f. Problem solving
      (1)   strategies of problem solving
3. Knowledge of sociological factors
   a. Effects of cultural deprivation
      (1)   specific theories of deprivation
      (2)   minority deprivation and teacher education
      (3)   awareness of deviate life-styles
      (4)   community response to educational needs
      (5)   specific learning styles of inner-city youth
   b. Race problem and racism
   c. Factors of the inner city
      (1)   problems of teaching specific subject matter in the inner city
      (2)   existent needs and available resources
      (3)   attitudes and aspirations of parents
      (4)   formal and informal institutions in inner city
      (5)   research findings about inner city
   d. Problems of specific ethnic groups
      (1)   blacks

          (a)   values and value system
      (2)   Chicanos
          (a)   values and value systems
      (3)   Indians
          (a)   on reservations
          (b)   off reservations
          (c)   cultural heritage of various tribes
          (d)   values
      (4)   Appalachia
          (a)   characteristics of Appalachian culture
   e. Contributions and problems of the business sector
 4. Knowledge of specific subject matter
 5. Knowledge of TTT philosophy
B. Skills
 1. Scholarly skills
   a. Discussion skills
      (1)   analyze and adapt pressures for change to home institution
      (2)   ability to discuss philosophic and socioeconomic developments in context of teacher education and ethnic education
      (3)   ability to apply educational-social theory to a practical situation
      (4)   ability to synthesize identified problems and solutions
      (5)   ability to compare cultural needs with educational opportunities
   b. Criticism skills
      (1)   ability to critique curriculum material with respect to treatment of minority groups
      (2)   ability to identify needs and weaknesses in current research
      (3)   ability to critique a graduate program
   c. Requirements
      (1)   completion of Ph.D. degree requirements
      (2)   completion of M.A. degree requirements
 2. Curriculum design
   a. Ability to apply knowledge of concept development to modify an instructional program
   b. Ability to design curricula for various cultural backgrounds
   c. Ability to write performance objectives in lesson planning
   d. Ability to design a conceptually based lesson
   e. Skills in program planning: objectives, budgeting, coordination of resources, and proposal writing
   f. Ability to relate subject matter to clinical education problems
   g. Skill in preparing materials for efficient use by elementary and secondary teachers
   h. Skills in designing new programs for paraprofessionals
   i. Ability to design programs for bilingual children
 3. Evaluation of teaching
   a. Demonstration of ability to analyze and assess teacher behavior
   b. Ability to suggest remedies for inappropriate teacher behavior

    c. Ability to adapt current techniques of evaluation to specific situations

    d. Ability to design new evaluation techniques

    e. Ability to analyze dialogue between supervisors and intern teachers

    f. Ability to evaluate arts and sciences programs in an educational system

    g. Ability to participate in a colloquium setting

    h. Skill in self-analysis of teaching

    i. Ability to adjust to the expressed needs of students

    j. Ability to evaluate performance in a role

4. Research design

    a. Ability to conduct and report research on influence of racism

    b. Ability to gain firsthand knowledge of the problems of the inner-city schools

    c. Ability to gather data about interaction

    d. Conducting studies on psychological education as a factor in personal growth

    e. Development of a model for research in a natural setting

    f. Ability to conduct research on school-university cooperation

    g. Ability to interpret research data

    h. Organization of research in accord with social concerns

    i. Analysis of professional problems into researchable questions

5. Classroom skills

    a. Ability to vary or limit verbal behavior to meet desired instructional goals

    b. Skill at using expository and inquiry modes of instruction

    c. Skills necessary for instruction in minority group settings

    d. Ability to supervise classroom interns

    e. Skills in teacher training

    f. Ability to teach well at the university level

    g. Ability to use principles of individualization

    h. Ability to prepare undergraduates for inner-city experiences

    i. Skill in working in an open classroom structure

    j. Ability to use a problem-solving approach in teaching

    k. Ability to define roles and responsibilities

6. Use of media

    a. Understanding the process of location and development of teaching aids from available local resources

    b. Skill and practice in using videotape as both a presentation device and a feedback device

    c. Skills in using microteaching

    d. Ability to use a multimedia approach to teaching

    e. Use of computer resources

    f. Ability to use film as a learning media and means of communication

C. Attitudes

1. Attitudes toward the disadvantaged

    a. Positive attitude toward competence and sophistication of minority students

b. "Realistic" attitude toward the university
c. Positive attitude toward the community as a participant in the educational process
d. Positive attitude toward community problems
e. Increased sensitivity to the problems of the schools
f. Positive attitude toward ethnic background as an important factor in teacher recruitment
g. Positive attitude toward cultures represented in the community
h. Positive attitude toward slow learners
i. Positive attitude toward the solving of children's learning problems
2. Attitudes toward professional concerns
a. Positive attitude toward new teaching methods
b. Positive attitude toward research as a means for solving bilingual problems
c. Positive attitude toward the goals of the TTT program
d. Positive attitude toward improving teacher education
e. Positive receptiveness to change information
f. Positive attitude toward concrete field experience as a part of teacher training
g. Positive attitude toward the need for individualization
h. Positive attitude toward an interdisciplinary approach to education
i. Positive attitude toward teaching undergraduates
j. Positive attitude toward establishment of a formal career development program and paraprofessionals
3. Attitudes toward other professionals
a. Attitudes toward others
(1) positive attitude toward other participants
(2) positive attitude toward each of the four parity sectors
(3) positive attitude toward high school teachers
b. Attitudes toward self
(1) positive self-concept
(2) awareness of personal attitudinal posture toward TTT
D. Relations outcomes
1. Relating with other professionals
a. Knowledge of ongoing efforts of the TTT project and program
b. Ability to interact with and elicit participation for T's and TT's
c. Working relationships in an interdisciplinary program
d. Influence brought to bear on emphasizing clinical experience as a part of the graduate program
e. Ability to work in a team evaluation using performance criteria
f. Participation with the parity board
g. Consortium effort to solve state-wide problems
h. Awareness of how the four parity sectors interact
i. Establish new alliances for developing and implementing new programs
j. Participation with consumers in TTT project planning and implementation

k. Continued improvement of the graduate program using feedback
l. Direct involvement of liberal arts departments in education-related issues
m. Changing communication patterns within and among departments and faculty
n. Cooperative strategies to identify, analyze, and solve learning problems
o. Systematic consultation with a corps of professional consultants

2. Classroom-instructional relations
   a. Ability to use interaction analysis as a basis for decision making
   b. Commitment to institutional change
   c. Openness to people of different social, ethnic, and economic backgrounds
   d. Working relationship as a student-teacher supervisor
   e. Direct participation in a training-oriented teacher education program
   f. Improved staffing arrangements to promote communications
   g. Provide feedback in evaluating individual performance
   h. Group consideration of practicum problems with students
   i. Ability to implement a plan of supervision using feedback
   j. Consideration of practicum problems with students
   k. Team participation to provide most effective guidance and supervision of each student
   l. Ability to work with students as a team
   m. Identification of specific relationships between teacher roles and subject matter
   n. Increased relevance of methods courses
   o. Joint planning for student needs
   p. Involvement in supervision of cooperating teachers
   q. Cooperative design of courses

3. Relations with schools
   a. Cooperative relationships with the schools
   b. Communication between education professors and public school staff
   c. Effective relations with minority group teachers and students
   d. Development of a plan for teaching TT's in cooperation with the public schools
   e. Use of group dynamics to improve relations with public school people
   f. Development of a sense of responsibility for effecting change in the public schools
   g. Increased understanding and respect for field personnel
   h. Collaboration with school personnel in training instructional leaders

4. Relations with the community
   a. Cooperative relationships with schools in teacher training activity
   b. Involvement in "reach-out" programs to involve the community
   c. Memberships in school-community programs
   d. Increased contacts with community members on a personal basis
   e. Effective interaction with the community in fieldwork
   f. Commitment of time and skill to day-care centers

    g. Formal and informal contact with parent groups

5. Dissemination of results
   a. Understanding of how the TTT project is meeting personal and professional needs
   b. Placement of graduates in key positions
   c. Interaction and interchange of ideas across programs
   d. Visibility to national and regional groups

6. Interpersonal skills
   a. Skill at working with people around group interaction and the dynamics of change
   b. Skills at team participation directed at a specified objective
   c. Identification with decisions as group consensus
   d. Ability to successfully work with teachers and students in inner-city schools
   e. Ability to work with other teachers in curriculum development
   f. Ability to work with high school students in studying and acting on community issues
   g. Skill in group dynamics
   h. Ability to organize and motivate for instructional change
   i. Ability to disseminate techniques of research
   j. Ability to interpret academic-professional knowledge to the four parity groups
   k. Proficiency in working with people possessing fewer skills

TABLE D.1—CROSS-PROJECT ANALYSIS OF INDIVIDUAL CHANGE VARIABLES AND PARTICIPANTS AFFECTED, IN ACCORD WITH OBJECTIVES

Objective	Project site	Variable (individual change)	Participants*																
			1	2	3	4	5	6	7	8	9	10	11	12	13	14	15	16	17
1. To bring about effective interdisciplinary relations among university components	Appalachian State University	Greater sensitivity to "learning climate" as a concept in effective teaching was developed in the TTT participants in the Pilot Project in Individualized Instruction					X	X											
		Greater understanding of self as teacher was developed in the participants in the Pilot Project					X												
	Auburn University	Professors in pilot programs served as diagnosticians, facilitators, interactors, and innovators, as well as promoters of interdepartmental change.	X		X	X													

*Participants:

1. Graduate faculty in education
2. Other graduate faculty
3. Undergraduate faculty in education
4. Other undergraduate faculty
5. Graduate students in education
6. Other graduate students

7. Undergraduate students in education
8. Other undergraduate students
9. University administrators
10. Public school teachers
11. Public school counselors
12. Public school administrators

13. Public school students
14. Community leaders
15. Private citizens in the community
16. Parents of public school students
17. Other

TABLE D.1—*continued.*

Objective	Project site	Variable (individual change)	Participants* 1	2	3	4	5	6	7	8	9	10	11	12	13	14	15	16	17
		As a result of involvement of two professors from industrial engineering in the TTT project, six professors in this department have devised some alternative ways of individualizing education.				X													
	George Peabody University	The Nashville TTT has brought into existence an inter-institutional, interdepartmental, interdisciplinary board as its decision-making body (coordinating council).	X	X	X		X	X		X	X					X	X		
		A new cooperative inter-institutional, interdepartmental, interdisciplinary program for doctoral study involving all Nashville area colleges and universities offering graduate programs in teacher education and the	X	X			X	X		X				X	X	X	X		

Description										
Metropolitan Nashville Schools has been established. The program emphasizes inner-city education and involves the community.										
College administrative units have approved new inter-institutional, interdepartmental, interdisciplinary programs and have assigned faculty to handle the responsibilities involved.	X	X	X	X	X					
A new cooperative inter-institutional, inner-city student teaching program involving all Nashville colleges and universities offering teacher education programs and the Metropolitan Nashville Schools has been established. The program involves community participation.	X	X	X	X	X	X	X	X	X	X
Indiana University — Student teachers taught unique content, that is, content they usually would not have been able to teach without the TTT program.					X			X		X

TABLE D.1—*continued.*

Objective	Project site	Variable (individual change)	Participants*																	
			1	2	3	4	5	6	7	8	9	10	11	12	13	14	15	16	17
		Knowledge of current innovative teacher education practice is increased by monthly meeting within school of education, other colleges, local school district, local schools, other universities, professional organizations, etc.	X	X	X	X	X	X	X	X	X	X	X	X						
		The attitude that university personnel are pragmatic educators offering relevant training to prospective teachers is developed.							X			X								
		Selected problems (and solutions) common to all elementary school teachers are discussed.							X											
		Instruction and materials of instruction are adapted to fit the reality of a particular school environment.			X				X											

Students learn to use principles from educational psychology in observing and interpreting teacher-pupil classroom behavior. — X

Michigan State University

Jane Dickie (1970-71 doctoral fellow) received experiences in TTT that had a profound effect or her perceptions of both the needs of the teacher and the needs of the student. — X

Dr. Dorothy West (MSU family ecology department) recognizes the need for a wider range of field experiences for undergraduate students in the schools, in the university, and in the community. This would provide greater awareness of what makes a good teacher and of the in-service experience to be encountered in secondary teaching. — X

Dr. Lois Bader (college of education) recognizes the need for field experiences in education courses. — X X

TABLE D.1—*continued.*

Objective	Project site	Variable (individual change)	Participants*																
			1	2	3	4	5	6	7	8	9	10	11	12	13	14	15	16	17
	Portland State University	TTT preservice teachers had significantly lower dogmatism scores than either a national norm or a comparison group from another college. (This characteristic may be due to selection rather than intervention.)							X										
		Knowledge of noninstructional as well as instructional activities conducted by elementary and secondary teachers increased.							X										
		After one year in the program, preservice teachers were more skilled in interpreting data, in formulating plans, and in avoiding unwarranted conclusions than a group just beginning preservice training, than a national norm group, or than a comparison group from another college.							X										

Knowledge in academic areas increased.	X	X	X					X						
Teaching skills improved.								X						
Professors modified their instructional procedures and, in some instances, the content of the courses they taught.														
San Jose State University														
The plan was to increase awareness of the changing needs in the development of educational personnel.	X	X		X			X							
Commitment to TTT goals by San Jose State staff not on the TTT staff increased through attendance at a planning and development conference and the formation of an ad hoc committee.	X	X												
Syracuse University														
The content of instructional programs was revised by developing new courses. New components were developed and implemented.	X	X	X	X	X	X	X	X	X	X				
A practicum component was developed to add to existing instructional programs. New components were developed and implemented.	X	X	X	X	X	X	X	X	X	X				

TABLE D.1—*continued.*

Objective	Project site	Variable (individual change)	*Participants 1	2	3	4	5	6	7	8	9	10	11	12	13	14	15	16	17
		New structures were developed to facilitate training of educational personnel, such as action teams, institutes, and a steering committee.	X	X	X	X	X	X			X	X		X	X	X			
		Improved institutional conditions were conducive to developing effective educational programs.	X	X	X	X	X	X			X	X		X	X	X			
	Texas Southern University	Potential TTT and TT individuals are identified and selected before assigning them to one of the three institutions for programs of training.					X												
		There is a validation or elimination of tentative operational assumptions in the training of teacher trainers.					X												
		TTT scholars and fellows are trained for leadership positions.				X		X											

University of
North
Dakota

Faculty with liberal arts background participate in the life of cooperating elementary schools, including two who spend an entire semester working with master's-level interns.

A clinic experience for doctoral students is conducted in close relationship to plan an individualized program of academic study.

University of
Pittsburgh

Contracts for five TTT slots were created at four sites: Oakdale, Mars, Penn-Trafford, Canevin (internships in teacher education).

University of
Washington

In-service training was provided for teachers of schools with predominantly Indian populations.

The college of education teacher preparation program moved steadily toward becoming field oriented.

TABLE D.1—*continued.*

Objective	Project site	Variable (individual change)	1	2	3	4	5	6	7	8	9	10	11	12	13	14	15	16	17
																		Participants*		
		TTT personnel were utilized by the curriculum and instruction department to serve on revision committees for all C&I masters and doctors degree programs.					X												
		New courses developed for and by TTT personnel have become regular offerings of the college of education.				X													
		A unique opportunity for a teacher training practicum is being provided.				X	X	X	X										
	University of Wisconsin	The level of enrollment of Ph.D. candidates in secondary social studies (department of curriculum and instruction) has been raised from an average of four per year to seventeen (1971-73).	X	X	X		X				X								
		A new program has been established whereby graduate students can work with high				X								X	X	X	X	X	X

school students on community issues.

A professor was hired, and a course in supervision for graduate students supervising interns in secondary social studies was established.

A new course offering established in the department of curriculum and instruction enabled students to get repeated variable credit for independent fieldwork.

There were plans to meet needs of Ph.D. fellows and the institutions to which they related.

Washington University

An arts and sciences advisory board was established to serve the instruction center.

A program was set up to improve the teaching skills of prospective college teachers.

An instruction center was established and charged with the improvement of undergraduate instruction.

TABLE D.1—*continued.*

Objective	Project site	Variable (individual change)	Participants*																
			1	2	3	4	5	6	7	8	9	10	11	12	13	14	15	16	17
		Program increased the use of media in undergraduate courses in arts and sciences.							X	X									
		An experimental teacher education program for preservice elementary students has been implemented at the Nathaniel Hawthorne School in University City, Missouri.			X							X							
		There was a new staffing arrangement for a preservice program that included TTT university faculty, non-TTT university faculty, public school teachers, college students, and community people.	X	X	X	X					X						X		
		Financial and human resources were reallocated to provide a preservice teacher education program.					X	X	X										
	Wayne State University	Teaching assistants and senior faculty in liberal arts, chemistry, and biology collabor-	X			X									X				

ated with public school science teachers and educational psychologists to analyze and discuss means of improving their college teaching.

Skills required for joint problem solving improved as a direct result of participation on the academic discipline teams.

Objective	Institution	Description						
		ated with public school science teachers and educational psychologists to analyze and discuss means of improving their college teaching.						
		Skills required for joint problem solving improved as a direct result of participation on the academic discipline teams.	X					X
2. To bring about effective relations with minority groups.	Auburn State	Members of a minority community group interacted with graduate students and faculty members and experienced growth in project.	X	X				X
	Indiana University	Faculty and administrative personnel of the university were encouraged to recognize that minority subgroups in the community have inputs to make to teacher education and that their expectations should be honored by educators.	X	X	X	X		X X

*See beginning of table for key to participants.

TABLE D.1 —*continued.*

Objective	Project site	Variable (individual change)	1	2	3	4	5	6	7	8	9	10	11	12	13	14	15	16	17
		Knowledge of current instructional practices, student characteristics, organizational features, and socio-economic problems in an inner-city school increased.							X										
		Awareness of urban dwellers' needs and of the social agencies and programs designed to assist them grew.							X										
		Participants were exposed to an environment that provided for a more realistic decision as to the feasibility of a career in inner-city schools and that suggested other available occupational directions in the field of education.							X										
		Rural poor community residents, faculty, staff, undergraduate and graduate students, and foreign students were exposed to inner-city culture.	X	X	X	X	X	X	X										

Participants became acquainted with the frustration and lack of personal freedom that results from material deprivation.   X

Participants gained firsthand knowledge of fears often associated with the inner city, and they could decide the extent to which such fears were based in reality.   X

Having been exposed to the variety of roles (student teacher, community agency worker, community resident, family member, low-income person, trainer of teachers) thrust upon inner-city residents and teachers, the participant could determine the extent to which these roles varied from roles assumed by people living in the dominant culture.   X X

Michigan State University   Dr. Jean Enochs (science-math teaching center) recognizes the importance of individualization of teaching to provide for the problems   X X

*See beginning of table for key to participants.

TABLE D.1—*continued.*

Objective	Project site	Variable (individual change)	Participants*																
			1	2	3	4	5	6	7	8	9	10	11	12	13	14	15	16	17
		and concerns of minority people.	X																
		Dr. Sam Reuschleiu (1969-70 professorial fellow) was motivated through his TTT experiences to become involved as a TTT internal evaluator for the following three years of the program. His commitment to the project and to his university department in the area of teacher education has been greatly increased as a result of his involvement in TTT. In addition, his teaching methods have been noticeably affected through his involvement with community people.													X		X	X	
	Portland State University	Professors became more realistic in their concepts regarding economic, cultural, and ethnic minorities.	X	X	X	X													

	San Jose State University	Syracuse University
	All TTT participants gained competence in planning curriculum content and materials for children from low-income, ethnic minority communities, particularly in the areas of individualized instruction, cultural awareness, problem-solving skills, and community involvement. Through a better understanding of school and community needs, an improved program for training education personnel was planned and implemented.	A parity situation was organized so a cooperative effort of graduate education and discipline faculties and students, community leaders, secondary school supervisors, and secondary school students could begin.

San Jose State University — X X | X X | | | X X X | X | | X X X | X X X | | | X | X X | | X X X X | X

Syracuse University — X X X | X X X X | X X X | | X X X | X X X | X X X | | | | | |

*See beginning of table for key to participants.

TABLE D.1—*continued.*

Objective	Project site	Variable (individual change)	*Participants 1	2	3	4	5	6	7	8	9	10	11	12	13	14	15	16	17
		Facilities, faculties, and students from the Maxwell graduate school and the school of education at Syracuse University, the Metropolitan Syracuse Unified School District and the East Syracuse-Minoa Central School District were used, as well as community leaders and monitors from agencies such as black youth united, neighborhood youth corps, and the New York human rights commission.	X	X	X	X	X	X			X	X	X	X	X	X			
	University of Washington	A new curriculum was set up in Washington State public schools for Indians.										X		X					
3. To develop cooperative relations between schools and universities.	Auburn State	A liaison person was working both in the public school and at the university (doctoral student in TTT program).	X																

Participant	Description				
Indiana University	Over eight graduate interns helped provide methods instruction in field settings with TTT professors. They acquired practical field skills in demonstration teaching, supervision, and consultation.			X		
	There was increased knowledge of the developmental levels of elementary school students and student teachers.	X	X		X	
Michigan State University	Dr. Justin Kestenbaum (1969-70 professorial fellow) was motivated as a result of his TTT experiences to return to a senior high school (Eastern) the following year and teach a U.S. history course for one year with no pay. His teaching experience was accomplished with four or five prestudent teachers and one graduate assistant on a team-teaching basis.			X	X	X
	TTT experiences motivated Dirk Horton (1969-70 doctoral fellow) to become a			X		X

*See beginning of table for key to participants.

TABLE D.1—*continued.*

Objective	Project site	Variable (individual change)	1	2	3	4	5	6	7	8	9	10	11	12	13	14	15	16	17
		secondary public school teacher (Sexton).																	
	San Jose State University	An in-service training program for site school personnel and college staff was implemented.	X	X							X	X	X	X				X	X
		Each site school developed specific objectives and made plans to implement these objectives. Individuals within each group developed specific competencies.					X				X	X	X	X				X	X
	Syracuse University	The ability to plan the complex interrelationships of the parity groups increases when feedback received from the evaluation unit process begins.	X	X	X	X	X	X			X	X	X	X	X	X			
	Texas Southern University	Each participant is to be placed in an assignment that promises the greatest returns for the institution and the individual.						X											

* Participants

University of Miami	Increased cooperation within the University of Miami included use of facilities and resources so as to provide a laboratory.	X							X		
Auburn State	Ability to discuss education problems in groups involving professional and lay persons developed.	X	X	X	X				X		
Indiana University	Community field experience modules were added to the list of alternative modules from which preservice teachers could select (modules open to all students, faculty, and staff). All of these modules were designed to provide an opportunity for the student to observe, participate, or interact with community agencies and as low-income persons.								X		
	The Office of Community Experiences was involved in decisions of the Human Relations Committee, a community-wide organization.							X	X		

4. To develop cooperative relations between university and community persons.

*See beginning of table for key to participants.

Objective	Project site	Variable (individual change)	Participants* 1	2	3	4	5	6	7	8	9	10	11	12	13	14	15	16	17
	San Jose State University	A program was designed to change according to the needs of the participants and the community. Continuous feedback from all participants provided information needed to adjust the program and activities.	X		X							X	X	X		X			X
	Syracuse University	Ability to plan the complex interrelationships of the parity groups increases with feedback received from the evaluation unit process.	X	X	X	X	X	X		X	X		X	X	X	X			
		The community liaison disseminates information about the TTT project and actively seeks cooperation from formal and informal community agencies in support of components leading to improved maintenance of new structures.	X	X	X	X	X	X		X	X		X	X	X				
		Improved relations with other	X	X	X	X	X	X		X	X		X	X	X	X			

Objective	Institution		
5. To develop cooperative relations between schools and communities.		organizations mean that channels of communication have been established.	X X X X X X X X X
	Indiana University	There was an attempt to develop the attitude among faculty and administrative personnel of the university that minority subgroups in the community have inputs to make to teacher education and expectations that should be honored by educators.	X X X X X X X X X X X
		Office of Community Experiences became involved in decisions of the Human Relations Committee, a community-wide organization.	X X X
	San Jose State University	Knowledge of educational practices appropriate for the implementation of TTT objectives increased.	X X X X X X X X X X X X
		There was more communication among individuals within the school, college, and community through participation in the planning and development institute.	X X

*See beginning of table for key to participants.

TABLE D.1—*continued.*

Objective	Project site	Variable (individual change)	Participants*																
			1	2	3	4	5	6	7	8	9	10	11	12	13	14	15	16	17
		A plan to provide clinical experiences included community and public school persons.																X	X
		The number of community persons who participated in planned career opportunity programs designed to prepare them for service in the public schools (Ind.) increased.	X		X		X				X	X	X	X	X			X	X
		All TTT participants gained competence in planning curriculum content for children from low-income, ethnic minority communities; particularly in the areas of individualized instruction, cultural awareness, problem-solving skills, and community involvement.											X	X	X	X	X	X	

				X
6. To make learning experiences more relevant to minority and disadvantaged children.	Appalachian State University	A greater appreciation for, and tolerance of, the sociocultural differences among children was developed in TTT participants in the Pilot Project.	X X	
	Auburn State	Participants assumed more responsibility in directing their own learning; initiated conferences with faculty members; interacted with faculty members in a different manner; participated in a modular program; set their own schedules; did laboratory work in public schools.		X
	Indiana University	Participants were able to gain firsthand knowledge of those fears often associated with the inner city and to form a personal opinion of the extent to which such fears are based in reality.		X
		The exposure of participants to the variety of roles (student teacher, community agency worker, community resident,		X X

Objective	Project site	Variable (individual change)	Participants*																
			1	2	3	4	5	6	7	8	9	10	11	12	13	14	15	16	17
		family member, low-income person, trainer of teachers) thrust upon inner-city residents and teachers and the extent to which those roles varied from the roles assumed by a person living in the dominant culture brought about a greater understanding.	X	X	X	X	X	X		X	X	X	X	X		X	X		
	George Peabody University	A new cooperative interinstitutional, inner-city student teaching program involving all Nashville colleges and universities offering teacher education programs and the Metropolitan Nashville Schools has been established. The program involves community participation.					X	X		X			X	X	X	X	X		
		A new cooperative interinstitutional, interdepartmental interdisciplinary program for doctoral study involving all Nashville-area colleges and	X	X			X	X		X			X	X	X				

universities offering graduate programs in teacher education and the Metropolitan Nashville Schools has been established. The program emphasizes inner-city education and involves the community.

San Jose State University — All TTT participants showed increased competence in planning curriculum content for children from low-income, ethnic minority communities, particularly in the areas of individualized instruction, cultural awareness, problem-solving skills, and community involvement.

Texas Southern University — Organizational resources were turned toward influencing programs of the schools. Bilingual conferences were held for an entire summer.

TABLE D.1—*continued.*

Objective	Project site	Variable (individual change)	*Participants																	
			1	2	3	4	5	6	7	8	9	10	11	12	13	14	15	16	17
7. To render learning a more meaningful "life-connected" experience.	Appalachian State University	TT participants in the Appalachian State University Pilot Project in Individualized Instruction in Math and Science for 1970-71 report professional advancement based on their experiences with the project.			X							X								
		The basic educational philosophies of the TT participants in the Pilot Project changed by their experiences in the program.			X							X								
		A major change in the TT's concept of the role of the teacher in the classroom occurred as a result of the experience which the Pilot Project provided.			X				X			X								
		A greater desire to search for new methods, to try new approaches, to experiment, to become innovative was stimulated by experiences in the Pilot Project.					X		X											

The sense of freedom achieved through interpersonal relationships of graduate faculty, TT participants, and children whom they worked with in the learning laboratory situation as a basis for more effective teaching was developed in many of the TT participants.   X X X

A greater realization that the "learning climate" comes closer to reality as traditional "artificialities" are removed from the classroom situation was experienced by TT participants in the Pilot Project.   X

A greater appreciation of educational problems in public schools on the part of the teachers from cooperating schools resulted from experience in the program.   X

Public school students involved in the Pilot Project carried their enthusiasm for the program into the homes and community served by the public school.   X X

*See beginning of table for key to participants.

Objective	Project site	Variable (individual change)	Participants*																
			1	2	3	4	5	6	7	8	9	10	11	12	13	14	15	16	17
		Public school teachers working in the schools that cooperated with the university in the Pilot Project were more firmly convinced that an individualized approach to teaching is more effective than traditional methods.										X								
	Auburn State	Skills in designing instructional materials were gained.	X									X								
		Materials were designed for individualized education in elementary and secondary schools (TT personnel directed a three-week workshop for teachers in Jackson, Mississippi).										X								
		Modules were designed for use in freshman English where compositions explored different ways individual differences can be dealt with in freshman composition.		X				X												
		Other models were designed for evaluating systems-based	X																	

individualized instruction.

There were alternate plans for teaching a course in American history, along with construction of diagnostic tests, seminars, and other activities. — X

Roles of elementary school teachers were redefined in order to plan the curriculum for a pilot program. — X

Faculty efforts to validate materials to be used in a pilot program could be evaluated. — X

There was a greater understanding of the nature of the pilot program. — X

Sessions on individualized instruction were held at the Annual Conference of American Society for Engineering Education. — X

Expertise was gained in designing and implementing an individualized education program in teacher education. — X

Harvard University — Emphasis on clinical practicum increased. — X

Course work was individualized. — X

*See beginning of table for key to participants.

TABLE D.1—*continued.*

Objective	Project site	Variable (individual change)	1	2	3	4	5	6	7	8	9	10	11	12	13	14	15	16	17
	Indiana University	Undergraduate students conceived and implemented innovative ideas as a result of TTT. They became more active in the teaching-learning process.							X						X				
		Staff training for those in charge of "core" teacher education courses improved.					X								X				
		There was an understanding of such concepts as sensitivity training, group dynamics, information communications patterns, TTT parity, etc.							X										
		Attitudes toward individualizing instruction, nondidactic teaching techniques, etc., improved.							X		X								
		Children obtained additional instructional benefits from the TTT program.										X							
	Michigan State University	TTT experiences motivated Stuart Wilson (1969-70 doctoral fellow) to become a reading coordinator in a					X												

public senior high school (Eastern).	X		
Dr. Virgil Scott (MSU English department) believes that English methods courses should be based in the schools.	X		X
Dr. Virgil Scott (MSU English department), as a result of experiences in TTT, has modified his own teaching methods to relate more to what students do in high school.	X		
Dr. Nancy Stackhouse (MSU art department), as a result of TTT experiences, believes that early undergraduate experience should be provided in schools on a continuing basis.	X	X	
Dr. J. Ludwig (MSU English department) uses supplementary materials available to high school students in teaching literature classes to undergraduates.			
Ron Santora (English department doctoral candidate), as	X		X X

*See beginning of table for key to participants.

Objective	Project site	Variable (individual change)	Participants*																
			1	2	3	4	5	6	7	8	9	10	11	12	13	14	15	16	17
		a result of TTT experiences, believes that curriculum should be organized to study through an inductive process and that a much greater emphasis needs to be placed on clinic experiences in the schools and in the community.																		
		Dr. Jeannette Haviland (psychology department) advocates more diversity in teaching to reduce prejudice through condescension shown to students in schools.			X	X														
		Virginia Koslowski (instructor in family ecology department) has modified her approach in conducting monthly seminars and her approach toward undergraduate university students majoring in family ecology.		X																
		Dr. Jean Enochs (Science-Math			X	X														

Teaching Center) recognizes the importance of using public school teachers in college methods classes for science.

San Fernando State — Knowledge learned in TTT transferred to the field situation.   X X

San Jose State — Commitment to TTT goals through early clinical experience increased.   X   X   X X X X   X

The staff of the six schools was committed to the goals of TTT.   X X X   X X   X

Syracuse University — The direction and planning of teacher training experience in formal university courses, in the community, and in the public school system in an attempt to stimulate teacher trainers to become continual experimenters and improvers of teaching process were begun.   X X X X X   X X   X X X X

Staff training techniques and practice conducive to internal maintenance of new structures—new cooperative   X X   X   X X   X

Objective	Project site	Variable (individual change)	Participants*																
			1	2	3	4	5	6	7	8	9	10	11	12	13	14	15	16	17
		techniques and arrangements—were developed.																	
		Members' rapport and morale were boosted through establishing effective working relationships, both between community, university, and public school and within each. Higher morale and rapport were needed to maintain internal structures and to plan the operation.	X	X	X	X	X				X	X		X	X	X			
		New structures and programs—action teams and institutes, and steering committees—were developed to facilitate training of educational personnel.	X	X	X	X	X				X	X		X	X	X			
	Texas Southern University	There was cooperation with Harlem School for apprentice teachers.						X											

Goal	University		
8. To recruit and involve innovative persons in the educational reform effort.	Appalachian State University	TTT participants in the Appalachian State University Pilot Project for Individualized Instruction in Math and Science for 1970-71 were prepared for new roles of responsibility in colleges and public schools.	X
		Through visitations to schools in which innovative practices are successful, TT participants were stimulated to examine, select from, and try out various programs of individualized instruction.	X
		Test data revealed that public school children achieved beyond normal expectations in classrooms in which individualized instruction techniques were used.	X
		Greater sensitivity to the needs of the learner on the part of the TT participants in the Pilot Project was developed by the experiences which it provided.	X

TABLE D.1—*continued.*

Objective	Project site	Variable (individual change)	*Participants 1	2	3	4	5	6	7	8	9	10	11	12	13	14	15	16	17
	Auburn State	There was participation in sessions on individualized instruction at Annual Conference of American Society for Engineering Education.		X		X													
	Indiana University	The ability to critique, counsel, guide, and evaluate student teachers was developed so that university supervisors were not necessary and so that student teachers could continually set and reach new professional performance goals.									X								
		The feeling developed that methods classes and student teaching are more effective if they occur simultaneously. Methods professors were brought into a follow-up supervisory relationship with the students in their methods classes.			X			X			X								

Statement						
The skill to modify and adapt educational theories and methods to child readiness, available materials, organization, and scheduling constraints of a full school year was developed.				X		
An awareness of which methods of instruction are relevant in schools today and which are not was increased.	X			X		
An improved collaborative relationship with school teachers featured an exchange of practices and knowledge.	X	X				
A close working relationship with public school personnel was encouraged.	X	X		X		
Participants were exposed to innovative units and given an opportunity to witness demonstrations of new curricular materials employed with regularly assigned sections of students.				X	X	
Participants developed knowledge of the socioeconomic, educational, and cultural problems faced by various community subgroups.				X	X	

*See beginning of table for key to participants.

TABLE D.1—*continued.*

Objective	Project site	Variable (individual change)	Participants*																
			1	2	3	4	5	6	7	8	9	10	11	12	13	14	15	16	17
	George Peabody University	A new cooperative interinstitutional, interdepartmental, interdisciplinary program for doctoral study involving all Nashville area colleges and universities offering graduate programs in teacher education and the Metropolitan Nashville Schools has been established. The program emphasizes inner-city education and involves the community.	X	X			X	X			X				X	X	X		
		A new cooperative, interinstitutional, inner-city student teaching program involving all Nashville colleges and universities offering teacher education programs and the Metropolitan Nashville Schools has been established. The program involves community participation.		X	X	X	X	X		X	X		X	X		X			
		The TTT program has involved	X	X	X	X				X					X	X	X	X	

community representatives in its policy decisions and program development considerations.												
Colleges and universities have begun to make shared assignments with the school system.	X	X	X	X			X	X				X
New interinstitutional practicum experiences for in-service college and school faculty have been established.	X	X	X	X			X					X
Members' rapport and morale were boosted through establishing effective working relationships, both between community, university, and public school and within each. Higher morale and rapport were needed to maintain internal structures and to plan the operation.	X	X	X	X			X	X				X X X
Syracuse University												
The TTT project, composed of members drawn from all parity groups, develops an improved image of the TTT Program conducive to co-	X	X	X	X			X	X				X X X

*See beginning of table for key to participants.

TABLE D.1—*continued.*

Objective	Project site	Variable (individual change)	1	2	3	4	5	6	7	8	9	10	11	12	13	14	15	16	17
		operative operations through implementation of curriculum innovations aimed at the economically disadvantaged inner-city students.																	
	Texas Southern University	TTT and District 3 cooperated in the preparation of teachers.					X		X										
	University of Miami	The Concept of Model Building sounded "gimmicky" originally, but, as a result of TTT participation, it became an important factor in my thinking.										X							
	University of Nebraska	The participants' ability to work cooperatively with members of the local committees seeking answers to educational problems increased.	X	X	X	X	X	X			X				X	X			
		There was an increase in participants' experience in a	X	X		X	X	X			X		X						

variety of practicum settings, particularly open class-rooms.	X	X		X	X	X		X		X X X	
The capacity of participants for directing and evaluating their own learning activity and for creating and working with groups of people (whether adults or children) in defining group goals and accomplishing them increased.	X	X	X	X	X	X	X	X	X	X X X X	
Participants felt responsible for becoming change agents in education.	X	X	X	X	X	X	X				
University of South Florida	Fourteen individuals shared experiences that broadened considerably their capabilities for effecting changes through working with teachers, professors, school administrators, and legislators.	X	X		X						
University of Washington	New curricula have been provided for the public schools.									X	

*See beginning of table for key to participants.

TABLE D.1—continued.

Objective	Project site	Variable (individual change)	Participants*																	
			1	2	3	4	5	6	7	8	9	10	11	12	13	14	15	16	17
	Wayne State University	There was increased participation in program planning and staff development, with representatives from education, liberal arts, public schools, undergraduate students, and the community working as a planning and learning team on a parity basis.	X	X	X	X	X			X	X	X	X	X		X		X	
9. To develop cooperative relationships among communities, schools, and universities.	Auburn State	Members of a minority community group interact with graduate students and faculty members and experience growth in project.													X				
	Indiana University	An urban semester program is being participated in for credit by students in disciplines other than education.						X	X										
	Michigan State University	Teachers of the English department of a senior high school (Eastern) and parents meet															X		

weekly to work with students and others with common concerns (twelve teachers and twelve parents involved).

Texas Southern University — The use of education as a scapegoat by the citizens of the community has been reduced.

A university-community-school teacher-training seminar was developed.

University of Miami — There is a deeper understanding of the relationships between various cultures and the role this relationship plays in the education of children and youth.

University of Nebraska — Participants' ability to work cooperatively with members of the local committees seeking answers to educational problems has increased.

*See beginning of table for key to participants.

TABLE D.1—*continued.*

Objective	Project site	Variable (individual change)	1	2	3	4	5	6	7	8	9	10	11	12	13	14	15	16	17
		Participants*																	
		There are opportunities for participants to become more sensitive to the integrity and worth of the so-called minority culture.	X	X		X	X					X				X	X	X	X
	University of Washington	The management board (steering committee) was actively involved in influencing and approving project components through evaluation.																	
	University of Wisconsin	There were more opportunities for high school students to learn through participation in community issues.												X					
	Washington University	A new relationship existed between school and community.						X	X										
		A planning model for a pre-service teacher education program that included university faculty, public school teachers, public school administrator, and college stu-																X	

dents developed.

Wayne State University

There was an increase in participation in program planning and staff development with representation from education, liberal arts, public schools, undergraduate students, and community working as a planning and learning team on a parity basis (Planning Conference for DITE). — X X X X X X X

At least four administrators from each of the eight regions of the Detroit Public School System have been given specific training in the use of a systems approach to problem solving. — X